UNCTAD/DTCI/30(Vol. III)

United Nations Conference on Trade and Development
Division on Transnational Corporations and Investment

International Investment Instruments: A Compendium

Volume III
Regional Integration, Bilateral and Non-governmental Instruments

United Nations
New York and Geneva, 1996

NOTE

The UNCTAD Division on Transnational Corporations and Investment serves as the focal point within the United Nations Secretariat for all matters related to foreign direct investment and transnational corporations. In the past, the Programme on Transnational Corporations was carried out by the United Nations Centre on Transnational Corporations (1975-1992) and the Transnational Corporations and Management Division of the United Nations Department of Economic and Social Development (1992-1993). In 1993, the Programme was transferred to the United Nations Conference on Trade and Development and became the Division on Transnational Corporations and Investment. The Division on Transnational Corporations and Investment seeks to further the understanding of the nature of transnational corporations and their contribution to development and to create an enabling environment for international investment and enterprise development. The work of the Division is carried out through intergovernmental deliberations, policy analysis and research, technical assistance activities, seminars, workshops and conferences.

The term "country", as used in the boxes added by the UNCTAD Secretariat at the beginning of the instruments reproduced in this volume, also refers, as appropriate, to territories or areas; the designations employed and the presentation of the material do not imply the expression of any opinion whatsoever on the part of the Secretariat of the United Nations concerning the legal status of any country, territory, city or area or of its authorities, or concerning the delimitation of its frontiers or boundaries. Moreover, the country or geographical terminology used in these boxes may occasionally depart from standard United Nations practice when this is made necessary by the nomenclature used at the time of negotiation, signature, ratification or accession of a given international instrument.

To preserve the integrity of the texts of the instruments reproduced in this volume, references to the sources of the instruments that are not contained in their original text are identified as "note added by the editor".

The texts of the instruments included in this volume are reproduced as they were written in one of their original languages or an official translation thereof. When an obvious linguistic mistake has been found, the word "sic" has been added in brackets.

The materials contained in this volume have been reprinted with special permission of the relevant institutions. For those materials under copyright protection, all rights are reserved by the copyright holders.

It should be further noted that this collection of instruments has been prepared for documentation purposes only, and their contents do not engage the responsibility of UNCTAD.

UNCTAD/DTCI/30. Vol. III

UNITED NATIONS PUBLICATION
Sales No. E.96.II.A.11
ISBN 92-1-104465-0
Complete set of three volumes: ISBN 92-1-104466-9

PREFACE

This selection of international instruments relating to foreign direct investment (FDI) and the activities of transnational corporations (TNCs), presented in three volumes, is intended to fill a gap in existing publications on the topic. In spite of the proliferation in recent years of multilateral and regional instruments dealing with various aspects of FDI, there has been no collection of texts that would make them conveniently available to interested policy-makers, scholars and business executives. Lately, this *lacuna* has become particularly apparent as new initiatives are underway to negotiate a multilateral agreement on investment. In response to this need, and in pursuance of its analytical and consensus-building function, UNCTAD has designed and prepared the present *International Investment Instruments: A Compendium (I.I.I. Compendium)*.

While by necessity selective, the present collection seeks to provide a faithful record of the evolution and present status of intergovernmental cooperation concerning FDI and TNCs. While the emphasis is on relatively recent documents (more than half of the instruments reproduced date from after 1980), it was deemed useful to include important early instruments as well, with a view towards providing some indications of the historical development of international concerns over FDI in the decades since the end of the Second World War.

The core of this collection consists of legally-binding international instruments, mainly multilateral conventions and regional agreements that have entered into force. In addition, a number of "soft law" documents, such as guidelines, declarations and resolutions adopted by intergovernmental bodies, have been included since these instruments also play a role in the elaboration of an international framework for FDI. In an effort to enhance the understanding of the efforts behind the elaboration of this framework, certain draft instruments that never entered into force, or texts of instruments the negotiations of which were not concluded, are also included; and, in an annex, several prototypes of bilateral investment treaties are reproduced. Included also are a number of influential documents prepared by professional associations, business, consumer and labour organizations. It is clear from the foregoing that no implications concerning the legal status or the legal effect of an instrument can be drawn from its inclusion in this collection.

In view of the great diversity of instruments -- in terms of subject matter, approach, legal form and extent of participation of States -- the simplest possible method of presentation was deemed the most appropriate. Thus, within each subdivision, instruments are reproduced in chronological order:

- Volume I is devoted to multilateral instruments, that is to say, multilateral conventions as well as resolutions and other documents issued by multilateral organizations.

- Volume II covers interregional and regional instruments, including agreements, resolutions and other texts from regional organisations within an inclusive geographical context.

Both volumes cover international instruments widely differing in scope and coverage. A few are designed to provide an overall, general framework for FDI and cover many, although rarely all, aspects of investment operations. Most instruments deal with particular aspects and issues concerning FDI. A significant number address core FDI issues, such as investment liberalization, the promotion and protection of investment, dispute settlement and insurance and guarantees. Others cover specific issues, of direct but not exclusive relevance to FDI and TNCs, such as international trade, transfer of technology, intellectual property, avoidance of double taxation, competition and the protection of consumers and the environment. A relatively small number of instruments of this last category has been reproduced, since each of these specific issues often involves an entire system of legal regulation of its own, whose proper coverage would require an extended exposition of many kinds of instruments and arrangements.

The three annexes in volume III cover three types of instruments that differ in their context or their origin from those included in the two main parts:

- Annex A reproduces investment-related provisions in regional free trade and integration agreements. The specific function and, therefore, the effect of such provisions is largely determined by the economic integration process which they are intended to promote and in the context of which they operate.

- Annex B (the only section that departs from the chronological pattern) offers the texts of prototype bilateral treaties for the promotion and protection of foreign investments of several developed and developing countries, and a list of these treaties concluded up to July 1995. The bilateral character of these treaties differentiates them from the bulk of the instruments included in the *I.I.I. Compendium*. Over 900 such treaties had been adopted by July 1995.

- Annex C supplies the texts of documents prepared by non-governmental organizations; these give an indication of the broader environment in which the instruments collected here are prepared.

The *I.I.I. Compendium* is meant to be a collection of instruments, not an anthology of relevant provisions. Indeed, to understand a particular instrument, it is normally necessary to take into consideration its entire text. An effort has been made, therefore, to reproduce complete instruments, even though, in a number of cases, reasons of space and relevance have dictated the inclusion of excerpts.

The texts collected are not offered as models. On the contrary, an effort has been made to select instruments that reflect a broad variety of political backgrounds, forms, attitudes towards FDI, preferred approaches and policies, and effectiveness of their provisions. The collection is intended as a record of international action, not as a codification of legal prescriptions.

For the same reason, the UNCTAD Secretariat has deliberately refrained from adding its own commentaries to the texts reproduced. The only exception to this rule are the boxes added at the beginning of each instrument which provide information on some basic facts, such as its date of adoption, date of entering into force, status as of 1995 and, where appropriate, signatory countries. Moreover, to facilitate the identification of each instrument in the table of contents, additional information has been added, in brackets, next to each title, on the year of its signature and the name of the institution involved.

UNCTAD hopes that the *I.I.I. Compendium* will help policy makers, business executives and researchers to understand better past developments and the current state of the regulatory framework relating to FDI.

Rubens Ricupero
Secretary-General of UNCTAD

Geneva, March 1996

ACKNOWLEDGEMENTS

The *I.I.I. Compendium* was prepared by Victoria Aranda and Michael Gestrin, with inputs from Anna Joubin-Bret, Vincent Casim, Mohamed Fayache and Letizia Salvini, and assisted by Mario Ardiri, Eric Gill, Per Kall, Christine Jeannet, and Liane Wolly, under the direction of Karl P. Sauvant. Arghyrios A. Fatouros prepared the Introduction and provided overall guidance and advice. Secretarial support was provided by Medarde Almario, Nayana Hein, Elisabeth Mahiga and Jenifer Tacardon.

CONTENTS

VOLUME II
REGIONAL INSTRUMENTS

VOLUME III
REGIONAL INTEGRATION, BILATERAL AND NON-GOVERNMENTAL INSTRUMENTS

ANNEX A. INVESTMENT-RELATED PROVISIONS IN FREE TRADE AND REGIONAL ECONOMIC INTEGRATION INSTRUMENTS

ANNEX B. PROTOTYPE BILATERAL INVESTMENT TREATIES AND LIST OF BILATERAL INVESTMENT TREATIES (1959-1995)

ANNEX C. NON-GOVERNMENTAL INSTRUMENTS

ANNEX A
Investment-Related Provisions in Free Trade and Regional Economic Integration Instruments

ANNEX A
Investment-Related Provisions in Free Trade and Regional
Economic Integration Instruments

TREATY ESTABLISHING THE EUROPEAN COMMUNITY[*][1]
[excerpts]

The Treaty Establishing the European Community (Treaty of Rome) was adopted on 25 March 1957 and entered into force on 1 January 1958. It was subsequently amended by the Single European Act and by the Treaty on European Union (Treaty of Maastricht). The Single European Act was signed on 17 and 28 February 1986 (in Luxembourg and The Hague, respectively) and entered into force on 1 July 1987. The Treaty on European Union was adopted in Maastricht on 7 February 1992 and entered into force on 1 November 1993. The member States of the European Community as of January 1995 were Austria, Belgium, Denmark, Finland, France, Germany, Greece, Ireland, Italy, Luxembourg, the Netherlands, Portugal, Spain, Sweden and the United Kingdom. The text reproduced in this volume is the latest version of the Treaty Establishing the European Community, after the Treaty on European Union.

Contents

---

[*] Source: European Commission (1993). "Treaty Establishing the European Community", *European Union: Selected Instruments Taken from the Treaties*, Book 1, Volume 1 (Luxembourg: Office for Official Publications of the European Communities). The footnotes in the original text are indicated by asterisks. For editorial reasons, these have been replaced by consecutively numbered footnotes. The acronym "TEU" in the footnotes stands for "Treaty on European Union" [Note added by the editor].

[1] Title as amended by Article G(1) TEU.

Final provisions

Annexes

Annex I -- Lists A to G referred to in Articles 19 and 20 of the Treaty
Annex II -- List referred to in Article 38 of the Treaty
Annex III -- List of invisible transactions referred to in Article 73h of the Treaty
Annex IV -- Overseas countries and territories to which the provisions of Part IV of the Treaty apply

II -- Protocols

Protocol (No A) on the Statute of the European Investment Bank
Protocol (No B) on the Statute of the Court of Justice of the European Community
Protocol (No 1) on the acquisition of property in Denmark
Protocol (No 2) concerning Article 119 of the Treaty establishing the European Community
Protocol (No 3) on the Statue of the European System of Central Banks and of the European Central Bank
Protocol (No 4) on the Statute of the European Monetary Institute
Protocol (No 5) on the excessive deficit procedure
Protocol (No 6) on the convergence criteria referred to in Article 109j of the Treaty establishing the European Communities
Protocol (No 7) amending the Protocol on the privileges and immunities of the European Communities
Protocol (No 8) on Denmark
Protocol (No 9) on Portugal
Protocol (No 10) on the transition to the third stage of economic and monetary union
Protocol (No 11) on certain provisions relating to the United Kingdom of Great Britain and Northern Ireland
Protocol (No 12) on certain provisions relating to Denmark
Protocol (No 13) on France
Protocol (No 14) on social policy
Protocol (No 15) on economic and social cohesion

PART ONE
PRINCIPLES

Article 1

By this Treaty, the HIGH CONTRACTING PARTIES establish among themselves a EUROPEAN COMMUNITY.

Article 2[2]

The Community shall have as its task, by establishing a common market and an economic and monetary union and by implementing the common policies or activities referred to in Articles 3 and 3a, to promote throughout the Community a harmonious and balanced development of economic activities, sustainable and non-inflationary growth respecting the environment, a high degree of convergence of economic performance, a high level of employment and of social protection, the raising of the standard of living and quality of life, and economic and social cohesion and solidarity among Member States.

Article 3[3]

For the purposes set out in Article 2, the activities of the Community shall include, as provided in this Treaty and in accordance with the timetable set out therein:

(a)   the elimination, as between Member States, of customs duties and quantitative restrictions on the import and export of goods, and of all other measures having equivalent effect;

(b)   a common commercial policy;

(c)   an internal market characterized by the abolition, as between Member States, of obstacles to the free movement of goods, persons, services and capital;

(d)   measures concerning the entry and movement of persons in the internal market as provided for in Article 100c;

(e)   a common policy in the sphere of agriculture and fisheries;

(f)   a common, policy in the sphere of transport;

(g)   a system ensuring that competition in the internal market is not distorted;

(h)   the approximation of the laws of Member States to the extent required for the functioning of the common market;

(i)   a policy in the social sphere comprising a European Social Fund;

(j)   the strengthening of economic and social cohesion;

(k)   a policy in the sphere of the environment;

---

[2]As amended by Article G(2) TEU.

[3]As amended by Article G(3) TEU.

(l)   the strengthening of the competitiveness of Community industry;

(m)   the promotion of research and technological development;

(n)   encouragement for the establishment and development of trans-European networks;

(o)   a contribution to the attainment of a high level of health protection;

(p)   a contribution to education and training of quality and to the flowering of the cultures of the Member States;

(q)   a policy in the sphere of development cooperation;

(r)   the association of the overseas countries and territories in order to increase trade and promote jointly economic and social development;

(s)   a contribution to the strengthening of consumer protection;

(t)   measures in the spheres of energy, civil protection and tourism.

Article 3a[4]

1.   For the purposes set out in Article 2, the activities of the Member States and the Community shall include, as provided in this Treaty and in accordance with the timetable set out therein, the adoption of an economic policy which is based on the close coordination of Member States' economic policies, on the internal market and on the definition of common objectives, and conducted in accordance with the principle of an open market economy with free competition.

2.   Concurrently with the foregoing, and as provided in this Treaty and in accordance with the timetable and the procedures set out therein, these activities shall include the irrevocable fixing of exchange rates leading to the introduction of a single currency, the ECU, and the definition and conduct of a single monetary policy and exchange-rate policy the primary objective of both of which shall be to maintain price stability and, without prejudice to this objective, to support the general economic policies in the Community, in accordance with the principle of an open market economy with free competition.

3.   These activities of the Member States and the Community shall entail compliance with the following guiding principles: stable prices, sound public finances and monetary conditions and a sustainable balance of payments.

---

[4]As inserted by Article G(4) TEU.

Article 3b[5]

The Community shall act within the limits of the powers conferred upon it by this Treaty and of the objectives assigned to it therein.

In areas which do not fall within its exclusive competence, the Community shall take action, in accordance with the principle of subsidiarity, only if and in so far as the objectives of the proposed action cannot be sufficiently achieved by the Member States and can therefore, by reason of the scale or effects of the proposed action, be better achieved by the Community.

Any action by the Community shall not go beyond what is necessary to achieve the objectives of this Treaty.

PART THREE
COMMUNITY POLICIES

TITLE III
FREE MOVEMENT OF PERSONS, SERVICES AND CAPITAL

CHAPTER 2
RIGHT OF ESTABLISHMENT

Article 52

Within the framework of the provisions set out below, restrictions on the freedom of establishment of nationals of a Member State in the territory of another Member State shall be abolished by progressive stages in the course of the transitional period. Such progressive abolition shall also apply to restrictions on the setting-up of agencies, branches or subsidiaries by nationals of any Member State established in the territory of any Member State.

Freedom of establishment shall include the right to take up and pursue activities as self-employed persons and to set up and manage undertakings, in particular companies or firms within the meaning of the second paragraph of Article 58, under the conditions laid down for its own nationals by the law of the country where such establishment is effected, subject to the provisions of the Chapter relating to capital.

Article 53

Member States shall not introduce any new restrictions on the right of establishment in their territories of nationals of other Member States, save as otherwise provided in this Treaty.

---

[5]As inserted by Article G(5) TEU.

Article 54

1.   Before the end of the first stage, the Council shall, acting unanimously on a proposal from the Commission and after consulting the Economic and Social Committee and the European Parliament, draw up a general programme for the abolition of existing restrictions on freedom of establishment within the Community. The Commission shall submit its proposal to the Council during the first two years of the first stage.

The programme shall set out the general conditions under which freedom of establishment iS to be attained in the case of each type of activity and in particular the stages by which it is to be attained.

2.   In order to implement this general programme or, in the absence of such a programme, in order to achieve a stage in attaining freedom of establishment as regards a particular activity, the Council, acting in accordance with the procedure referred to in Article 189b and after consulting the Economic and Social Committee, shall act by means of directives.[6]

3.   The Council and the Commission shall carry out the duties devolving upon them under the preceding provisions, in particular:

(a)   by according, as a general rule, priority treatment to activities where freedom of establishment makes a particularly valuable contribution to the development of production and trade;

(b)   by ensuring close cooperation between the competent authorities in the Member States in order to ascertain the particular situation within the Community of the various activities concerned;

(c)   by abolishing those administrative procedures and practices, whether resulting from national legislation or from agreements previously concluded between Member States, the maintenance of which would form an obstacle to freedom of establishment;

(d)   by ensuring that workers of one Member State employed in the territory of another Member State may remain in that territory for the purpose of taking up activities therein as self-employed persons, where they satisfy the conditions which they would be required to satisfy if they were entering that State at the time when they intended to take up such activities;

(e)   by enabling a national of one Member State to acquire and use land and buildings situated in the territory of another Member State, in so far as this does not conflict with the principles laid down in Article 39(2);

---

[6]Paragraph 2 as amended by Article G(11) TEU.

(f)   by effecting the progressive abolition of restrictions on freedom of establishment in every branch of activity under consideration, both as regards the conditions for setting up agencies, branches or subsidiaries in the territory of a Member State and as regards the subsidiaries in the territory of a Member State and as regards the conditions governing the entry of personnel belonging to the main establishment into managerial or supervisory posts in such agencies, branches or subsidiaries;

(g)   by coordinating to the necessary extent the safeguards which, for the protection of the interests of members and other, are required by Member States of companies or firms within the meaning of the second paragraph of Article 58 with a view to making such safeguards equivalent throughout the Community;

(h)   by satisfying themselves that the conditions of establishment are not distorted by aids granted by Member States.

Article 55

The provisions of this Chapter shall not apply, so far as any given Member State is concerned, to activities which in that State are connected, even occasionally, with the exercise of official authority.

The Council may, acting by a qualified majority on a proposal from the Commission, rule that the provisions of this Chapter shall not apply to certain activities.

Article 56

1.   The provisions of this Chapter and measures taken in pursuance thereof shall not prejudice the applicability of provisions laid down by law, regulation or administrative action providing for special treatment for foreign nationals on grounds of public policy, public security or public health.

2.   Before the end of the transitional period, the Council shall, acting unanimously on a proposal from the Commission and after consulting the European Parliament, issue directives for the coordination of the above-mentioned provisions laid down by law, regulation or administrative action. After the end of the second stage, however, the Council shall, acting in accordance with the procedure referred to in Article 189b, issue directives for the coordination of such provisions as, in each Member State, are a matter for regulation or administrative action.[7]

---

[7]Paragraph 2 as amended by Article G(12) TEU.

Article 57[8]

1.   In order to make it easier for persons to take up and pursue activities as self-employed persons, the Council shall, acting in accordance with the procedure referred to in Article 189b, issue directives for the mutual recognition of diplomas, certificates and other evidence of formal qualifications.

2.   For the same purpose, the Council shall, before the end of the transitional period, issue directives for the coordination of the provisions laid down by law, regulation or administrative action in Member States concerning the taking-up and pursuit of activities as self-employed persons. The Council, acting unanimously on a proposal from the Commission and after consulting the European Parliament, shall decide on directives the implementation of which involves in at least one Member State amendment of the existing principles laid down by law governing the professions with respect to training and conditions of access for natural persons. In other cases the Council shall act in accordance with the procedure referred to in Article 189b.

3.   In the case of the medical and allied and pharmaceutical professions, the progressive abolition of restrictions shall be dependent upon coordination of the conditions for their exercise in the various Member States.

Article 58

Companies or firms formed in accordance with the law of a Member State and having their registered office, central administration or principal place of business within the Community shall, for the purposes of this Chapter, be treated in the same way as natural persons who are nationals of Member States.

'Companies or firms' means companies or firms constituted under civil or commercial law, including cooperative societies, and other legal persons governed by public or private law, save for those which are non-profitmaking.

CHAPTER 3
SERVICES

Article 59

Within the framework of the provisions set out below, restrictions on freedom to provide services within the Community shall be progressively abolished during the transitional period in respect of nationals of Member States who are established in a State of the Community other than that of the person for whom the services are intended.

---

[8]As amended by Article G(13) TEU.

The Council may, acting by a qualified majority on a proposal from the Commission, extend the provisions of the Chapter to nationals of a third country who provide services and who are established within the Community.

Article 60

Services shall be considered to be 'services' within the meaning of this Treaty where they are normally provided for remuneration, in so far as they are not governed by the provisions relating to freedom of movement for goods, capital and persons.

'Services' shall in particular include:

(a)   activities of an industrial character;

(b)   activities of a commercial character;

(c)   activities of craftsmen;

(d)   activities of the professions.

Without prejudice to the provisions of the Chapter relating to the right of establishment, the person providing a service may, in order to do so, temporarily pursue his activity in the State where the service is provided, under the same conditions as are imposed by that State on its own nationals.

Article 61

1.   Freedom to provide services in the field of transport shall be governed by the provisions of the Title relating to transport.

2.   The liberalization of banking and insurance services connected with movements of capital shall be effected in step with the progressive liberalization of movement of capital.

Article 62

Save as otherwise provided in this Treaty, Member States shall not introduce any new restrictions on the freedom to provide services which have in fact been attained at the date of the entry into force of this Treaty.

Article 63

1.   Before the end of the first stage, the Council shall, acting unanimously on a proposal from the Commission and after consulting the Economic and Social Committee and the European Parliament, draw up a general programme for the abolition of existing restrictions on freedom

to provide services within the Community. The Commission shall submit its proposal to the Council during the first two years of the first stage.

The programme shall set out the general conditions under which and the stages by which each type of service is to be liberalized.

2.   In order to implement this general programme or, in the absence of such a programme, in order to achieve a stage in the liberalization of a specific service, the Council shall, on a proposal from the Commission and after consulting the Economic and Social Committee and the European Parliament, issue directives acting unanimously until the end of the first stage and by a qualified majority thereafter.

3.   As regards the proposals and decisions referred to in paragraphs 1 and 2, priority shall as a general rule be given to those services which directly affect production costs or the liberalization of which helps to promote trade in goods.

Article 64

The Member States declare their readiness to undertake the liberalization of services beyond the extent required by the directives issued pursuant to Article 63(2), if their general economic situation and the situation of the economic sector concerned so permit.

To this end, the Commission shall make recommendations to the Member States concerned.

Article 65

As long as restrictions on freedom to provide services have not been abolished, each Member State shall apply such restrictions without distinction on grounds of nationality or residence to all persons providing services within the meaning of the first paragraph of Article 59.

Article 66

The provisions of Articles 55 to 58 shall apply to the matters covered by this Chapter.

CHAPTER 4
CAPITAL AND PAYMENTS[9]

Article 67

1.   During the transitional period and to the extent necessary to ensure the proper functioning

---

[9]Title as amended by Article G(14) TEU.

---

of the common market, Member States shall progressively abolish between themselves all restrictions on the movement of capital belonging to persons resident in Member States and any discrimination based on the nationality or on the place of residence of the parties or on the place where such capital is invested.

2.   Current payments connected with the movement of capital between Member States shall be freed from all restrictions by the end of the first stage at the latest.

Article 68

1.   Member States shall, as regards the matters dealt with in this Chapter, be as liberal as possible in granting such exchange authorizations as are still necessary after the entry into force of this Treaty.

2.   Where a Member State applies to the movements of capital liberalized in accordance with the provisions of this Chapter the domestic rules governing the capital market and the credit system, it shall do so in a nondiscriminatory manner.

3.   Loans for the direct or indirect financing of a Member State or its regional or local authorities shall not be issued or placed in other Member States unless the States concerned have reached agreement thereon. This provision shall not preclude the application of Article 22 of the Protocol on the statute of the European Investment Bank.

Article 69

The Council shall, on a proposal from the Commission, which for its purpose shall consult the Monetary Committee provided for in Article 109c, issue the necessary directives for the progressive implementation of the provisions of Article 67, acting unanimously during the first two stages and by a qualified majority thereafter.

Article 70

1.   The Commission shall propose to the Council measures for the progressive coordination of the exchange policies of Member States in respect of the movement or capital between those States and third countries. For this purpose the Council shall issue directives, acting by a qualified majority. It shall endeavour to attain the highest possible degree of liberalization. Unanimity shall be required for measures which constitute a step back as regards the liberalization of capital movements.

2.   Where the measures taken in accordance with paragraph 1 do not permit the elimination of differences between the exchange rules of Member States and where such differences could lead persons resident in one of the Member States to use the freer transfer facilities within the Community which are provided for in Article 67 in order to evade the rules of one of the Member States concerning the movement of capital to or from third countries, that State may, after consulting the other Member States and the Commission, take appropriate measures to

overcome these difficulties.

Should the Council find that these measures are restricting the free movement of capital within the Community to a greater extent than is required for the purpose of overcoming the difficulties, it may, acting by a qualified majority on a proposal from the Commission, decide that the State concerned shall amend or abolish these measures.

Article 71

Member States shall endeavour to avoid introducing within the Community any new exchange restrictions on the movement of capital and current payments connected with such movements, and shall endeavour not to make existing rules more restrictive.

They declare their readiness to go beyond the degree of liberalization of capital movements provided for in the preceding Articles in so far as their economic situation, in particular the situation of their balance of payments, so permits.

The commission may, after consulting the Monetary Committee, make recommendations to Member States on this subject.

Article 72

Member States shall keep the Commission informed of any movements of capital to and from third countries which come to their knowledge. The Commission may deliver to Member States any opinions which it considers appropriate on this subject.

Article 73

1.   If movements of capital lead to disturbances in the functioning of the capital market in any Member State, the Commission shall, after consulting the Monetary Committee, authorize that State to take protective measures in the field of capital movements, the conditions and details of which the Commission shall determine.

The Council may, acting by a qualified majority, revoke this authorization or amend the conditions or details thereof.

2.   A Member State which is in difficulties may, however, on grounds of secrecy or urgency, take the measures mentioned above, where this proves necessary, on its own initiative. The Commission and the other Member States shall be informed of such measures by the date of their entry into force at the latest. In this event the Commission may, after consulting the Monetary Committee, decide that the State concerned shall amend or abolish the measures.

Article 73a[10]

As from 1 January 1994, Articles 67 to 73 shall be replaced by Articles 73b, c, d, e, f and g.

Article 73b

1.   Within the framework of the provisions set out in this Chapter, all restrictions on the movement of capital between Member States and between Member States and third countries shall be prohibited.

2.   Within the framework of the provisions set out in this Chapter, all restrictions on payments between Member States and between Member States and third countries shall be prohibited.

Article 73c

1.   The provisions of Article 73b shall be without prejudice to the application to third countries of any restrictions which exist on 31 December 1993 under national or Community law adopted in respect of the movement of capital to or from third countries involving direct investment -- including in real estate -- establishment, the provision of financial services or the admission of securities to capital markets.

2.   Whilst endeavouring to achieve the objective of free movement of capital between Member States and third countries to the greatest extent possible and without prejudice to the other Chapters of this Treaty, the Council may, acting by a qualified majority on a proposal from the Commission, adopt measures on the movement or capital to or from third countries involving direct investment --including investment in real estate -- establishment, the provision of financial services or the admission of securities to capital markets. Unanimity shall be required for measures under this paragraph which constitute a step back in Community law as regards the liberalization or the movement of capital to or from third countries.

Article 73d

1.   The provisions of Article 73b shall be without prejudice to the right of Member States:

(a)   to apply the relevant provisions of their tax law which distinguish between taxpayers who are not in the same situation with regard to their place of residence or with regard to the place where their capital is invested;

(b)   to take all requisite measures to prevent infringements of national law and regulations, in particular in the field of taxation and the prudential supervision of financial

---

[10]Articles 73a to 73h as inserted by Article G(15) TEU [Note by the editor: this footnote is repeated for Articles 73a through 73h in the original source document].

institutions, or to lay down procedures for the declaration of capital movements for purposes of administrative or statistical information, or to take measures which are justified on grounds of public policy or public security.

2.   The provisions of this Chapter shall be without prejudice to the applicability of restrictions on the right of establishment which are compatible with this Treaty.

3.   The measures and procedures referred to in paragraphs 1 and 2 shall not constitute a means of arbitrary discrimination or a disguised restriction on the free movement of capital and payments as defined in Article 73b.

Article 73e

By way of derogation from Article 73b, Member States which, on 31 December 1993, enjoy a derogation on the basis of existing Community law, shall be entitled to maintain, until 31 December 1995 at the latest, restrictions on movements of capital authorized by such derogations as exist on that date.

Article 73f

Where, in exceptional circumstances, movements of capital to or from third countries cause, or threaten to cause, serious difficulties for the operation of economic and monetary union, the Council, acting by a qualified majority on a proposal from the Commission and after consulting the ECB, may take safeguard measures with regard to third countries for a period not exceeding six months if such measures are strictly necessary.

Article 73g

1.   If, in the cases envisaged in Article 228a, action by the Community is deemed necessary, the Council may, in accordance with the procedure provided for in Article 228a, take the necessary urgent measures on the movement of capital and on payments as regards the third countries concerned.

2.   Without prejudice to Article 224 and as long as the Council has not taken measures pursuant to paragraph 1, a Member State may, for serious political reasons and on grounds of urgency, take unilateral measures against a third country with regard to capital movements and payments. The Commission and the other Member States shall be informed of such measures by the date of their entry into force at the latest.

The Council may, acting by a qualified majority on a proposal from the Commission, decide that the Member State concerned shall amend or abolish such measures. The President of the Council shall inform the European Parliament of any such decision taken by the Council.

Article 73h

Until 1 January 1994, the following provisions shall be applicable:

(1)   Each Member State undertakes to authorize, in the currency of the Member State in which the creditor or the beneficiary resides, any payments connected with the movement of goods, services or capital, and any transfers of capital and earnings, to the extent that the movement of goods, services, capital and persons between Member States has been liberalized pursuant to this Treaty.

The Member States declare their readiness to undertake the liberalization of payments beyond the extent provided in the preceding subparagraph, in so far as their economic situation in general and the state of their balance of payments in particular so permit.

(2)   In so far as movements of goods, services and capital are limited only by restrictions on payments connected therewith, these restrictions shall be progressively abolished by applying, *mutatis mutandis*, the provisions of this Chapter and the Chapters relating to the abolition of quantitative restrictions and to the liberalization of services.

(3)   Member States undertake not to introduce between themselves any new restrictions on transfers connected with the invisible transactions listed in Annex III to this Treaty.

The progressive abolition of existing restrictions shall be effected in accordance with the provisions of Articles 63 to 65, in so far as such abolition is not governed by the provisions contained in points (1) and (2) or by the other provisions of this Chapter.

(4)   If need be, Member States shall consult each other on the measures to be taken to enable the payments and transfers mentioned in this Article to be effected; such measures shall not prejudice the attainment of the objectives set out in this Treaty.

TITLE V
COMMON RULES ON COMPETITION, TAXATION AND
APPROXIMATION OF LAWS[11]

CHAPTER 1
RULES ON COMPETITION

Section 1
Rules applying to undertakings

Article 85

1.   The following shall be prohibited as incompatible with the common market: all agreements between undertakings, decisions by associations of undertakings and concerted practices which may affect trade between Member States and which have as their object or effect the prevention, restriction or distortion of competition within the common market, and in particular those which:

(a)   directly or indirectly fix purchase or selling prices or any other trading conditions;

(b)   limit or control production, markets, technical development, or investment;

(c)   share markets or sources of supply;

(d)   apply dissimilar conditions to equivalent transactions with other trading parties, thereby placing them at a competitive disadvantage;

(e)   make the conclusion of contracts subject to acceptance by the other parties of supplementary obligations which, by their nature or according to commercial usage, have no connection with the subject of such contracts.

2.   Any agreements or decisions prohibited pursuant to this Article shall be automatically void.

3.   The provisions of paragraph 1 may, however, be declared inapplicable in the case of:

--   any agreement or category of agreements between undertakings:

--   any decision or category of decisions by associations of undertakings:

--   any concerted practice or category of concerted practices;

---

[11]Title introduced by Article G(17) TEU.

---

which contributes to improving the production or distribution of goods or to promoting technical or economic progress, while allowing consumers a fair share of the resulting benefit, and which does not:

(a)   impose on the undertakings concerned restrictions which are not indispensable to the attainment of these objectives;

(b)   afford such undertakings the possibility of eliminating competition in respect of a substantial part of the products in question.

Article 86

Any abuse by one or more undertakings of a dominant position within the common market or in a substantial part of it shall be prohibited as incompatible with the common market in so far as it may affect trade between Member States.

Such abuse may, in particular, consist in:

(a)   directly or indirectly imposing unfair purchase or selling prices or other unfair trading conditions;

(b)   limiting production, markets or technical development to the prejudice of consumers;

(c)   applying dissimilar conditions to equivalent transactions with other trading parties, thereby placing them at a competitive disadvantage;

(d)   making the conclusion of contracts subject to acceptance by the other parties of supplementary obligations which, by their nature or according to commercial usage, have no connection with the subject of such contracts.

Article 87

1.   Within three years of the entry into force of this Treaty the Council shall, acting unanimously on a proposal from the Commission and after consulting the European Parliament, adopt any appropriate regulations or directives to give effect to the principles set out in Articles 85 and 86.

If such provisions have not been adopted within the period mentioned, they shall be laid down by the Council, acting by a qualified majority on a proposal from the Commission and after consulting the European Parliament.

2.   The regulations or directives referred to in paragraph 1 shall be designed in particular:

(a)   to ensure compliance with the prohibitions laid down in Article 85(1) and in Article 86 by making provision for fines and periodic penalty payments;

(b) to lay down detailed rules for the application of Article 85(3), taking into account the need to ensure effective supervision on the one hand, and to simplify administration to the greatest possible extent on the other;

(c) to define, if need be, in the various branches of the economy, the scope of the provisions of Articles 85 and 86;

(d) to define the respective functions of the Commission and of the Court of Justice in applying the provisions laid down in this paragraph;

(e) to determine the relationship between national laws and the provisions contained in this Section or adopted pursuant to this Article.

Article 88

Until the entry into force of the provisions adopted in pursuance of Article 87, the authorities in Member States shall rule on the admissibility of agreements, decisions and concerted practices and on abuse of a dominant position in the common market in accordance with the law of their country and with the provisions of Article 85, in particular paragraph 3, and of Article 86.

Article 89

1. Without prejudice to Article 88, the Commission shall as soon as it takes up its duties, ensure the application of the principles laid down in Articles 85 and 86. On application by a Member State or on its own initiative, and in cooperation with the competent authorities in the Member States, who shall give it their assistance, the Commission shall investigate cases of suspected infringement of these principles. If it finds that there has been an infringement, it shall propose appropriate measures to bring it to an end.

2. If the infringement is not brought to an end, the Commission shall record such infringement of the principles in a reasoned decision. The Commission may publish its decision and authorize Member States to take the measures, the conditions and details of which it shall determine, needed to remedy the situation.

Article 90

1. In the case of public undertakings and undertakings to which Member States grant special or exclusive rights, Member States shall neither enact nor maintain in force any measure contrary to the rules contained in this Treaty, in particular to those rules provided for in Article 6 and Articles 85 to 94.

2. Undertakings entrusted with the operation of services of general economic interest or having the character of a revenue-producing monopoly shall be subject to the rules contained in this Treaty, in particular to the rules on competition, in so far as the application of such rules

does not obstruct the performance, in law or in fact, of the particular tasks assigned to them. The development of trade must not be affected to such an extent as would be contrary to the interests of the Community.

3.   The Commission shall ensure the application of the provisions of this Article and shall, where necessary, address appropriate directives or decisions to Member States.

*   *   *

AGREEMENT ON ARAB ECONOMIC UNITY[*]
[excerpts]

The Agreement on Arab Economic Unity was signed on 3 June 1957 and came into force on 30 April 1964. The original signatory States were Iraq, Jordan, Kuwait, Lebanon, Libyan Arab Jamahirija, Morocco, Saudi Arabia, Sudan, Syrian Arab Republic, Tunisia, United Arab Republic, and the Arab Republic of Yemen. Mauritania, Palestine and Somalia subsequently also became signatories to the Agreement.

The Governments of: the Hashemite Kingdom of Jordan; the Tunisian Republic; the Republic of Sudan; the Republic of Iraq; the Saudi Arabian Kingdom; the Syrian Arab Republic; the United Arab Republic; the Lebanese Republic; the United Libyan Kingdom; the Yemenite Kingdom; the Kingdom of Morocco; and the State of Kuwait;

In pursuance of their desire to organize and consolidate economic relations among the Arab League States on principles conforming with the natural and historical ties among them, and with view to creating the best conditions for the advancement for their economy, for promoting their wealths and ensuring the welfare of their peoples, have agreed on setting up a complete unity among themselves to be achieved gradually with the speed commensurate with effecting their transfer from the present to the desired situation without detriment to its vital interests, in accordance with the following stipulations:

CHAPTER I
OBJECTIVES AND METHODS

Article 1

A complete economic unity shall be established among the Arab League States. The member states and their nationals are guaranteed the following on equal footing:

1. Freedom of movement of persons and capital.

2. Freedom of exchange of domestic and foreign goods and products.

3. Freedom of transport and transit and of using means of transport, ports and civil airports.

4. Freedom of residence, work, employment and exercise of economic activities.

---

[*]Source: Council of Arab Economic Unity, General Secretariat (1957). *Agreement on Arab Economic Unity*, mimeo. [Note added by the editor].

5.   Rights of ownership, of making one's will and of inheritance.

Article 2

For attaining the unity mentioned in Article (1) the contracting states shall work for accomplishing the following:

1.   The Arab States should be made one customs zone subject to a single administration. Customs' tariffs, legislation and regulations applied in these states should be standardized.

2.   The Arab States should work for standardizing regulations thereof.

3.   Standardizing transport and transit systems.

4.   Concluding collective trade agreements and payments agreements with third countries.

5.   Co-ordinating policies related to agriculture, industry, and internal trade. Economic legislations should be standardized in a manner ensuring equal terms to all nationals of the contracting countries with respect to work in agriculture, industry, and other professions.

6.   Co-ordinating labour and social insurance legislation.

7.   a.   Co-ordinating legislation concerning government and municipal taxes and duties and all other taxes pertaining to agriculture, industry, trade, real estate, and capital investments in a manner ensuring equal opportunities.

        b.   Avoiding double taxation and duties levied on the nationals of the contracting parties.

8.   The co-ordination of monetary and fiscal policies and all regulations thereof [in] the contracting countries should be undertaken as a prerequisite for the standardization of the currency.

9.   Standardizing the methods of the classification of statistics.

10.   All necessary measures should be taken to ensure the attainment of the goals specified in Article (1) and (2) of the Agreement.

It is, however, possible to circumvent the principle of standardization in respect of certain circumstances and certain countries subject to the approval of the Council of Arab Economic Unity.

* * *

AGREEMENT ON ANDEAN SUBREGIONAL INTEGRATION*
[excerpts]

The Cartagena Agreement, creating the Andean Common Market, was signed on 26 May 1969 by Bolivia, Colombia, Chile, Ecuador, and Peru. Venezuela signed the Agreement in 1973 and Chile withdrew in 1976. The Agreement entered into force in October 1969. The Lima Protocol Amending the Cartagena Agreement on Andean Subregional Integration was signed on 30 October 1976. The version of the Cartagena Agreement reproduced in this volume reflects changes incorporated in the Agreement in accordance with the Quito Protocol of 25 May 1988 and Decision 236 of 15 July 1988, which codified these changes.

DECISION 236

Codification of the Cartagena Agreement

THE COMMISSION OF THE CARTAGENA AGREEMENT

IN VIEW OF Article 79 of the Quito Protocol and Proposal 179 of the Board;

CONSIDERING that the Quito Protocol entered into effect on May 25, 1988;

That it is necessary and suitable to have a new codification of the Cartagena Agreement and its instruments of modification -- Additional Instrument for the Adherence of Venezuela, Protocol of Lima, Protocol of Arequipa, Protocol of Quito and Decision 102 -- in order to facilitate knowledge about, the publication of and the application of the basic norms that govern the Andean subregional integration process;

DECIDES:

Article 1. Approve the codification of the Cartagena Agreement in the manner presented in the Annex to this Decision.

Article 2. This Decision substitutes Decision 147 of September 7, 1979.

Done at the city of Lima, Peru on the fifteenth day of the month of July of one thousand nine hundred eighty-eight.

---

*Source: International Legal Materials (1989). "Decision 236. Codification of the Cartagena Agreement", vol. 28, p. 1169. English translation by John R. Pate. The original Spanish text appears in Gaceta Oficial del Acuerdo de Cartagena, Year V, No. 32 (July 26, 1988) [Note added by the editor].

ANNEX

CARTAGENA AGREEMENT

Official Codified Text
1988

THE GOVERNMENTS of Bolivia, Colombia, Ecuador, Peru and Venezuela,

INSPIRED by the Declaration of Bogota and the Declaration of the Presidents of America;

RESOLVED to strengthen the union of their peoples and to establish the bases for advancing toward the formation of an Andean subregional community;

CONSCIOUS that integration constitutes an historical, political, economic, social and cultural mandate for their countries in order to preserve their sovereignty and independence;

BASED on the principles of equality, justice, peace, solidarity and democracy;

DECIDED to achieve these goals through the formation of a system of integration and cooperation that promotes an economic development that is balanced, harmonious and shared by their countries;

AGREE UPON, through their duly authorized plenipotentiary representatives, the execution of the following **SUBREGIONAL INTEGRATION AGREEMENT:**

Chapter I: Objectives and Mechanisms

Article 1

The objectives of this Agreement are to promote the balanced and harmonious development of the Member Countries under conditions of equality through integration and economic and social cooperation; accelerate their development and the generation of employment; facilitate their participation in the regional integration process, with a view to the gradual formation of a Latin American common market.

Likewise, objectives of this Agreement are to procure a reduction in external vulnerability and to improve the position of the Member Countries in the international economic context; strengthen subregional solidarity and reduce the existing differences in development among the Member Countries.

These objectives are intended to achieve a continual improvement in the standard of living of the inhabitants of the Subregion.

Article 2

The balanced and harmonious development must lead to an equitable distribution of the benefits deriving from integration among the Member Countries so as to reduce the existing differences among them. The results of this process must be evaluated periodically, taking into account, among other factors, the effects on the expansion of global exports of each country, the situation of its trade balance with the Subregion, the evolution of its gross territorial product, the generation of new employment and the formation of capital.

Article 3

In order to achieve the objectives of this Agreement the following mechanisms and measures, among others, shall be used:

(a)   The gradual harmonization of economic and social policies, and the approximation of national legislation in pertinent areas;

(b)   Joint programming, intensification of the subregional industrialization process and the execution of industrial programs and other means of industrial integration;

(c)   A Liberation Program for commercial interchange that is more advanced than the commitments deriving from the Montevideo Treaty of 1980;

(d)   A Common External Tariff the previous stage of which shall be the adoption of a Minimum Common External Tariff;

(e)   Programs to accelerate the development of the agricultural and agroindustrial sectors;

(f)   The channeling of internal and external resources to the Subregion in order to provide financing for the investments that are necessary for the integration process;

(g)   Physical integration; and

(h)   Preferential treatment for Bolivia and Ecuador.

Complementary to the preceding mechanisms, the following programs, and economic and social cooperation efforts shall be advanced as mutually agreed upon:

(a)   External efforts in the economic field in areas of mutual interest;

(b)   Programs intended to stimulate scientific and technological development;

(c)   Efforts in the area of frontier integration;

(d)   Programs in the tourism area;

(e)   Efforts for the rational exploitation and conservation of natural resources and the environment;

(f)   Programs in the service area;

(g)   Social development programs; and

(h)   Efforts in the area of social communication.

Chapter III: Harmonization of Economic Policies and Coordination of Development Plans

Article 25

The Member Countries shall progressively adopt a strategy for achieving the development objectives of the Subregion contemplated in this Agreement.

Article 26

The Member Countries shall coordinate their development plans in specific sectors and shall gradually harmonize their economic and social policies, with a view to achieving the integrated development of the area through planned efforts.

This process shall be fulfilled parallel to and in coordination with the formation of the subregional market through the following mechanisms, among others:

(a)   Industrial Development Programs;

(b)   Agricultural and Agroindustrial Development Programs;

(c)   Physical Infrastructure Development Programs;

(d)   The harmonization of exchange, monetary, financial and fiscal policies, including the treatment accorded to subregional and foreign capital;

(e)   A common commercial policy vis-a-vis third countries; and

(f)   The harmonization of planning methods and techniques.

Article 27

Prior to December 31, 1970 the Commission, upon the proposal of the Board, shall approve and submit for the consideration of the Member Countries a common code for the treatment of foreign investment and, among others, on trademarks, patents, licenses and royalties.

The Member Countries agree to adopt the measures necessary to put this code into effect within the six months following its approval by the Commission.

Article 28

Prior to December 31, 1971 the Commission, upon the proposal of the Board, shall approve and propose to the Member Countries the uniform code to govern Andean multinational enterprises.

Chapter IV: Industrial Development Programs

Article 32

The Member Countries agree to promote a joint industrial development process in order to achieve, among others, the following objectives:

(a)   The expansion, specialization, diversification and promotion of industrial activities;

(b)   To take advantage of economies of scale;

(c)   Optimize the utilization of available resources in the area, especially through the industrialization of natural resources;

(d)   Improve productivity;

(e)   A greater degree of relations, ties and complementation among the industrial enterprises of the subregion;

(f)   The equitable distribution of benefits; and

(g)   A greater participation of subregional industry in the international context.

Article 33

For the purposes indicated in the preceding article the mechanisms of industrial integration are the following:

(a)   Industrial Integration Programs;

(b)   Industrial Complementation Agreements; and

(c)   Industrial Integration Projects.

Section A -- Industrial Integration Programs

Article 34

The Commission, upon the proposal of the Board, shall adopt Industrial Integration Programs, preferably to promote new sectoral or intersectoral industrial production involving the participation of, at least, four Member Countries.

These programs must contain provisions on

(a)   Specific Objectives;

(b)   Identification of the products of the Program;

(c)   Location of plants in the countries of the subregion when the characteristics of the sector or sectors so require, in which case norms must be included regarding the commitment not to encourage production in those countries not receiving the assignment;

(d)   Liberation Program, which may contemplate different schedules by country and by product;

(e)   Common External Tariff;

(f)   Coordination of new investments at the subregional level and measures to assure their financing;

(g)   Harmonization of policies in those areas that directly affect the Program;

(h)   Complementary measures that stimulate greater industrial ties and that facilitate the fulfillment of the objectives of the Program; and

(i)   The periods for which the rights and obligations arising from the Program must be maintained in the event of a renunciation of the Agreement.

Section B -- Industrial Complementation Agreements

Article 37

The object of Industrial Complementation Agreements shall be to promote industrial specialization among the Member Countries. They may be entered into and executed by two or more countries. These Agreements must be communicated to the Commission.

For the purposes indicated in the preceding paragraph, these Agreements may contain measures such as the distribution of production, co-production, subcontracting production capacity, marketing agreements and joint foreign trade operations, and others that facilitate more intensive productive processes and entrepreneurial activity.

Industrial Complementation Agreements shall be temporary by nature and, in addition to the determination of the products included in them and the period of application of the rights and obligations of the participating Member Countries, they may contain special measures with respect to tariff treatment, trade regulations and the establishment of preferential margins that are not extensive to the nonparticipating countries, provided that said measures create equal or better conditions that those existing for reciprocal trade. In this case, the tariffs applicable to third countries shall be determined.

Section C -- Industrial Integration Projects

Article 40

The Commission, upon the proposal of the Board, shall approve Industrial Integration Projects, which shall be executed with respect to preferably new specific products or families of products by means of collective cooperative actions and with the participation of all the Member Countries.

The following measures among others, shall be begun for the execution of these projects:

(a)   Undertaking of feasibility and design studies;

(b)   Supply of equipment, technical assistance, technology and other goods and services, preferably of subregional origin;

(c)   Support from the Andean Development Corporation through financing or equity participation; and

(d)   Joint contacts and negotiations with entrepreneurs and international governmental agencies for obtaining external resources and the transfer of technology.

Industrial Integration Projects shall include provisions regarding the location of plants in the Member Countries when the corresponding characteristics of the sector or sectors so require and they may include provisions intended to facilitate the access of products to the subregional market.

In the case of specific projects located in Bolivia or Ecuador, the Commission shall establish temporary, non-extensive tariff treatment that improves and the conditions for the access of said products to the subregional market. Regarding those products not produced, if these are included in this scheme, they shall contemplate exceptions to the principle of irrevocability of the first paragraph of Article 45.

Section D -- Other Provisions

Article 40A

In applying the different schemes of industrial integration the Commission and the Board shall take into account the situation and requirements of small and medium industries, particularly those regarding the following aspects:

(a) The installed capacity of existing companies;

(b) The requirements for financial and technical assistance for the installation, expansion, modernization or conversion of plants;

(c) The prospects for establishing joint systems for commercialization, technological investigation and other forms of cooperation among like enterprises; and

(d) The requirements for labor training.

Article 40B

The industrial integration schemes may contemplate actions related to industrial rationalization, with a view to achieving the optimum utilization of productive factors and achieving greater levels of productivity and efficiency.

Article 40C

The Board may undertake or promote cooperation efforts, including those of industrial rationalization and modernization, on behalf of any activity of this sector and, especially, for the small and medium industries of the Subregion, for the purpose of assisting with the industrial development of the Member Countries. These efforts shall be carried out on a priority basis in Bolivia and Ecuador.

Chapter V: Liberation Program

Article 41

The objective of the Liberation Program is to eliminate the charges and restrictions of any nature affecting the importation of products that originate in the territory of any Member Country.

Article 42

By "charges" shall be understood customs duties and any other fees of like effect, whether of a tax, monetary or foreign exchange nature that affect imports. Not included in this category are fees and other analogous charges when they correspond to the approximate cost of the services provided.

The term "restrictions of any nature" shall mean any measure of an administrative, financial or foreign exchange nature by which a Member Country impedes or creates difficulties for imports by unilateral decision. Not contemplated in this concept are the adoption of and compliance with measures intended to

(a)   Protect public morality;

(b)   Apply laws and regulations related to security;

(c)   Regulate the importation or exportation of arms, munitions and other materials of war and, under exceptional circumstances, all other types of military items, provided that they do not interfere with treaties on unrestricted, free transit in effect among the Member Countries;

(d)   Protect the lives and health of people, animals and vegetable products;

(e)   Importation and exportation of metallic gold and silver;

(f)   Protect the national assets of artistic, historical or archaeological value; and

(g)   Export, utilize and consume nuclear materials, radioactive products and any other material used in the development and exploitation of nuclear energy.

Article 44

With respect to domestic taxes, fees and other charges, products that originate in a Member Country shall enjoy in the territory of another Member Country a treatment no less favorable than that applied to similar national products.

Article 45

The Liberation Program shall be automatic and irrevocable, and shall include the universe of products, except for the provisions of exception established in this Agreement, in order to achieve total liberation in the periods and under the mechanisms indicated in this Agreement.

This Program shall be applied, through its different mechanisms, to

(a)   Products included in Industrial Integration Programs;

(b)   Products included in the Common List indicated in Article 4 of the Treaty of Montevideo of 1960;

(c)   Products not produced in any country of the Subregion and that are included in the corresponding list; and

(d)   Products not included in any of the preceding categories.

Chapter VIII: Commercial Competition

Article 75

Before December 31, 1971 the Commission shall adopt, upon the proposal of the board, the norms essential for preventing or correcting practices that may distort competition within the Subregion, such as dumping, improper price manipulation, actions intended to interfere with the normal supply of raw materials and others of an equivalent effect. In this regard the Commission shall contemplate the difficulties that may derive from the application of charges and other restrictions on exports.

The Board shall be responsible for monitoring the application of said norms in the particular cases that are denounced.

Chapter IX: Safeguard Clauses

Article 78

A Member Country that has adopted measures to correct an imbalance in its global balance of payments may extend said measures, upon the prior authorization of the Board, temporarily and in a nondiscriminatory manner, to the intrasubregional trade of products incorporated in the Liberation Program.

The Member Countries shall endeavor not to affect trade within the Subregion of products incorporated in the Liberation Program when imposing restrictions by virtue of balance of payments situations.

When the situation contemplated in this article requires immediate action, the affected Member Country may, on an emergency basis, apply the measures contemplated; it must then communicate them immediately to the Board, which shall issue its ruling within the following thirty days as to whether to authorize, modify or suspend them.

If the application of the measures contemplated in this article is extended for more than one year, the Board shall propose to the Commission, on its own initiative or at the request of any Member Country, the immediate initiation of negotiations intended to attempt to eliminate the restrictions adopted.

Article 79

If the compliance with the Liberation Program of the Agreement causes or threatens to cause grave prejudice to the economy of a Member Country or to a significant sector of its economy, said country may, upon the prior authorization of the Board, apply corrective measures of a temporary nature and in a nondiscriminatory manner. When necessary the Board shall propose to the Commission measures of collective cooperation intended to overcome such difficulties.

The Board shall periodically analyze the evolution of the situation with a view to preventing the restrictive measures from being prolonged beyond the period strictly necessary or to consider new formulas for cooperation, if appropriate.

When the prejudice referred to in this article is so grave as to require immediate action, the affected Member Country may provisionally apply corrective measures of an emergency nature, subject to the subsequent ruling of the Board.

Said measures must cause the least possible prejudice to the Liberation Program and, while they are applied unilaterally, they may not signify a reduction in the importation of the product or products involved based on the average of the preceding 12 months.

The Member Country that adopts such measures must communicate them immediately to the Board and the Board shall decide within the following 30 days, regarding whether to authorize, modify or suspend them.

Article 79A

Whenever there are imports of products originating in the Subregion in quantities or in conditions that cause harm for the national production of specific products of a Member Country, said country may apply corrective, nondiscriminatory measures of a provisional nature, subject to the subsequent ruling of the Board.

The Member Country applying corrective measures must communicate them to the Board in a term of not more than sixty days and present a report regarding its reasons for such application. The Board, within the term of sixty days following the date of receipt of said report, shall verify the harm and the origin of the imports causing it, and shall issue its ruling as to whether to suspend, modify or authorize said measures, which may only be applied to the products of the Member Country in which the harm originated. The corrective measures applied must assure a trade flow that is not less than the average of the preceding three years.

Article 80

If a monetary devaluation undertaken by one of the Member Countries alters the normal conditions of competition, the country that considers itself prejudiced may present its case to the board, which shall decide promptly and summarily. If the harm is verified by the Board, the prejudiced country may adopt corrective measures of a temporary nature for as long as the variation persists, within the recommendations of the Board. In any event, said measures may not signify a reduction of import levels existing prior to the devaluation.

Without prejudice to the application of the referred to temporary measures, any of the Member Countries may request the Commission to definitively decide on the matter.

The Member Country that devalued may request the Board, at any time, to review the situation in order to relax or suppress the referred to corrective measures. The ruling of the Board may be amended by the Commission.

In the situations contemplated in this article the country that considers that it is being prejudiced, at the time of presenting its case to the Board, may propose protective measures proportionate to the magnitude of the alleged variation, accompanying its request with the technical data on which it is based. The Board may request such complementary information as it deems appropriate.

The brief and summary decision of the Board must be issued within the term of one month from the date of receipt of the request. If the Board does not decide in this period and the requesting country considers that the delay in the decision may cause it harm, it may adopt the initial measures proposed by it, immediately communicating this fact to the Board, which in its subsequent ruling must decide about maintaining, modifying or suspending the measures applied.

In its ruling the Board shall take into account, among other factors, the economic indicators related to the conditions of commercial competition in the Subregion that the Commission has adopted of a general nature, upon the proposal of the Board, the particular characteristics of the exchange systems of the Member Countries and the studies that in this respect are undertaken by the Monetary and Foreign Exchange Council.

Until the adoption of the system of economic indicators by the Commission, the Board shall proceed based on its own criteria.

Notwithstanding that provided in the preceding paragraphs, if during the period between the referred to presentation and the ruling of the Board in the judgment of the requesting Member Country there exist precedents that justify fears that as a consequence of the devaluation immediate harm will be caused of the indicated gravity for its economy, thereby requiring on an emergency basis the adoption of protective measures, it may present this situation to the Board which, if it considers the request well founded, may authorize the application of adequate measures, for which it shall have a period of seven continuous days. The definitive ruling of the Board on the variation of normal conditions of competition shall determine, in any case, the continuation, modification or suspension of the authorized emergency measures.

The measures adopted in accordance with this article may not signify a reduction of trade flows existing prior to the devaluation.

With respect to all of these measures the provisions of the second and third paragraphs of this article shall be fully applicable.

Article 81

No safeguard clauses of any type shall be applied to imports of products originating in the Subregion included in Industrial Integration Programs and Projects.

Chapter X: Origin

Article 82

The Commission, upon the proposal of the Board, shall adopt the special norms that are necessary for qualifying the origin of goods. These norms must constitute a dynamic instrument for the development of the Subregion and be adequate to facilitate the achievement of the objectives of the Agreement.

Chapter XI: Physical Integration

Article 86

The Member Countries shall develop joint efforts to achieve a better exploitation of their physical space, improve the infrastructure and the services necessary for advancing the economic integration process of the Subregion. This action shall be undertaken principally in the areas of energy, transportation and communications, and shall include the measures necessary in order to facilitate frontier traffic among the Member Countries.

For this purpose, the Member Countries shall stimulate the establishment of entities or companies of a multinational nature, when this is possible and suitable in order to facilitate the execution and administration of said projects.

Chapter XII: Financial Aspects

Article 89

The Member Countries shall execute programs and coordinate their policies in financial and payment matters to the extent necessary to facilitate achieving the objectives of the Agreement.

For these purposes, the Commission, upon the proposal of the Board, shall adopt the following measures:

(a)   Recommendations for channeling financial resources through pertinent entities for the development requirements of the Subregion;

(b)   Promotion of investments for Andean integration programs;

(c)   Financing trade between the Member Countries and with those outside of the Subregion;

(d)   Measures that facilitate the flow of capital within the Subregion and particularly the promotion of Andean multinational enterprises;

(e)   Coordination of positions for strengthening the reciprocal payments and credit mechanisms in the context of LAIA;

(f)   Establishing an Andean system for finance and payments that includes the Andean Reserve Fund, a common unit of account, trade financing lines, a subregional compensation clearinghouse and a system of reciprocal credits;

(g)   Cooperation and coordination of positions regarding foreign financial problems of the Member Countries; and

(h)   Coordination with the Andean Development Corporation and the Andean Reserve Fund for the purposes contemplated in the preceding provisions.

Article 90

If as a result of compliance with the Liberation Program of the Agreement a member Country suffers difficulties related to fiscal income, the Board may propose to the Commission, upon the request of the affected country, measures to resolve said problems. In its proposals, the Board shall take into account the relative degrees of economic development of the Member Countries.

Chapter XIII: Special Norms for Bolivia and Ecuador

Section A -- Harmonization of Economic Policies and Coordination of Development Plans

Article 92

With respect to the harmonization of economic and social policies, and the coordination of the plans referred to in Chapter III, a differential treatment and sufficient incentives to compensate the structural deficiencies of Bolivia and Ecuador, and assure the availability and allocation of the resources essential for fulfilling the objectives contemplated for them in the Agreement must be established.

Chapter XIV: Economic and Social Cooperation

Article 108

The Member Countries may undertake programs and actions in the area of economic and social cooperation, which must be agreed upon by the Commission and shall be limited to that contemplated in this Agreement.

Article 108A

The Member Countries shall undertake actions at the international level in areas of common interest for the purpose of improving their participation in the international economy.

Article 108B

For the purposes contemplated in the preceding article, the Commission shall adopt programs to orient the joint external efforts of the Member Countries, particularly with respect to negotiations with third countries and groups of countries, as well as for the participation in forums and specialized organizations in areas related to the international economy.

Article 108C

The Member Countries shall promote a joint process of scientific and technological development in order to achieve the following objectives:

(a)   Creation of subregional capabilities responsive to the challenges of the present scientific-technological revolution;

(b)   Contribution of science and technology to the conceptualization and execution of strategies and programs for Andean development; and

(c)   Utilization of the mechanisms of economic integration to stimulate technological innovation and productive modernization.

Article 108D

For the purposes indicated in the preceding article, the Member Countries shall adopt in fields of common interest:

(a)   Programs for cooperation and joint efforts in scientific and technological development that at the subregional level can be more efficacious for preparing human resources and obtaining research results;

(b)   Technological development programs that contribute to achieving solutions to common problems of the productive sectors; and

(c)   Programs to take advantage of the expanded market and the joint physical, human and financial capabilities to propitiate technological development in sectors of common interest.

Article 108E

The Member Countries shall undertake actions to stimulate the integral development of the frontier regions and to effectively incorporate them into the national and Andean subregional economies.

Article 108F

In the field of tourism, the Member Countries shall develop joint programs intended to achieve a greater knowledge of the Subregion and to stimulate economic activities related to this sector.

Article 108G

The Member Countries shall undertake joint actions that permit a greater utilization of their renewable and nonrenewable natural resources, and the conservation and improvement of the environment.

Article 108H

The Member Countries shall undertake cooperation projects in the area of services. In this regard the Commission shall adopt programs and projects in selected areas of the service sector, defining in each case the mechanisms and instruments to be applied.

*   *   *

TREATY ESTABLISHING THE CARIBBEAN COMMUNITY*
[excerpts]

The Treaty Establishing the Caribbean Community was signed in Chaguaramas, Trinidad and Tobago, on 4 July 1973 and entered into force on 1 August 1973. Member States of the Caribbean Common Market (CARICOM) are Antigua and Barbuda, the Bahamas, Barbados, Belize, Dominica, Grenada, Guyana, Jamaica, Montserrat, Saint Kitts and Nevis, Saint Lucia, Saint Vincent and the Grenadines, Trinidad and Tobago.

ANNEX TO THE TREATY
THE CARIBBEAN COMMON MARKET

Chapter I: PRINCIPLES

Article 3
Objectives of the Common Market

The Common Market shall have as its objectives:

(a)   the strengthening, co-ordination and regulation of the economic and trade relations among Member States in order to promote their accelerated harmonious and balanced development;

(b)   the sustained expansion and continuing integration of economic activities, the benefits of which shall be equitably shared taking into account the need to provide special opportunities for the Less Developed Countries;

(c)   the achievement of a greater measure of economic independence and effectiveness of its Member States in dealing with states, groups of states and entities of whatever description.

Chapter III: TRADE LIBERALISATION

Article 30
Restrictive Business Practices

1.   Member States recognize that the following practices are incompatible with this Annex in so far as they frustrate the benefits expected from such removal or absence of duties and

---

*Source: Caribbean Common Market Secretariat (1973). *Treaty Establishing the Caribbean Community* (Georgetown: Caribbean Community Secretariat) [Note added by the editor].

43

quantitative restrictions as is required by this Annex:

(a)   agreements between enterprises, decisions by associations of enterprises and concerted practices between enterprises which have as their object or result the prevention, restriction or distortion of competition within the Common Market;

(b)   actions by which one or more enterprises take unfair advantage of a dominant position within the Common Market or a substantial part of it.

2.   If any practice of the kind described in paragraph 1 of this Article is referred to the Council in accordance with Article 11 of this Annex the Council may, in any recommendation in accordance with paragraph 3 or in any decision in accordance with paragraph 4 of that Article, make provision for publication of a report on the circumstances of the matter.

3.   (a)   In the light off experience, the Council shall, as soon as practicable, consider whether further or different provisions are necessary to deal with the effect of restrictive business practices or dominant enterprises on the trade within the Common Market.

(b)   Such review shall include consideration of the following matters:

(i)   specification of restrictive business practices or dominant enterprises with which the Council should be concerned;

(ii)   methods of securing information about restrictive business practices or dominant enterprises;

(iii)   procedures for investigation;

(iv)   whether the right to initiate inquiries should be conferred on the Council.

(c)   The Council may decide to make the provisions found necessary as a result of the review envisaged in sub-paragraphs (a) and (b) of this paragraph.

4.   Member States undertake to introduce as soon as practicable uniform legislation for the control of restrictive practices by business enterprises giving particular attention to the practices referred to in paragraph 1 of this Article.

Chapter V: ESTABLISHMENT, SERVICES, AND MOVEMENT OF CAPITAL

Article 35
Establishment

1.   Each Member State recognises that restrictions on the establishment and operation of economic enterprises therein by nationals of other Member States should not be applied, through

accord to such persons of treatment which is less favourable than that accorded in such matters to nationals of that Member State, in such a way as to frustrate the benefits expected from such removal or absence of duties and quantitative restrictions as is required by this Annex.

2.   Member States shall not apply new restrictions in such a way that they conflict with the principle set out in paragraph 1 of this Article.

3.   A Member State shall notify the Council within such period as the Council may decide of particulars of any restrictions which it applies in such a way that persons belonging to another Member State are accorded in the first-mentioned State less favourable treatment in respect of the matters set out in paragraph 1 of this Article than is accorded to persons belonging thereto.

4.   The Council shall consider from time to time, whether further or different provisions are necessary to give effect to the principles set out in paragraph 1 of this Article.

5.   Nothing in this Article shall prevent the adoption and enforcement by a Member State of measures for the control of entry, residence, activity and departure of persons where such measures are justified by reasons of public order, public health or morality, or national security of that Member State.

6.   For the purposes of this Article and Articles 36 and 38 of this Annex:

(a)   a person shall be regarded as a national of a Member State if such person

(i)   is a citizen of that State;

(ii)   has a connection with that State of a kind which entitles him to be regarded as belonging to, or, if it be so expressed, as being a native or resident of the State for purposes of such laws thereof relating to immigration as are for the time being in force; or

(iii)   is a company or other legal person constituted in the Member State in conformity with the law thereof and which that State regards as belonging to it, provided that such company or other legal person has been formed for gainful purposes and has its registered office and central administration, and carries on substantial activity, within the Common Market and which is substantially owned and effectively controlled by persons falling under (i) and (ii) above.

(b)   "economic enterprises" means any type of economic enterprises for production of or commerce in goods which are of Common Market origin, whether conducted by individuals or through agencies, branches or companies or other legal persons.

Article 36

Right to Provide Services

1.　　Each Member State agrees as far as practicable to extend to persons belonging to other Member States preferential treatment over persons belonging to States outside the Common Market with regard to the provision of services.

2.　　For the purposes of this Article the term "services" shall be considered as services for remuneration provided that they are not governed by provisions relating to trade, the right of establishment or movement of capital and includes, in particular, activities of an industrial or commercial character, artisan activities and activities of the professions, excluding activities of employed persons.

Article 37

Movement of Capital

The Council shall examine ways and means for the introduction of a scheme for the regulated movement of capital within the Common Market, giving particular attention to the development needs of the Less Developed Countries and shall recommend to Member States proposals for the establishment of such a scheme.

Article 38

Saving in respect of Movement of Persons

Nothing in this Treaty shall be construed as requiring, or imposing any obligation on a Member State to grant freedom of movement in persons into its territory whether or not such persons are nationals of other Member States of the Common Market.

Chapter VI: CO-ORDINATION OF ECONOMIC POLICIES AND DEVELOPMENT PLANNING

Article 39

Consultation on Economic Policies

1.　　Member States recognise that the economic and financial policies of each of them affect the economies of other Member States and intend to pursue those policies in a manner which serves to promote the objectives of the Common Market. In particular but without prejudice to the generality of the foregoing, Member States shall seek as far as practicable to:

　　(i)　　co-ordinate their economic policies and for this purpose facilitate collaboration between appropriate ministries, administrative departments and agencies;

　　(ii)　　co-ordinate their statistical services in matters affecting the operation of the Common Market; and

(iii) co-ordinate their positions and presentations at all international economic, financial and trade meetings at which they are represented.

2. The Council may make recommendations to Member States on matters relating to those policies and on how best to achieve such co-ordination and collaboration.

Article 40
Harmonisation of Fiscal Incentives

1. Member States shall seek to harmonise such legislation and practices as directly affect fiscal incentives to industry.

2. Member States shall seek also to establish regimes for the harmonisation of fiscal incentives to agriculture and tourism with appropriate differentials in favour of the Less Developed Countries.

3. Member States agree to study the possibility of approximating income tax systems and rates with respect to companies and individuals.

Article 41
Intra-Regional and Extra-Regional Double Taxation Agreements

1. Member States shall approach their negotiations for agreements for the avoidance of double taxation with countries outside the Common Market on the basis of a set of mutually agreed principles.

2. With a view to encouraging the regulated movement of capital within the Common Market, particularly to the Less Developed Countries, Member States agree to adopt among themselves agreements for the avoidance of double taxation.

Article 42
Harmonisation of Laws

1. Member States recognise the desirability to harmonise as soon as practicable such provisions imposed by law or administrative practices as effect the establishment and operation of the Common Market in the following areas:

    (a)   companies;
    (b)   trade marks;
    (c)   patents;
    (d)   designs and copyrights;
    (e)   industrial standards;
    (f)   marks of origin;
    (g)   labelling of food and drugs;
    (h)   plant and animal quarantine restrictions;

       (i)   restrictive business practices;

       (j)   dumping and subsidisation of exports.

2.   The Council shall keep the provisions of this Article under review and may make recommendations for the achievement of this objective.

Article 43
Monetary, Payments and Exchange-Rate Policies

1.   Member States undertake to permit within the Common Market freedom of payments on:

    (a)   current account; and

    (b)   capital account

necessary to further the objectives of the Common Market.

2.   Member States recognising that exchange-rate stability as between themselves is necessary to promote the smooth functioning of the Common Market agree to:

    (a)   a policy of continuing consultation and the fullest possible exchange of relevant information on monetary payments and exchange-rate matters, and

    (b)   to examine ways and means of harmonising their monetary and exchange-rate and payment policies in the interest of the smooth functioning of the Common Market.

3.   Member States further agree:

    (a)   to the policy whereby through arrangements by their Central Banks or Monetary Authorities the notes and coins of other Member States shall be exchanged within their own States at official par value without exchange commission;

    (b)   to develop arrangements for co-operation in other monetary matters including the operation of a clearing arrangement by their Central Monetary Authorities.

Article 44
Ownership and Control of Regional Resources

1.   Member States recognise the need for continuing inflows of extra-regional capital and the urgent necessity to promote development in the Less Developed Countries.

2.   Member States shall keep under review the question of ownership and control of their resources with a view to increasing the extent of national participation in their economies and working towards the adoption as far as possible of a common policy on foreign investment.

Article 45
Co-ordination of National Development Planning

1.   Member States recognise the desirability of a long-term Common Market Perspective Plan as a framework for co-ordinating their development efforts and agree to work jointly in the formulation of such a Plan.

2.   In order to promote maximum complementarity between industries and economic sectors of Member States, each Member State agrees to consult with other Member States in drawing up its national medium-term operational development plans. Member States shall establish a Committee of Officials in charge of national planning agencies for the purpose of promoting collaboration in development planning.

Article 46
Common Market Industrial Programming

1.   Member States undertake to promote a process of industrial development through industrial programming aimed at achieving the following objectives:

   (a)   the greater utilisation of the raw materials of the Common Market;

   (b)   the creation of production linkages both within and between the national economies of the Common Market;

   (c)   to minimise product differentiation and achieve economies of large scale production, consistent with the limitations of market size;

   (d)   the encouragement of greater efficiency in industrial production;

   (e)   the promotion of exports to markets both within and outside the Common Market;

   (f)   an equitable distribution of the benefits of industrialisation paying particular attention to the need to locate more industries in the Less Developed States.

2.   The Council may make recommendations from time to time to promote achievement of the objectives stated in paragraph 1 of this Article.

Article 47
Joint Development of Natural Resources

1.   Member States agree to a policy of regular exchange of information on their natural resources with a view to the development of joint projects for the increased utilisation of these resources within the Common Market and to collaborate in promoting research in these areas.

2.   With a view to facilitating negotiations with mining companies, Member States agree to

exchange information on exploration leases, exploitation licences and on taxation of mining companies.

3. The Council advised by the Standing Committee of Ministers responsible for Mines and Natural Resources may make recommendations for achieving the objectives stated in paragraphs 1 and 2 of this Article.

Chapter VII: SPECIAL REGIME FOR THE LESS DEVELOPED COUNTRIES

Article 59
Financial Assistance from More Developed Countries

1. With a view to promoting the flow of investment capital to the Less Developed Countries, the More Developed Countries agree to co-operate in:

   (a) facilitating, whether by means of private investment capital or otherwise, joint ventures in those States;

   (b) negotiating double taxation agreements in respect of the income from investments in the Less Developed Countries by residents of other Member States; and

   (c) facilitating the flow of loan capital to the Less Developed Countries.

2. In furtherance of the objectives stated in paragraph 1 above, primary consideration should be given to ventures which are substantially owned and effectively controlled by nationals of Member States within the meaning of Article 35 of this Annex.

3. Member States agree that in order to promote the development of industries in the Less Developed Countries an appropriate investment institution shall be established.

* * *

TREATY ESTABLISHING THE LATIN AMERICAN INTEGRATION ASSOCIATION (LAIA)* [excerpts]

The Treaty of Montevideo Establishing the Latin American Integration Association was signed on 12 August 1980. It entered into force on 18 March 1981, replacing the Treaty that created the Latin American Free Trade Association (1960). The member States of the Latin American Integration Association are Argentina, Bolivia, Brazil, Chile, Colombia, Ecuador, Mexico, Paraguay, Peru, Uruguay and Venezuela.

The Governments of the Argentine Republic, the Republic of Bolivia, the Federative Republic of Brazil, the Republic of Chile, the Republic of Colombia, the Republic of Ecuador, the United Mexican States, the Republic of Paraguay, the Republic of Peru, the Eastern Republic of Uruguay, and the Republic of Venezuela,

INSPIRED by the purpose of strengthening the friendship and solidarity links between their peoples.

PERSUADED that economic regional integration is one of the principal means for the Latin American countries to speed up their economic and social development process in order to ensure better standards of life for their peoples.

DECIDED to renew the Latin American integration process and establish objectives and mechanisms consistent with the region's real situation.

CERTAIN that the continuation of such process requires taking advantage of the positive experience obtained in the implementation of the Montevideo Treaty dated 18 February 1960.

AWARE that it is necessary to ensure a special treatment for countries at a relatively less advanced stage of economic development.

WILLING to encourage the development of solidarity and cooperation ties with other countries and integration areas of Latin America in order to promote a process converging towards the establishment of a regional common market.

---

*Source: LAFTA Secretariat (1981). *1980 Montevideo Treaty: Instrument Establishing the Latin American Integration Association (LAIA)*, (Montevideo: LAFTA Secretariat) [Note added by the editor].

CONVINCED of the need to contribute towards obtaining a new scheme of horizontal cooperation between developing countries and their integration areas, inspired by the principles of international law regarding development.

BEARING IN MIND the decision adopted by the Contracting Parties to the General Agreement on Tariffs and Trade whereby regional or general agreements may be drawn up between developing countries in order to mutually reduce or eliminate obstacles to their reciprocal trade,

THEY HEREBY AGREE to sign the present Treaty which, concurrent with the provisions herein contained, shall substitute the Treaty instituting the Latin American Free Trade Association.

CHAPTER I
Objectives, duties and principles

Article 1

By the present Treaty the Contracting Parties pursue the integration process leading to promote the harmonious and balanced socio-economic development of the region, and to that effect they hereby institute the Latin American Integration Association (hereinafter referred to as the "Association"), with headquarters in the city of Montevideo, Eastern Republic of Uruguay.

The long-term objective of such process shall be the gradual and progressive establishment of a Latin American common market.

Article 2

The rules and mechanisms of the present Treaty, as well as those which may be established within its framework by member countries, shall have as their purpose the performance of the following basic duties of the Association: promotion and regulation of reciprocal trade, economic complementation, and development of economic cooperation actions encouraging market expansion.

Article 3

In the implementation of the present Treaty and the evolution towards its final objective, member countries shall bear in mind the following principles:

a)   Pluralism, sustained by the will of member countries to integrate themselves, over and above the diversity which might exist in political and economic matters in the region;

b)   Convergence, meaning progressive multilateralization of partial scope agreements by means of periodical negotiations between member countries, with a view to establish the Latin American common market;

c) Flexibility, characterized by the capacity to allow the conclusion of partial scope agreements, ruled in a form consistent with the progressive attainment of their convergence and the strengthening of integration ties;

d) Differential treatments, as determined in each case, both in regional and partial scope mechanisms, on the basis of three categories of countries, which will be set up taking into account their economic-structural characteristics. Such treatments shall be applied in a determined scale to intermediate developed countries, and in a more favorable manner to countries at a relatively less advanced stage of economic development; and

e) Multiple, to make possible various forms of agreements between member countries, following the objectives and duties of the integration process, using all instruments capable of activating and expanding markets at regional level.

CHAPTER II
Mechanisms

Article 4

In order to fulfill the basic duties of the Association set forth in article 2 of the present Treaty, member countries hereby establish an area of economic preferences, comprising a regional tariff preference, regional scope agreements, and partial scope agreements.

Second section - Regional scope agreements

Article 6

Regional scope agreements are those in which all member countries participate.

They shall be drawn up within the framework of the objectives and provisions of the present Treaty, and may refer to the same matters and include those instruments foreseen for the partial scope agreements provided for in the third section of the present chapter.

Third section - Partial scope agreements

Article 7

Partial scope agreements are those wherein all member countries do not participate. These agreements shall tend to create the conditions necessary to deepen the regional integration process by means of their progressive multilateralization.

Rights and obligations to be established in partial scope agreements shall exclusively bind the signatory member countries or those adhered thereto.

Article 8

Partial scope agreements may refer to trade, economic complementation, agriculture, trade promotion, or adopt other modalities concurring with article 14 of the present Treaty.

Article 9

Partial scope agreements shall be governed by the following general rules:

a) They shall be open for accession to the other member countries, prior negotiation;

b) They shall contain clauses promoting convergence in order that their benefits reach all member countries;

c) They may contain clauses promoting convergence with other Latin American countries, in concurrence with the mechanisms established in the present Treaty;

d) They shall include differential treatments depending on the three categories of countries recognized by the present Treaty. The implementation of such treatments as well as negotiation procedures for their periodical revision at the request of any member country which may consider itself at a disadvantage shall be determined in each agreement;

e) Tariff reductions may be applied to the same products or tariff sub-items and on the basis of a percentage rebate regarding the tariffs applied to imports originating from non-participating countries;

f) They shall be in force for a minimum term of one year; and

g) They may include, among others, specific rules regarding origin, safeguard clauses, non-tariff restrictions, withdrawal of concessions, renegotiation of concessions, denouncement, coordination and harmonization of policies. Should these specific rules not have been adopted, the general provisions to be established by member countries on the respective matters shall be taken into account.

Article 10

Trade agreements are exclusively aimed towards trade promotion among member countries, and shall be subject to the specific rules to be established for that purpose.

Article 11

Economic complementation agreements are aimed, among other objectives, to promote maximum utilization of production factors, stimulate economic complementation, ensure equitable conditions for competition, facilitate entry of products into the international market, and encourage the balanced and harmonious development of member countries.

These agreements shall be subject to the specific rules to be established for that purpose.

Article 12

Agricultural agreements are aimed to promote and regulate intraregional trade of agricultural and livestock products. They shall contemplate flexibility elements bearing in mind the participating countries' socio-economic characteristics of production. These agreements may refer to specific products or groups of products, and may be based on temporary, seasonal, per quota or mixed concessions, or on contracts between State or para-State organizations. They shall be subject to the specific rules to be established for that purpose.

Article 13

Trade promotion agreements shall refer to non-tariff matters and tend to promote intraregional trade flows. They shall be subject to the specific rules to be established for that purpose.

Article 14

Member countries may establish, through the corresponding regulations, specific rules to conclude other modalities of partial scope agreements.

For this purpose, they shall take into consideration, among other matters, scientific and technological cooperation, tourism promotion and preservation of the environment.

Chapter III
System in favor of countries at a relatively
less advanced stage of economic development

Article 15

Member countries shall establish conditions favoring participation of countries at a relatively less advanced stage of economic development in the economic integration process, based on the principles of non-reciprocity and community cooperation.

Article 16

For the purpose of ensuring them an effective preferential treatment, member countries shall establish market openings as well as set up programs and other specific forms of cooperation.

Article 17

Actions favoring relatively less developed countries shall be concluded through regional scope and partial scope agreements.

In order to ensure the effectiveness of such agreements, member countries shall execute negotiated rules concerning preservation of preferences, elimination of non-tariff restrictions and application of safeguard clauses in justified cases.

First section - Regional scope agreements

Article 18

For each relatively less developed country, member countries shall approve negotiated lists of preferably industrial products originating from each relatively less developed country, for which total elimination of customs duties and other restrictions shall be accorded, without reciprocity, by all other member countries of the Association.

Member countries shall set up the necessary procedures to achieve progressive extension of the respective liberalization lists. Corresponding negotiations may be carried out when deemed convenient.

At the same time, member countries shall endeavour to set up effective compensation mechanisms to take care of negative effects which might influence intra-regional trade of the relatively less developed land-locked countries.

Second section - Partial scope agreements

Article 19

Partial scope agreements negotiated by the relatively less developed countries with other member countries shall conform, wherever pertinent, with the provisions contained in articles 8 and 9 of the present Treaty.

Article 20

In order to encourage effective and collective cooperation in favor of relatively less developed countries, member countries shall negotiate Special Cooperation Programs with each one of them.

Article 21

In order to facilitate utilization of tariff cuts, member countries may set up cooperation programs and actions in the fields of preinvestment, financing and technology, mainly directed towards supporting the relatively less developed countries, with special regard, among them, to land-locked countries.

Article 22

Notwithstanding the preceding articles, treatments in favor of relatively less developed countries may include collective and partial cooperation actions calling for effective mechanisms meant to compensate the disadvantageous situation faced by Bolivia and Paraguay due to their land-locked location.

Provided that criteria referred to gradual timing are adopted within the regional tariff preference referred to in article 5 of the present Treaty, attempts shall be made to preserve the margins granted in favor of land-locked countries by means of cumulative tariff cuts.

At the same time, attempts shall be made to establish compensation formulae, both as regards the regional tariff preference when deepened, and regional and partial scope agreements.

Article 23

Member countries shall endeavor to grant land-locked countries facilities to establish free zones, warehouses or ports and other administrative international transit facilities in their territories.

CHAPTER IV
Convergence and cooperation with other Latin American countries
and areas of economic integration

Article 24

Member countries may establish multilateral association or relationship systems encouraging convergence with other countries and areas of economic integration of Latin America, including the possibility of agreeing with these countries or areas the establishment of a Latin American tariff preference.

Member countries shall in due course regulate the characteristics of these systems.

Article 25

Likewise, member countries may draw up partial scope agreements with other Latin American countries and areas of economic integration, in accordance with the various modalities foreseen in the third section of chapter II of the present Treaty, and under the terms of the respective regulative provisions.

Notwithstanding the above, these agreements shall be subject to the following rules:

a)   Concessions granted by participating member countries shall not be extensive to the others, excepting the relatively less developed countries;

b)   When a member country includes products already negotiated in partial agreements with other member countries, concessions granted may be higher than those agreed with the former; in this case, consultation with the affected member countries shall be carried out in order to find mutually satisfactory solutions, unless the respective partial agreements include clauses concerning automatic extension or waiver of preferences contained in the partial agreements referred to in the present article; and

c)   They shall be multilaterally assessed by the member countries within the Committee in order to acknowledge the scope of the agreements drawn up and facilitate participation of other member countries in same.

CHAPTER V
Cooperation with other areas of economic integration

Article 26

Member countries shall undertake the actions necessary to establish and develop solidarity and cooperation links with other integration areas outside Latin America, through the Association's participation in horizontal cooperation programs carried out at international level, thus implementing the basic principles and commitments adopted within the context of the Declaration and Action Program on the establishment of a New International Economic Order and of the Charter of Economic Rights and Duties of States.

The Committee shall adopt adequate measures to facilitate compliance with the objectives set forth.

Article 27

At the same time, member countries may draw up partial scope agreements with other developing countries or respective economic integration areas outside Latin America, following the various modalities foreseen in the third section of chapter II of the present Treaty, and under the terms of the pertinent regulative provisions.

Notwithstanding the above, these agreements shall be subject to the following rules:

a)   Concessions granted by member countries participating in them shall not be extended to other members, with the exception of the relatively less developed countries;

b)   When products already negotiated with other member countries in partial scope agreements are included, concessions granted may not be higher than those agreed with the former, and in such case they shall be automatically extended to those countries; and

c)   They shall be declared consistent with the commitments undertaken by member countries within the frame of the present Treaty, in accordance with captions a) and b) of the present article.

CHAPTER VII
General provisions

Article 44

Any advantages, favorable treatments, franchises, immunities and privileges which member countries apply to products originating from or bound to any other member country or non-member country, pursuant to decisions or agreements not foreseen in the present Treaty or the Cartagena Agreement, shall be immediately and unconditionally extended to the other member countries.

Article 45

Any advantages, favorable treatments, franchises, immunities and privileges already granted or to be granted under agreements between member countries or between these and third countries to facilitate border traffic shall be exclusively applicable to the countries which sign or may have signed them.

Article 46

As regards taxes, charges and other internal duties, products originating from the territory of a member country shall be entitled within the territory of the other member countries to a treatment not less favorable than that applied to similar national products.

Member countries shall adopt such steps as may be required to comply with the preceding provision, in accordance with their respective National Constitutions.

Article 47

In the case of products included in the regional tariff preference or in regional or partial scope agreements which are not produced or will not be produced in substantial quantities in its territory, each member country shall endeavor to avoid that taxes or other internal measures applied result in annulment or reduction of any concession or advantage obtained by any member country as a result of the respective negotiations.

If a member country considers itself at a disadvantage by the measures contained in the preceding paragraph, it may resort to the Committee so that the situation raised may be examined and pertinent recommendations issued.

Article 48

Within the territory of other member countries, capitals originating from member countries shall have the right to a treatment not less favorable than that granted to capitals coming from any other non-member country, notwithstanding the provisions set out in agreements which might be concluded on this matter by member countries under the terms of the present Treaty.

Article 49

Member countries may establish supplementary rules on trade policy regulating, among other matters, the application of non-tariff restrictions, a system of origin, the adoption of safeguard clauses, export promotion systems and border traffic.

Article 50

No provision under the present Treaty shall be interpreted as precluding the adoption and observance of measures regarding:

a)   Protection of public morality;

b)   Implementation of security laws and regulations;

c)   Regulation of imports and exports of arms, munitions, and other war materials and, under exceptional circumstances, all other military equipments;

d)   Protection of human, animal and plant life and health;

e)   Imports and exports of gold and silver in bullion form;

f)   Protection of national treasures of artistic, historical or archeological value; and

g)   Exportation, use and consumption of nuclear materials, radioactive products or any other material used for the development and exploitation of nuclear energy.

Article 51

Products imported and exported by any member country shall have the right to free transit throughout the territory of the other member countries, and be exclusively subject to payment of charges normally applicable for services rendered.

*   *   *

TREATY FOR THE ESTABLISHMENT OF THE ECONOMIC COMMUNITY OF CENTRAL AFRICAN STATES[*1]
[excerpts]

> The Treaty for the Establishment of the Economic Community of Central African States was signed on 18 October 1983. It came into force in December 1984. The member States of the ECCAS (also known by the French acronym CEEAC) are: Burundi, Cameroon, Central African Republic, Chad, Congo, Equatorial Guinea, Gabon, Rwanda, Sao Tome and Principe, and Zaire.

PREAMBLE

The President of the Republic of Burundi,

The President of the United Republic of Cameroon,

The President of the Central African Republic,

The President of the People's Republic of the Congo,

The President of the Republic of Gabon,

The President of the Republic of Equatorial Guinea,

The President of the Republic of Rwanda,

The President of the Democratic Republic of Sao Tome and Principe,

The President of the Republic of Chad,

The President of the Republic of Zaire,

---

[*]Source: Secretariat of the Economic Community of Central African States (1984). *Treaty for the Establishment of the Economic Community of Central African States* (Libreville: Secretariat of the Economic Community of Central African States). See also United Nations Conference on Trade and Development (1988). Economic Co-operation and Integration Among Developing Countries: A Review of Recent Developments in Subregional, Regional and Interregional Organizations and Arrangements, vol. iv (TD/B/C.7/51(Part II)/Add.1(vol.IV)) [Note added by the editor].

[1]United Nations Economic Commission for Africa, *Treaty for the establishment of the Economic Community of Central African States*, 1983, pp. vii-59.

Conscious of the need to promote the economic and social development of their States in order to improve the living standards of their peoples,

Recalling:

- the aims expressed in the Charter of the Organization of African Unity, particularly Article 2, paragraph 1 (b) and paragraph 2,

- the African Declaration on Co-operation, Development and Economic Independence adopted by the tenth Assembly of Heads of State and Government of the Organization of African Unity (May 1973),

- the Declaration of Commitment of Monrovia (July 1979) on the guidelines to be observed and the measures to be taken to achieve national and collective self-sufficiency in the economic and social fields in order to initiate a new international economic order,

- the Plan of Action and Final Act of Lagos (April 1980), notably the measures aimed at the economic, social and cultural development of Africa and defining *inter alia* those relating to the establishment of subregional structures and the strengthening of existing structures with a view to the gradual and progressive establishment of an African common market as a prelude to an African economic community,

- their solemn commitment in the Declaration of Libreville (December 1981) to do everything in their power to set up an Economic Community of Central African States,

Bearing in mind the principles of international law governing relationships between States, notably the principles of sovereignty, equality and independence of all States, non-interference in their internal affairs and the principle of the rule of law in their mutual relations,

Convinced that efficient co-operation in large groups, backed up by a resolute and concerted policy, will foster the accelerated and harmonious economic development of their States,

Conscious that progress towards subregional economic co-operation can be achieved only by having regard to the situation and interests of every State,

Conscious of the different levels of development in the countries of the subregions, more particularly of the situation in countries which are land-locked or semi-land-locked, islands and/or belong to the category of the least advanced countries,

Convinced that present forms of economic co-operation in the subregion are decisive stages on the way to broader co-operation,

Recognizing that efforts at subregional co-operation should not conflict with or hamper similar efforts being made to foster wider co-operation in Africa,

Determined to lay the foundations for a greater subregional economic zone,

Undertaking to collaborate sincerely and effectively in pursuance of the aims defined by this Treaty *inter alia* by abstaining from any measures likely to jeopardize the achievement of such aims,

Resolved to make every effort and take the necessary steps to secure the enactment of such legislation as is necessary to implement the obligations arising from this Treaty or from the institutions of the Community,

Deciding to establish an Economic Community of Central African States,

HEREBY AGREE AS FOLLOWS:

CHAPTER II
ESTABLISHMENT, PRINCIPLES, AIMS AND PROCEDURES

ARTICLE 2
Establishment of the Community

THE HIGH CONTRACTING PARTIES hereby establish between them an Economic Community of Central African States (ECCAS), hereinafter called "the Community".

ARTICLE 3
Principles

THE HIGH CONTRACTING PARTIES undertake to observe the principles of international law governing relations between States, notably the principles of sovereignty, equality and independence of all States, good neighbourliness, non-interference in their internal affairs, non-use of force to settle disputes and the respect of the rule of law in their mutual relations.

ARTICLE 4
Aims of the Community

1.   It shall be the aim of the Community to promote and enhance a harmonious co-operation and a balanced and self-maintaining development in all fields of economic and social activity particularly in the fields of industry, transport and communications, energy, agriculture, natural resources, trade, customs, monetary and financial questions, human resources, tourism, education, further training, culture, science, technology and the movement of people in order to achieve collective self-reliance, raise the standards of living of its peoples, increase and maintain economic stability, foster close peaceful relations between Member States and contribute to the progress and development of the African continent.

2.   For the purposes set out in paragraph 1 of this Article and in accordance with the relevant

provisions of this Treaty, the aims of the Community are as follows:

(a)   the elimination between Member States of customs duties and any other equivalent charges levied on the import and export of goods;

(b)   the abolition between Member States of quantitative restrictions and other hindrances to trade;

(c)   the establishment and maintenance of a common external customs tariff;

(d)   the establishment of a trade policy *vis-à-vis* third States;

(e)   the gradual abolition between Member States of obstacles to the free movement of people, goods, services and capital and to the rights of establishment;

(f)   the harmonization of national policies in order to promote Community activities, notably in the industry, transport and communications, energy, agriculture, natural resources, trade, currency and finance, human resources, tourism, education and culture, science and technology;

(g)   the setting-up of a Co-operation and Development Fund;

(h)   the rapid development of States which are fully or partly land-locked and fully or partly islands and/or belong to the category of the least advanced countries;

(i)   any other joint activities by Member States for achieving Community aims.

ARTICLE 5
General undertaking

1.   The Member States shall direct their endeavours with a view to creating favourable conditions for the development of the Community and the achievements of its aims and the harmonization of their policies for achievement of such aims through Community institutions. Member States shall refrain from any unilateral action likely to impair such achievement.

2.   Each Member State shall take all steps under its constitutional procedures to secure the enactment and circulation of such legislation as is necessary to give effect to this Treaty.

ARTICLE 6
Procedures for establishing the Community

1.   The Economic Community of Central African States shall be established progressively over a twelve-year period subdivided into three four-year stages.

2.   Each stage shall have allotted to it a schedule of actions to be undertaken and pursued

concurrently, as follows:

(a)   first stage: stability of the fiscal and customs regime existing at the date of entry into force of the Treaty, and the carrying out of studies to determine the timetable for the gradual removal of tariff and non-tariff obstacles to intra-Community trade; setting a timetable for increases or decreases in the customs tariffs of Member States in adaptation to a common external tariff;

(b)   second stage: setting up a free trade zone (application of the timetable for the gradual elimination of tariff and non-tariff obstacles to intra-Community trade);

(c)   third stage: establishment of the customs union (adoption of the common external tariff).

3.   Change-overs between stages shall be subject to confirmation that the essential elements of the specific aims of this Treaty or the Conference have been achieved and undertakings observed.

At the proposal of the Council the Conference shall confirm that the aims allotted to a stage have been achieved and shall decide on the change-over to the next stage.

4.   The total duration of the stages may be lengthened or shortened only by a consensual decision. However, decisions taken shall not be effective to shorten the transition period to ten years or prolong it for more than twenty years from the entry into force of this Treaty.

CHAPTER V
FREEDOM OF MOVEMENT, RESIDENCE AND RIGHT OF ESTABLISHMENT

ARTICLE 40

1.   Citizens of Member States shall be deemed to be citizens of the Community. Accordingly, Member States agree, in accordance with the Protocol on Freedom of Movement and Right of Establishment annexed hereto as Annex VII, gradually to facilitate procedures for the freedom of movement and right of establishment within the Community.

2.   For the purposes of Protocol VII legal persons complying with existing legislation in a Member State shall be deemed to be natural persons.

CHAPTER VI
CO-OPERATION IN THE CURRENCY, FINANCIAL AND PAYMENTS FIELD

ARTICLE 41
Currency, finance and payments

1.   Member States agree to harmonize their currency, financial and payments policies in order to create confidence in their respective currencies, to ensure satisfactory operation of the Community and to further the achievement of its aims and to improve currency and financial co-operation between them and the other African countries.

2.   For the purposes of paragraph 1 of this Article the General Secretariat acting in liaison with the particular subregional committees concerned with the Association of Central African Banks shall:

(a)   prepare for the Council's attention recommendations on harmonization of the economic and financial policies of Member States;

(b)   give continuous attention to the balance-of-payments problems of Member States and undertake any studies relating thereto;

(c)   study the development of the economies of Member States;

(d)   make recommendations to the Council about the short-term creation of bilateral clearing systems among Member States and the long-term establishment of a multilateral clearing system and monetary union.

3.   Under the Protocol on the Clearing House annexed hereto as Annex VIII, Member States undertake to boost intra-Community trading in goods and services through the channel of a compensation chamber.

ARTICLE 42
Movement of capital

Upon the entry into force hereof the Conference shall, at the proposal of the Council and subject to the approval of the Consultative Commission, take steps for the progressive co-ordination of national exchange policies with regard to movements of capital between Member States and third States.

CHAPTER VIII
CO-OPERATION IN INDUSTRY

ARTICLE 45

1. In order to integrate their economies Member States agree to harmonize their industrialization policies in the subregion.

2. Accordingly, they undertake to:

   (a) inform the General Secretariat of their development plans and corresponding action programmes with a view to the preparation of basic programmes for the harmonious development of the subregion;

   (b) exchange information on any industrial project for the subregion;

   (c) inform one another of their industrial experiences;

   (d) exchange experts and information on industrial, commercial and technological research.

ARTICLE 46

1. To achieve a rational and harmonious industrial development the Member States agree to:

   (a) harmonize measures for stimulating industrial development by gradually establishing a homogeneous industrial environment in the subregion, *inter alia* by the preparation of a common investment code;

   (b) promote the establishment of large industrial units of a Community character and of an industrial development centre;

   (c) distribute Community projects in a balanced and harmonious manner among all Member States;

   (d) refuse permission to national industries which might compete with Community industries meeting the demands of Member States of the Community satisfactorily;

   (e) create subregional training and further training centres at all levels of skill to satisfy their personnel requirements in industry, trade and technology.

2. For the purposes of this Chapter the Member States shall agree to co-operate under Protocol X annexed hereto.

CHAPTER IX
CO-OPERATION IN INFRASTRUCTURE AND EQUIPMENT, TRANSPORT AND COMMUNICATIONS

ARTICLE 47
Transport and communications

1.   To achieve a harmonious and integrated development of the subregional transport and communications network and gradually to prepare a common policy, the Member States agree to:

(a)   promote the integration of transport and communications infrastructures;

(b)   co-ordinate the various modes of transport in order to increase their effectiveness;

(c)   progressively harmonize their transport and communications laws and regulations;

(d)   encourage the use of local material and human resources, the standardization of networks and equipment, the research and publicizing of appropriate technologies for constructing appropriate infrastructures and equipment;

(e)   expand and modernize transport and communications infrastructures by mobilizing the necessary technological and financial resources;

(f)   promote subregional industry in the field of equipment for transport and communications;

(g)   organize, structure and promote subregional sector of passenger and freight transport activities.

2.   The Member States shall accordingly:

(a)   prepare co-ordinated programmes for structuring the road transport sector;

(b)   prepare plans for improving and re-organizing different railways systems of Member States with a view to their interconnection, and construct new railways;

(c)   harmonize:

their policies on international sea and river transport;

their air transport policies;

their work on basic and further training of specialist cadres in transport and communications;

(d)   modernize and standardize their equipment in order that all Member States may be linked with one another and with the exterior by scheduled flights.

ARTICLE 48

Member States shall make every effort to establish Community sea, river and airline companies.

ARTICLE 49
Post and telecommunications

Member States undertake to:

- reorganize, modernize and develop their telecommunications systems, in order to meet the requirements of international traffic and to provide reliable interconnection between Member States;

- devise as soon as possible a regional satellite communication system to complete the Pan-African Telecommunications Network in Central Africa;

- provide rapid and frequent postal services within the Community and develop close collaboration between postal administrations.

ARTICLE 50

For the purposes of this Chapter Member States shall agree to co-operate in accordance with Protocol XI annexed hereto.

CHAPTER X
CO-OPERATION IN SCIENCE AND TECHNOLOGY

ARTICLE 51

1.   The Member States agree:

(a)   to develop an adequate scientific and technological base able to initiate the socio-economic changes needed to improve the quality of life of their populations, particularly rural populations;

(b)   to arrange for an appropriate application of science and technology in the development of agriculture, transport and communications, industry, health and hygiene, energy, education and manpower and preservation of the environment;

(c)   to reduce their dependence and promote their individual and collective technological self-reliance by seeking a favourable socio-economic balance between foreign contributions and contributions from local technology.

2.   In the implementation of this co-operation the Member States shall:

(a)   harmonize their national policies on scientific and technological research with a view to improving their integration at national levels of economic and social development;

(b)   co-ordinate their applied research, research and development and scientific and technological services programmes;

(c)   harmonize their national technological development plans by placing special emphasis on local technologies and their control of industrial property and the transfer of foreign technologies;

(d)   co-ordinate their positions on all scientific and technological questions forming the subject of international negotiations;

(e)   arrange for a permanent exchange of information and documentation and the establishment of Community data networks and data bank;

(f)   develop joint programmes for training scientific and technological cadres including the basic and further training of skilled manpower;

(g)   promote exchange of researchers and specialists among Member States in order to make full use of the technical skills available in the Community.

ARTICLE 52

1.   The Member States shall take all the necessary measures to prepare and implement a joint scientific research and technological development programme.

2.   The General Secretariat shall therefore undertake jointly with the competent national and subregional bodies the technical studies needed to define priority sectors and sectors of joint interest and shall submit its conclusions to the Council.

ARTICLE 53

For the purposes of this Chapter the Member States agree to co-operate in accordance with Protocol XII annexed hereto.

CHAPTER XI
CO-OPERATION IN ENERGY AND NATURAL RESOURCES

ARTICLE 54

1. The Member States agree to:

    (a) rapidly increase the Community's energy resources availabilities;

    (b) establish the appropriate trade machinery to ensure a regular supply of hydrocarbons;

    (c) promote renewable energy sources in connection with the policy of diversification of energy sources.

2. To achieve the aims of paragraph 1 of this Article, the Member States shall:

    (a) harmonize their national energy development plans;

    (b) establish a joint energy policy more particularly for exploitation, production and distribution;

    (c) establish an adequate system of concertation and co-ordination for jointly solving the Community's energy development problems, notably those relating to energy transmission, shortage of skilled cadres and the shortage of funds for implementing their energy projects;

    (d) promote the basic and further training of cadres.

ARTICLE 55

The Member States shall agree to assess and upgrade the mineral and hydraulic resources *inter alia* by:

    (a) endeavours to improve their knowledge of their natural resource potentialities;

    (b) gradually reducing their dependence on transnational companies for upgrading such resources, notably by mastering exploitation technologies;

    (c) improving methods of pricing and marketing raw materials.

ARTICLE 56

To promote this co-operation the Member States shall:

(a)   harmonize their policies of prospecting for producing and processing mineral resources and prospecting, exploiting and distributing hydraulic resources;

(b)   co-ordinate their development and utilization programmes for mineral and hydraulic resources in order to exploit similarities and complementarities within the Community and promote vertical and horizontal interindustrial relationships arising between Member States subsequently to the upgrading of such resources;

(c)   co-ordinate their positions in all international negotiations on raw materials in order to safeguard their interests;

(d)   develop a system of transfer of know-how and exchange of scientific, technical and economic data among Member States;

(e)   prepare and implement joint basic and further training programmes for cadre in order to develop the human resources and the appropriate local technological capacities needed for the exploration, exploitation and processing of mineral and hydraulic resources.

ARTICLE 57

To implement the co-operation activities under Articles 54-56 hereof the Secretary-General shall submit proposals to the Council for preparing a joint policy for upgrading mineral and hydraulic resources.

ARTICLE 58

For the purposes of this Chapter the Member States shall agree to co-operate in accordance with the Protocols XIII and XIV annexed hereto.

* * *

NORTH AMERICAN FREE TRADE AGREEMENT[*]
[excerpts]

The North American Free Trade Agreement (NAFTA) was signed by Canada, Mexico, and the United States of America on 17 September 1992. It entered into force on 1 January 1994.

Chapter Eleven

Investment

Section A - Investment

Article 1101: Scope and Coverage

1.   This Chapter applies to measures adopted or maintained by a Party relating to:

   (a)   investors of another Party;

   (b)   investments of investors of another Party in the territory of the Party; and

   (c)   with respect to Articles 1106 and 1114, all investments in the territory of the Party.

2.   A Party has the right to perform exclusively the economic activities set out in Annex III and to refuse to permit the establishment of investment in such activities.

3.   This Chapter does not apply to measures adopted or maintained by a Party to the extent that they are covered by Chapter Fourteen (Financial Services).

4.   Nothing in this Chapter shall be construed to prevent a Party from providing a service or performing a function such as law enforcement, correctional services, income security or insurance, social security or insurance, social welfare, public education, public training, health, and child care, in a manner that is not inconsistent with this Chapter.

---

[*]Source: Government of Canada (1994). *North American Free Trade Agreement* [Note added by the editor].

Article 1102: National Treatment

1.   Each Party shall accord to investors of another Party treatment no less favorable than that it accords, in like circumstances, to its own investors with respect to the establishment, acquisition, expansion, management, conduct, operation, and sale or other disposition of investments.

2.   Each Party shall accord to investments of investors of another Party treatment no less favorable than that it accords, in like circumstances, to investments of its own investors with respect to the establishment, acquisition, expansion, management, conduct, operation, and sale or other disposition of investments.

3.   The treatment accorded by a Party under paragraphs 1 and 2 means, with respect to a state or province, treatment no less favorable than the most favorable treatment accorded, in like circumstances, by that state or province to investors, and to investments of investors, of the Party of which it forms a part.

4.   For greater certainty, no Party may:

   (a)   impose on an investor of another Party a requirement that a minimum level of equity in an enterprise in the territory of the Party be held by its nationals, other than nominal qualifying shares for directors or incorporators of corporations; or

   (b)   require an investor of another Party, by reason of its nationality, to sell or otherwise dispose of an investment in the territory of the Party.

Article 1103: Most-Favored-Nation Treatment

1.   Each Party shall accord to investors of another Party treatment no less favorable than that it accords, in like circumstances, to investors of any other Party or of a non-Party with respect to the establishment, acquisition, expansion, management, conduct, operation, and sale or other disposition of investments.

2.   Each Party shall accord to investments of investors of another Party treatment no less favorable than that it accords, in like circumstances, to investments of investors of any other Party or of a non-Party with respect to the establishment, acquisition, expansion, management, conduct, operation, and sale or other disposition of investments.

Article 1104: Standard of Treatment

Each Party shall accord to investors of another Party and to investments of investors of another Party the better of the treatment required by Articles 1102 and 1103.

Article 1105: Minimum Standard of Treatment

1. Each Party shall accord to investments of investors of another Party treatment in accordance with international law, including fair and equitable treatment and full protection and security.

2. Without prejudice to paragraph 1 and notwithstanding Article 1108(7)(b), each Party shall accord to investors of another Party, and to investments of investors of another Party, non-discriminatory treatment with respect to measures it adopts or maintains relating to losses suffered by investments in its territory owing to armed conflict or civil strife.

3. Paragraph 2 does not apply to existing measures relating to subsidies or grants that would be inconsistent with Article 1102 but for Article 1108(7)(b).

Article 1106: Performance Requirements

1. No Party may impose or enforce any of the following requirements, or enforce any commitment or undertaking, in connection with the establishment, acquisition, expansion, management, conduct or operation of an investment of an investor of a Party or of a non-Party in its territory:

    (a) to export a given level or percentage of goods or services;

    (b) to achieve a given level or percentage of domestic content;

    (c) to purchase, use or accord a preference to goods produced or services provided in its territory, or to purchase goods or services from persons in its territory;

    (d) to relate in any way the volume or value of imports to the volume or value of exports or to the amount of foreign exchange inflows associated with such investment;

    (e) to restrict sales of goods or services in its territory that such investment produces or provides by relating such sales in any way to the volume or value of its exports or foreign exchange earnings;

    (f) to transfer technology, a production process or other proprietary knowledge to a person in its territory, except when the requirement is imposed or the commitment or undertaking is enforced by a court, administrative tribunal or competition authority to remedy an alleged violation of competition laws or to act in a manner not inconsistent with other provisions of this Agreement; or

    (g) to act as the exclusive supplier of the goods it produces or services it provides to a specific region or world market.

2.   A measure that requires an investment to use a technology to meet generally applicable health, safety or environmental requirements shall not be construed to be inconsistent with paragraph 1(f). For greater certainty, Articles 1102 and 1103 apply to the measure.

3.   No Party may condition the receipt or continued receipt of an advantage, in connection with an investment in its territory of an investor of a Party or of a non-Party, on compliance with any of the following requirements:

(a)   to achieve a given level or percentage of domestic content;

(b)   to purchase, use or accord a preference to goods produced in its territory, or to purchase goods from producers in its territory;

(c)   to relate in any way the volume or value of imports to the volume or value of exports or to the amount of foreign exchange inflows associated with such investment; or

(d)   to restrict sales of goods or services in its territory that such investment produces or provides by relating such sales in any way to the volume or value of its exports or foreign exchange earnings.

4.   Nothing in paragraph 3 shall be construed to prevent a Party from conditioning the receipt or continued receipt of an advantage, in connection with an investment in its territory of an investor of a Party or of a non-Party, on compliance with a requirement to locate production, provide a service, train or employ workers, construct or expand particular facilities, or carry out research and development, in its territory.

5.   Paragraphs 1 and 3 do not apply to any requirement other than the requirements set out in those paragraphs.

6.   Provided that such measures are not applied in an arbitrary or unjustifiable manner, or do not constitute a disguised restriction on international trade or investment, nothing in paragraph 1(b) or (c) or 3(a) or (b) shall be construed to prevent any Party from adopting or maintaining measures, including environmental measures:

(a)   necessary to secure compliance with laws and regulations that are not inconsistent with the provisions of this Agreement;

(b)   necessary to protect human, animal or plant life or health; or

(c)   necessary for the conservation of living or non-living exhaustible natural resources.

Article 1107: Senior Management and Boards of Directors

1.   No Party may require that an enterprise of that Party that is an investment of an investor of another Party appoint to senior management positions individuals of any particular nationality.

2.   A Party may require that a majority of the board of directors, or any committee thereof, of an enterprise of that Party that is an investment of an investor of another Party, be of a particular nationality, or resident in the territory of the Party, provided that the requirement does not materially impair the ability of the investor to exercise control over its investment.

Article 1108: Reservations and Exceptions

1.   Articles 1102, 1103, 1106 and 1107 do not apply to:

   (a)   any existing non-conforming measure that is maintained by

      (i)   a Party at the federal level, as set out in its Schedule to Annex I or III,

      (ii)   a state or province, for two years after the date of entry into force of this Agreement, and thereafter as set out by a Party in its Schedule to Annex I in accordance with paragraph 2, or

      (iii)   a local government;

   (b)   the continuation or prompt renewal of any non-conforming measure referred to in subparagraph (a); or

   (c)   an amendment to any non-conforming measure referred to in subparagraph (a) to the extent that the amendment does not decrease the conformity of the measure, as it existed immediately before the amendment, with Articles 1102, 1103, 1106 and 1107.

2.   Each Party may set out in its Schedule to Annex I, within two years of the date of entry into force of this Agreement, any existing non-conforming measure maintained by a state or province, not including a local government.

3.   Articles 1102, 1103, 1106 and 1107 do not apply to any measure that a Party adopts or maintains with respect to sectors, subsectors or activities, as set out in its Schedule to Annex II.

4.   No Party may, under any measure adopted after the date of entry into force of this Agreement and covered by its Schedule to Annex II, require an investor of another Party, by reason of its nationality, to sell or otherwise dispose of an investment existing at the time the measure becomes effective.

5.   Articles 1102 and 1103 do not apply to any measure that is an exception to, or derogation from, the obligations under Article 1703 (Intellectual Property - National Treatment) as specifically provided for in that Article.

6.   Article 1103 does not apply to treatment accorded by a Party pursuant to agreements, or with respect to sectors, set out in its Schedule to Annex IV.

7.   Articles 1102, 1103 and 1107 do not apply to:

(a)   procurement by a Party or a state enterprise; or

(b)   subsidies or grants provided by a Party or a state enterprise, including government-supported loans, guarantees and insurance.

8.   The provisions of:

(a)   Article 1106(1)(a), (b) and (c), and (3)(a) and (b) do not apply to qualification requirements for goods or services with respect to export promotion and foreign aid programs;

(b)   Article 1106(1)(b), (c), (f) and (g), and (3)(a) and (b) do not apply to procurement by a Party or a state enterprise; and

(c)   Article 1106(3)(a) and (b) do not apply to requirements imposed by an importing Party relating to the content of goods necessary to qualify for preferential tariffs or preferential quotas.

Article 1109: Transfers

1.   Each Party shall permit all transfers relating to an investment of an investor of another Party in the territory of the Party to be made freely and without delay. Such transfers include:

(a)   profits, dividends, interest, capital gains, royalty payments, management fees, technical assistance and other fees, returns in kind and other amounts derived from the investment;

(b)   proceeds from the sale of all or any part of the investment or from the partial or complete liquidation of the investment;

(c)   payments made under a contract entered into by the investor, or its investment, including payments made pursuant to a loan agreement;

(d)   payments made pursuant to Article 1110; and

(e)   payments arising under Section B.

2.   Each Party shall permit transfers to be made in a freely usable currency at the market rate of exchange prevailing on the date of transfer with respect to spot transactions in the currency to be transferred.

3.   No Party may require its investors to transfer, or penalize its investors that fail to transfer, the income, earnings, profits or other amounts derived from, or attributable to, investments in the territory of another Party.

4.   Notwithstanding paragraphs 1 and 2, a Party may prevent a transfer through the equitable, non-discriminatory and good faith application of its laws relating to:

(a)   bankruptcy, insolvency or the protection of the rights of creditors;

(b)   issuing, trading or dealing in securities;

(c)   criminal or penal offenses;

(d)   reports of transfers of currency or other monetary instruments; or

(e)   ensuring the satisfaction of judgments in adjudicatory proceedings.

5.   Paragraph 3 shall not be construed to prevent a Party from imposing any measure through the equitable, non-discriminatory and good faith application of its laws relating to the matters set out in subparagraphs (a) through (e) of paragraph 4.

6.   Notwithstanding paragraph 1, a Party may restrict transfers of returns in kind in circumstances where it could otherwise restrict such transfers under this Agreement, including as set out in paragraph 4.

Article 1110: Expropriation and Compensation

1.   No Party may directly or indirectly nationalize or expropriate an investment of an investor of another Party in its territory or take a measure tantamount to nationalization or expropriation of such an investment ("expropriation"), except:

(a)   for a public purpose;

(b)   on a non-discriminatory basis;

(c)   in accordance with due process of law and Article 1105(1); and

(d)   on payment of compensation in accordance with paragraphs 2 through 6.

2.   Compensation shall be equivalent to the fair market value of the expropriated investment immediately before the expropriation took place ("date of expropriation"), and shall not reflect

any change in value occurring because the intended expropriation had become known earlier. Valuation criteria shall include going concern value, asset value including declared tax value of tangible property, and other criteria, as appropriate, to determine fair market value.

3.   Compensation shall be paid without delay and be fully realizable.

4.   If payment is made in a G7 currency, compensation shall include interest at a commercially reasonable rate for that currency from the date of expropriation until the date of actual payment.

5.   If a Party elects to pay in a currency other than a G7 currency, the amount paid on the date of payment, if converted into a G7 currency at the market rate of exchange prevailing on that date, shall be no less than if the amount of compensation owed on the date of expropriation had been converted into that G7 currency at the market rate of exchange prevailing on that date, and interest had accrued at a commercially reasonable rate for that G7 currency from the date of expropriation until the date of payment.

6.   On payment, compensation shall be freely transferable as provided in Article 1109.

7.   This Article does not apply to the issuance of compulsory licenses granted in relation to intellectual property rights, or to the revocation, limitation or creation of intellectual property rights, to the extent that such issuance, revocation, limitation or creation is consistent with Chapter Seventeen (Intellectual Property).

8.   For purposes of this Article and for greater certainty, a non-discriminatory measure of general application shall not be considered a measure tantamount to an expropriation of a debt security or loan covered by this Chapter solely on the ground that the measure imposes costs on the debtor that cause it to default on the debt.

Article 1111: Special Formalities and Information Requirements

1.   Nothing in Article 1102 shall be construed to prevent a Party from adopting or maintaining a measure that prescribes special formalities in connection with the establishment of investments by investors of another Party, such as a requirement that investors be residents of the Party or that investments be legally constituted under the laws or regulations of the Party, provided that such formalities do not materially impair the protections afforded by a Party to investors of another Party and investments of investors of another Party pursuant to this Chapter.

2.   Notwithstanding Articles 1102 or 1103, a Party may require an investor of another Party, or its investment in its territory, to provide routine information concerning that investment solely for informational or statistical purposes. The Party shall protect such business information that is confidential from any disclosure that would prejudice the competitive position of the investor or the investment. Nothing in this paragraph shall be construed to prevent a Party from otherwise obtaining or disclosing information in connection with the equitable and good faith application of its law.

Article 1112: Relation to Other Chapters

1.   In the event of any inconsistency between this Chapter and another Chapter, the other Chapter shall prevail to the extent of the inconsistency.

2.   A requirement by a Party that a service provider of another Party post a bond or other form of financial security as a condition of providing a service into its territory does not of itself make this Chapter applicable to the provision of that cross-border service. This Chapter applies to that Party's treatment of the posted bond or financial security.

Article 1113: Denial of Benefits

1.   A Party may deny the benefits of this Chapter to an investor of another Party that is an enterprise of such Party and to investments of such investor if investors of a non-Party own or control the enterprise and the denying Party:

(a)   does not maintain diplomatic relations with the non-Party; or

(b)   adopts or maintains measures with respect to the non-Party that prohibit transactions with the enterprise or that would be violated or circumvented if the benefits of this Chapter were accorded to the enterprise or to its investments.

2.   Subject to prior notification and consultation in accordance with Articles 1803 (Notification and Provision of Information) and 2006 (Consultations), a Party may deny the benefits of this Chapter to an investor of another Party that is an enterprise of such Party and to investments of such investors if investors of a non-Party own or control the enterprise and the enterprise has no substantial business activities in the territory of the Party under whose law it is constituted or organized.

Article 1114: Environmental Measures

1.   Nothing in this Chapter shall be construed to prevent a Party from adopting, maintaining or enforcing any measure otherwise consistent with this Chapter that it considers appropriate to ensure that investment activity in its territory is undertaken in a manner sensitive to environmental concerns.

2.   The Parties recognize that it is inappropriate to encourage investment by relaxing domestic health, safety or environmental measures. Accordingly, a Party should not waive or otherwise derogate from, or offer to waive or otherwise derogate from, such measures as an encouragement for the establishment, acquisition, expansion or retention in its territory of an investment of an investor. If a Party considers that another Party has offered such an encouragement, it may request consultations with the other Party and the two Parties shall consult with a view to avoiding any such encouragement.

**Section B - Settlement of Disputes between a Party and
an Investor of Another Party**

Article 1115: Purpose

Without prejudice to the rights and obligations of the Parties under Chapter Twenty (Institutional Arrangements and Dispute Settlement Procedures), this Section establishes a mechanism for the settlement of investment disputes that assures both equal treatment among investors of the Parties in accordance with the principle of international reciprocity and due process before an impartial tribunal.

Article 1116: Claim by an Investor of a Party on Its Own Behalf

1.   An investor of a Party may submit to arbitration under this Section a claim that another Party has breached an obligation under:

      (a)   Section A or Article 1503(2) (State Enterprises), or

      (b)   Article 1502(3)(a) (Monopolies and State Enterprises) where the monopoly has acted in a manner inconsistent with the Party's obligations under Section A,

and that the investor has incurred loss or damage by reason of, or arising out of, that breach.

2.   An investor may not make a claim if more than three years have elapsed from the date on which the investor first acquired, or should have first acquired, knowledge of the alleged breach and knowledge that the investor has incurred loss or damage.

Article 1117: Claim by an Investor of a Party on Behalf of an Enterprise

1.   An investor of a Party, on behalf of an enterprise of another Party that is a juridical person that the investor owns or controls directly or indirectly, may submit to arbitration under this Section a claim that the other Party has breached an obligation under:

      (a)   Section A or Article 1503(2) (State Enterprises), or

      (b)   Article 1502(3)(a) (Monopolies and State Enterprises) where the monopoly has acted in a manner inconsistent with the Party's obligations under Section A,

and that the enterprise has incurred loss or damage by reason of, or arising out of, that breach.

2.   An investor may not make a claim on behalf of an enterprise described in paragraph 1 if more than three years have elapsed from the date on which the enterprise first acquired, or should have first acquired, knowledge of the alleged breach and knowledge that the enterprise has incurred loss or damage.

3.   Where an investor makes a claim under this Article and the investor or a non-controlling investor in the enterprise makes a claim under Article 1116 arising out of the same events that gave rise to the claim under this Article, and two or more of the claims are submitted to arbitration under Article 1120, the claims should be heard together by a Tribunal established under Article 1126, unless the Tribunal finds that the interests of a disputing party would be prejudiced thereby.

4.   An investment may not make a claim under this Section.

Article 1118: Settlement of a Claim through Consultation and Negotiation

The disputing parties should first attempt to settle a claim through consultation or negotiation.

Article 1119: Notice of Intent to Submit a Claim to Arbitration

The disputing investor shall deliver to the disputing Party written notice of its intention to submit a claim to arbitration at least 90 days before the claim is submitted, which notice shall specify:

(a)   the name and address of the disputing investor and, where a claim is made under Article 1117, the name and address of the enterprise;

(b)   the provisions of this Agreement alleged to have been breached and any other relevant provisions;

(c)   the issues and the factual basis for the claim; and

(d)   the relief sought and the approximate amount of damages claimed.

Article 1120: Submission of a Claim to Arbitration

1.   Except as provided in Annex 1120.1, and provided that six months have elapsed since the events giving rise to a claim, a disputing investor may submit the claim to arbitration under:

(a)   the ICSID Convention, provided that both the disputing Party and the Party of the investor are parties to the Convention;

(b)   the Additional Facility Rules of ICSID, provided that either the disputing Party or the Party of the investor, but not both, is a party to the ICSID Convention; or

(c)   the UNCITRAL Arbitration Rules.

2.   The applicable arbitration rules shall govern the arbitration except to the extent modified by this Section.

Article 1121: Conditions Precedent to Submission of a Claim to Arbitration

1.   A disputing investor may submit a claim under Article 1116 to arbitration only if:

    (a)   the investor consents to arbitration in accordance with the procedures set out in this Agreement; and

    (b)   the investor and, where the claim is for loss or damage to an interest in an enterprise of another Party that is a juridical person that the investor owns or controls directly or indirectly, the enterprise, waive their right to initiate or continue before any administrative tribunal or court under the law of any Party, or other dispute settlement procedures, any proceedings with respect to the measure of the disputing Party that is alleged to be a breach referred to in Article 1116, except for proceedings for injunctive, declaratory or other extraordinary relief, not involving the payment of damages, before an administrative tribunal or court under the law of the disputing Party.

2.   A disputing investor may submit a claim under Article 1117 to arbitration only if both the investor and the enterprise:

    (a)   consent to arbitration in accordance with the procedures set out in this Agreement; and

    (b)   waive their right to initiate or continue before any administrative tribunal or court under the law of any Party, or other dispute settlement procedures, any proceedings with respect to the measure of the disputing Party that is alleged to be a breach referred to in Article 1117, except for proceedings for injunctive, declaratory or other extraordinary relief, not involving the payment of damages, before an administrative tribunal or court under the law of the disputing Party.

3.   A consent and waiver required by this Article shall be in writing, shall be delivered to the disputing Party and shall be included in the submission of a claim to arbitration.

4.   Only where a disputing Party has deprived a disputing investor of control of an enterprise:

    (a)   a waiver from the enterprise under paragraph 1(b) or 2(b) shall not be required; and

    (b)   Annex 1120.1(A)(b) shall not apply.

Article 1122: Consent to Arbitration

1.   Each Party consents to the submission of a claim to arbitration in accordance with the procedures set out in this Agreement.

2.   The consent given by paragraph 1 and the submission by a disputing investor of a claim to arbitration shall satisfy the requirement of:

(a)   Chapter II of the ICSID Convention (Jurisdiction of the Centre) and the Additional Facility Rules for written consent of the parties;

(b)   Article II of the New York Convention for an agreement in writing; and

(c)   Article I of the Inter-American Convention for an agreement.

Article 1123: Number of Arbitrators and Method of Appointment

Except in respect of a Tribunal established under Article 1126, and unless the disputing parties otherwise agree, the Tribunal shall comprise three arbitrators, one arbitrator appointed by each of the disputing parties and the third, who shall be the presiding arbitrator, appointed by agreement of the disputing parties.

Article 1124: Constitution of a Tribunal When a Party Fails to Appoint an Arbitrator or the Disputing Parties Are Unable to Agree on a Presiding Arbitrator

1.   The Secretary-General shall serve as appointing authority for an arbitration under this Section.

2.   If a Tribunal, other than a Tribunal established under Article 1126, has not been constituted within 90 days from the date that a claim is submitted to arbitration, the Secretary-General, on the request of either disputing party, shall appoint, in his discretion, the arbitrator or arbitrators not yet appointed, except that the presiding arbitrator shall be appointed in accordance with paragraph 3.

3.   The Secretary-General shall appoint the presiding arbitrator from the roster of presiding arbitrators referred to in paragraph 4, provided that the presiding arbitrator shall not be a national of the disputing Party or a national of the Party of the disputing investor. In the event that no such presiding arbitrator is available to serve, the Secretary-General shall appoint, from the ICSID Panel of Arbitrators, a presiding arbitrator who is not a national of any of the Parties.

4.   On the date of entry into force of this Agreement, the Parties shall establish, and thereafter maintain, a roster of 45 presiding arbitrators meeting the qualifications of the Convention and rules referred to in Article 1120 and experienced in international law and investment matters. The roster members shall be appointed by consensus and without regard to nationality.

Article 1125: Agreement to Appointment of Arbitrators

For purposes of Article 39 of the ICSID Convention and Article 7 of Schedule C to the ICSID Additional Facility Rules, and without prejudice to an objection to an arbitrator based on

Article 1124(3) or on a ground other than nationality:

(a)   the disputing Party agrees to the appointment of each individual member of a Tribunal established under the ICSID Convention or the ICSID Additional Facility Rules;

(b)   a disputing investor referred to in Article 1116 may submit a claim to arbitration, or continue a claim, under the ICSID Convention or the ICSID Additional Facility Rules, only on condition that the disputing investor agrees in writing to the appointment of each individual member of the Tribunal; and

(c)   a disputing investor referred to in Article 1117(1) may submit a claim to arbitration, or continue a claim, under the ICSID Convention or the ICSID Additional Facility Rules, only on condition that the disputing investor and the enterprise agree in writing to the appointment of each individual member of the Tribunal.

Article 1126: Consolidation

1.   A Tribunal established under this Article shall be established under the UNCITRAL Arbitration Rules and shall conduct its proceedings in accordance with those Rules, except as modified by this Section.

2.   Where a Tribunal established under this Article is satisfied that claims have been submitted to arbitration under Article 1120 that have a question of law or fact in common, the Tribunal may, in the interests of fair and efficient resolution of the claims, and after hearing the disputing parties, by order:

(a)   assume jurisdiction over, and hear and determine together, all or part of the claims; or

(b)   assume jurisdiction over, and hear and determine one or more of the claims, the determination of which it believes would assist in the resolution of the others.

3.   A disputing party that seeks an order under paragraph 2 shall request the Secretary-General to establish a Tribunal and shall specify in the request:

(a)   the name of the disputing Party or disputing investors against which the order is sought;

(b)   the nature of the order sought; and

(c)   the grounds on which the order is sought.

4.   The disputing party shall deliver to the disputing Party or disputing investors against

which the order is sought a copy of the request.

5.   Within 60 days of receipt of the request, the Secretary-General shall establish a Tribunal comprising three arbitrators. The Secretary-General shall appoint the presiding arbitrator from the roster referred to in Article 1124(4). In the event that no such presiding arbitrator is available to serve, the Secretary-General shall appoint, from the ICSID Panel of Arbitrators, a presiding arbitrator who is not a national of any of the Parties. The Secretary-General shall appoint the two other members from the roster referred to in Article 1124(4), and to the extent not available from that roster, from the ICSID Panel of Arbitrators, and to the extent not available from that Panel, in the discretion of the Secretary-General. One member shall be a national of the disputing Party and one member shall be a national of a Party of the disputing investors.

6.   Where a Tribunal has been established under this Article, a disputing investor that has submitted a claim to arbitration under Article 1116 or 1117 and that has not been named in a request made under paragraph 3 may make a written request to the Tribunal that it be included in an order made under paragraph 2, and shall specify in the request:

(a)   the name and address of the disputing investor;

(b)   the nature of the order sought; and

(c)   the grounds on which the order is sought.

7.   A disputing investor referred to in paragraph 6 shall deliver a copy of its request to the disputing parties named in a request made under paragraph 3.

8.   A Tribunal established under Article 1120 shall not have jurisdiction to decide a claim, or a part of a claim, over which a Tribunal established under this Article has assumed jurisdiction.

9.   On application of a disputing party, a Tribunal established under this Article, pending its decision under paragraph 2, may order that the proceedings of a Tribunal established under Article 1120 be stayed, unless the latter Tribunal has already adjourned its proceedings.

10.   A disputing Party shall deliver to the Secretariat, within 15 days of receipt by the disputing Party, a copy of:

(a)   a request for arbitration made under paragraph (1) of Article 36 of the ICSID Convention;

(b)   a notice of arbitration made under Article 2 of Schedule C of the ICSID Additional Facility Rules; or

(c)   a notice of arbitration given under the UNCITRAL Arbitration Rules.

11.   A disputing Party shall deliver to the Secretariat a copy of a request made under paragraph 3:

(a)   within 15 days of receipt of the request, in the case of a request made by a disputing investor;

(b)   within 15 days of making the request, in the case of a request made by the disputing Party.

12.   A disputing Party shall deliver to the Secretariat a copy of a request made under paragraph 6 within 15 days of receipt of the request.

13.   The Secretariat shall maintain a public register of the documents referred to in paragraphs 10, 11 and 12.

Article 1127: Notice

A disputing Party shall deliver to the other Parties:

(a)   written notice of a claim that has been submitted to arbitration no later than 30 days after the date that the claim is submitted; and

(b)   copies of all pleadings filed in the arbitration.

Article 1128: Participation by a Party

On written notice to the disputing parties, a Party may make submissions to a Tribunal on a question of interpretation of this Agreement.

Article 1129: Documents

1.   A Party shall be entitled to receive from the disputing Party, at the cost of the requesting Party a copy of:

(a)   the evidence that has been tendered to the Tribunal; and

(b)   the written argument of the disputing parties.

2.   A Party receiving information pursuant to paragraph 1 shall treat the information as if it were a disputing Party.

Article 1130: Place of Arbitration

Unless the disputing parties agree otherwise, a Tribunal shall hold an arbitration in the territory of a Party that is a party to the New York Convention, selected in accordance with:

(a)   the ICSID Additional Facility Rules if the arbitration is under those Rules or the ICSID Convention; or

(b)   the UNCITRAL Arbitration Rules if the arbitration is under those Rules.

Article 1131: Governing Law

1.   A Tribunal established under this Section shall decide the issues in dispute in accordance with this Agreement and applicable rules of international law.

2.   An interpretation by the Commission of a provision of this Agreement shall be binding on a Tribunal established under this Section.

Article 1132: Interpretation of Annexes

1.   Where a disputing Party asserts as a defense that the measure alleged to be a breach is within the scope of a reservation or exception set out in Annex I, Annex II, Annex III or Annex IV, on request of the disputing Party, the Tribunal shall request the interpretation of the Commission on the issue. The Commission, within 60 days of delivery of the request, shall submit in writing its interpretation to the Tribunal.

2.   Further to Article 1131(2), a Commission interpretation submitted under paragraph 1 shall be binding on the Tribunal. If the Commission fails to submit an interpretation within 60 days, the Tribunal shall decide the issue.

Article 1133: Expert Reports

Without prejudice to the appointment of other kinds of experts where authorized by the applicable arbitration rules, a Tribunal, at the request of a disputing party or, unless the disputing parties disapprove, on its own initiative, may appoint one or more experts to report to it in writing on any factual issue concerning environmental, health, safety or other scientific matters raised by a disputing party in a proceeding, subject to such terms and conditions as the disputing parties may agree.

Article 1134: Interim Measures of Protection

A Tribunal may order an interim measure of protection to preserve the rights of a disputing party, or to ensure that the Tribunal's jurisdiction is made fully effective, including an order to preserve evidence in the possession or control of a disputing party or to protect the Tribunal's jurisdiction. A Tribunal may not order attachment or enjoin the application of the measure alleged to constitute a breach referred to in Article 1116 or 1117. For purposes of this paragraph, an order includes a recommendation.

Article 1135: Final Award

1.   Where a Tribunal makes a final award against a Party, the Tribunal may award, separately or in combination, only:

(a)   monetary damages and any applicable interest;

(b)   restitution of property, in which case the award shall provide that the disputing Party may pay monetary damages and any applicable interest in lieu of restitution,

A tribunal may also award costs in accordance with the applicable arbitration rules.

2.   Subject to paragraph 1, where a claim is made under Article 1117(1):

(a)   an award of restitution of property shall provide that restitution be made to the enterprise;

(b)   an award of monetary damages and any applicable interest shall provide that the sum be paid to the enterprise; and

(c)   the award shall provide that it is made without prejudice to any right that any person may have in the relief under applicable domestic law.

3.   A Tribunal may not order a Party to pay punitive damages.

Article 1136: Finality and Enforcement of an Award

1.   An award made by a Tribunal shall have no binding force except between the disputing parties and in respect of the particular case.

2.   Subject to paragraph 3 and the applicable review procedure for an interim award, a disputing party shall abide by and comply with an award without delay.

3.   A disputing party may not seek enforcement of a final award until:

(a)   in the case of a final award made under the ICSID Convention

(i)   120 days have elapsed from the date the award was rendered and no disputing party has requested revision or annulment of the award, or

(ii)   revision or annulment proceedings have been completed; and

(b)   in the case of a final award under the ICSID Additional Facility Rules or the UNCITRAL Arbitration Rules

      (i)   three months have elapsed from the date the award was rendered and no disputing party has commenced a proceeding to revise, set aside or annul the award, or

      (ii)   a court has dismissed or allowed an application to revise, set aside or annul the award and there is no further appeal.

4.   Each Party shall provide for the enforcement of an award in its territory.

5.   If a disputing Party fails to abide by or comply with a final award, the Commission, on delivery of a request by a Party whose investor was a party to the arbitration, shall establish a panel under Article 2008 (Request for an Arbitral Panel). The requesting Party may seek in such proceedings:

(a)   a determination that the failure to abide by or comply with the final award is inconsistent with the obligations of this Agreement; and

(b)   a recommendation that the Party abide by or comply with the final award.

6.   A disputing investor may seek enforcement of an arbitration award under the ICSID Convention, the New York Convention or the Inter-American Convention regardless of whether proceedings have been taken under paragraph 5.

7.   A claim that is submitted to arbitration under this Section shall be considered to arise out of a commercial relationship or transaction for purposes of Article I of the New York Convention and Article I of the Inter-American Convention.

Article 1137: General

Time when a Claim is Submitted to Arbitration

1.   A claim is submitted to arbitration under this Section when:

(a)   the request for arbitration under paragraph (1) of Article 36 of the ICSID Convention has been received by the Secretary-General;

(b)   the notice of arbitration under Article 2 of Schedule C of the ICSID Additional Facility Rules has been received by the Secretary-General; or

(c)   the notice of arbitration given under the UNCITRAL Arbitration Rules is received by the disputing Party.

Service of Documents

2.   Delivery of notice and other documents on a Party shall be made to the place named for that Party in Annex 1137.2.

Receipts under Insurance or Guarantee Contracts

3.   In an arbitration under this Section, a Party shall not assert, as a defense, counterclaim, right of setoff or otherwise, that the disputing investor has received or will receive, pursuant to an insurance or guarantee contract, indemnification or other compensation for all or part of its alleged damages.

Publication of an Award

4.   Annex 1137.4 applies to the Parties specified in that Annex with respect to publication of an award.

Article 1138: Exclusions

1.   Without prejudice to the applicability or non-applicability of the dispute settlement provisions of this Section or of Chapter Twenty (Institutional Arrangements and Dispute Settlement Procedures) to other actions taken by a Party pursuant to Article 2102 (National Security), a decision by a Party to prohibit or restrict the acquisition of an investment in its territory by an investor of another Party, or its investment, pursuant to that Article shall not be subject to such provisions.

2.   The dispute settlement provisions of this Section and of Chapter Twenty shall not apply to the matters referred to in Annex 1138.2.

Section C - Definitions

Article 1139: Definitions

For purposes of this Chapter:

disputing investor means an investor that makes a claim under Section B;

disputing parties means the disputing investor and the disputing Party;

disputing party means the disputing investor or the disputing Party;

disputing Party means a Party against which a claim is made under Section B;

enterprise means an "enterprise" as defined in Article 201 (Definitions of General Application), and a branch of an enterprise;

enterprise of a Party means an enterprise constituted or organized under the law of a Party, and a branch located in the territory of a Party and carrying out business activities there.

equity or debt securities includes voting and non-voting shares, bonds, convertible debentures, stock options and warrants;

G7 Currency means the currency of Canada, France, Germany, Italy, Japan, the United Kingdom of Great Britain and Northern Ireland or the United States;

ICSID means the International Centre for Settlement of Investment Disputes;

ICSID Convention means the *Convention on the Settlement of Investment Disputes between States and Nationals of other States*, done at Washington, March 18, 1965;

Inter-American Convention means the *Inter-American Convention on International Commercial Arbitration*, done at Panama, January 30, 1975;

investment means:

    (a)   an enterprise;

    (b)   an equity security of an enterprise;

    (c)   a debt security of an enterprise

        (i)   where the enterprise is an affiliate of the investor, or

        (ii)   where the original maturity of the debt security is at least three years,

    but does not include a debt security, regardless of original maturity, of a state enterprise;

    (d)   a loan to an enterprise

        (i)   where the enterprise is an affiliate of the investor, or

        (ii)   where the original maturity of the loan is at least three years,

    but does not include a loan, regardless of original maturity, to a state enterprise;

    (e)   an interest in an enterprise that entitles the owner to share in income or profits of the enterprise;

(f)   an interest in an enterprise that entitles the owner to share in the assets of that enterprise on dissolution, other than a debt security or a loan excluded from subparagraph (c) or (d);

(g)   real estate or other property, tangible or intangible, acquired in the expectation or used for the purpose of economic benefit or other business purposes; and

(h)   interests arising from the commitment of capital or other resources in the territory of a Party to economic activity in such territory, such as under

    (i)   contracts involving the presence of an investor's property in the territory of the Party, including turnkey or construction contracts, or concessions, or

    (ii)   contracts where remuneration depends substantially on the production, revenues or profits of an enterprise;

but investment does not mean,

(i)   claims to money that arise solely from

    (i)   commercial contracts for the sale of goods or services by a national or enterprise in the territory of a Party to an enterprise in the territory of another Party, or

    (ii)   the extension of credit in connection with a commercial transaction, such as trade financing, other than a loan covered by subparagraph (d); or

(j)   any other claims to money, that do not involve the kinds of interests set out in subparagraphs (a) through (h);

investment of an investor of a Party means an investment owned or controlled directly or indirectly by an investor of such Party;

investor of a Party means a Party or state enterprise thereof, or a national or an enterprise of such Party, that seeks to make, is making or has made an investment;

investor of a non-Party means an investor other than an investor of a Party, that seeks to make, is making or has made an investment;

New York Convention means the *United Nations Convention on the Recognition and Enforcement of Foreign Arbitral Awards*, done at New York, June 10, 1958;

Secretary-General means the Secretary-General of ICSID;

transfers means transfers and international payments;

Tribunal means an arbitration tribunal established under Article 1120 or 1126; and

UNCITRAL Arbitration Rules means the arbitration rules of the United Nations Commission on International Trade Law, approved by the United Nations General Assembly on December 15, 1976.

Annex 1120.1
Submission of a Claim to Arbitration

Mexico

With respect to the submission of a claim to arbitration:

(a)   an investor of another Party may not allege that Mexico has breached an obligation under:

(i)   Section A or Article 1503(2) (State Enterprises), or

(ii)   Article 1502(3)(a) (Monopolies and State Enterprises) where the monopoly has acted in a manner inconsistent with the Party's obligations under Section A,

both in an arbitration under this Section and in proceedings before a Mexican court or administrative tribunal; and

(b)   where an enterprise of Mexico that is a juridical person that an investor of another Party owns or controls directly or indirectly alleges in proceedings before a Mexican court or administrative tribunal that Mexico has breached an obligation under:

(i)   Section A or Article 1503(2) (State Enterprises), or

(ii)   Article 1502(3)(a) (Monopolies and State Enterprises) where the monopoly has acted in a manner inconsistent with the Party's obligations under Section A,

the investor may not allege the breach in an arbitration under this Section.

Annex 1137.2
Service of Documents on a Party Under Section B

Each Party shall set out in this Annex and publish in its official journal by January 1, 1994, the place for delivery of notice and other documents under this Section.

Annex 1137.4
Publication of an Award

Canada

Where Canada is the disputing Party, either Canada or a disputing investor that is a party to the arbitration may make an award public.

Mexico

Where Mexico is the disputing Party, the applicable arbitration rules apply to the publication of an award.

United States

Where the United States is the disputing Party, either the United States or a disputing investor that is a party to the arbitration may make an award public.

Annex 1138.2
Exclusions from Dispute Settlement

Canada

A decision by Canada following a review under the *Investment Canada Act*, with respect to whether or not to permit an acquisition that is subject to review, shall not be subject to the dispute settlement provisions of Section B or of Chapter Twenty (Institutional Arrangements and Dispute Settlement Procedures).

Mexico

A decision by the National Commission on Foreign Investment ("Comisión Nacional de Inversiones Extranjeras") following a review pursuant to Annex I, page I-M-4, with respect to whether or not to permit an acquisition that is subject to review, shall not be subject to the dispute settlement provisions of Section B or of Chapter Twenty (Institutional Arrangements and Dispute Settlement Procedures).

Chapter Twelve
Services
[excerpts]

Article 1201: Scope and Coverage

1.   This Chapter applies to measures adopted or maintained by a Party relating to cross-border trade in services by service providers of another Party, including measures respecting:

    (a)   the production, distribution, marketing, sale and delivery of a service;

    (b)   the purchase or use of, or payment for, a service;

    (c)   the access to and use of distribution and transportation systems in connection with the provision of a service;

    (d)   the presence in its territory of a service provider of another Party; and

    (e)   the provision of a bond or other form of financial security as a condition for the provision of a service.

2.   This Chapter does not apply to:

    (a)   financial services, as defined in Chapter Fourteen (Financial Services);

    (b)   air services, including domestic and international air transportation services, whether scheduled or non-scheduled, and related services in support of air services, other than

        (i)   aircraft repair and maintenance services during which an aircraft is withdrawn from service, and

        (ii)   specialty air services;

    (c)   procurement by a Party or a state enterprise; or

    (d)   subsidies or grants provided by a Party or a state enterprise, including government-supported loans, guarantees and insurance.

3.   Nothing in this Chapter shall be construed to:

    (a)   impose any obligation on a Party with respect to a national of another Party seeking access to its employment market, or employed on a permanent basis in its territory, or to confer any right on that national with respect to that access or employment; or

    (b)   prevent a Party from providing a service or performing a function such as law enforcement, correctional services, income security or insurance, social security or insurance, social welfare, public education, public training, health, and child care, in a manner that is not inconsistent with this Chapter.

Article 1205: Local Presence

No Party may require a service provider of another Party to establish or maintain a representative office or any form of enterprise, or to be resident, in its territory as a condition for the cross-border provision of a service.

Chapter Fourteen
Financial Services
[excerpts]

Article 1401: Scope and Coverage

1.   This Chapter applies to measures adopted or maintained by a Party relating to:

    (a)   financial institutions of another Party;

    (b)   investors of another Party, and investments of such investors, in financial institutions in the Party's territory; and

    (c)   cross-border trade in financial services.

2.   Articles 1109 through 1111, 1113, 1114 and 1211 are hereby incorporated into and made a part of this Chapter. Articles 1115 through 1138 are hereby incorporated into and made a part of this Chapter solely for breaches by a Party of Articles 1109 through 1111, 1113 and 1114, as incorporated into this Chapter.

3.   Nothing in this Chapter shall be construed to prevent a Party, including its public entities, from exclusively conducting or providing in its territory:

    (a)   activities or services forming part of a public retirement plan or statutory system of social security; or

(b)   activities or services for the account or with the guarantee or using the financial resources of the Party, including its public entities.

4.   Annex 1401.4 applies to the Parties specified in that Annex.

Article 1408: Senior Management and Boards of Directors

1.   No Party may require financial institutions of another Party to engage individuals of any particular nationality as senior managerial or other essential personnel.

2.   No Party may require that more than a simple majority of the board of directors of a financial institution of another Party be composed of nationals of the Party, persons residing in the territory of the Party, or a combination thereof.

*   *   *

Treaty Establishing the Common Market for Eastern and Southern Africa
and
Treaty for the Establishment of the Preferential Trade Area for Eastern and Southern African States[*]
[excerpts]

The Treaty for the Establishment of a Preferential Trade Area for the Eastern and Southern African States (PTA) was signed on 21 December 1981 and came into force on 30 September 1982. The States members of the PTA were Angola, Botswana, Comoros, Djibouti, Ethiopia, the Republic of Kenya, Lesotho, Madagascar, Malawi, Mauritius, Mozambique, Seychelles, Somalia, Swaziland, the United Republic of Tanzania, Uganda, Zambia, and Zimbabwe. The PTA was superseded by the Treaty Establishing the Common Market for Eastern and Southern Africa (COMESA), which was signed on 5 November 1993 and came into force in December 1994. The States members of COMESA are Angola, Botswana, Comoros, Djibouti, Ethiopia, Kenya, Lesotho, Madagascar, Malawi, Mauritius, Mozambique, Seychelles, Somalia, Swaziland, United Republic of Tanzania, Uganda, Zambia, and Zimbabwe.

Treaty Establishing the Common Market for Eastern and Southern Africa
[excerpts]

CHAPTER TWELVE
CO-OPERATION IN INDUSTRIAL DEVELOPMENT

Article 99
Scope of Co-operation in Industrial Development

The objectives of co-operation in industrial development in the Common Market are to:

(a)   promote self-sustained and balanced growth;

(b)   increase the availability of industrial goods and services for intra-Common Market trade;

---

[*]Source: International Legal Materials (1994). "Treaty Establishing the Common Market for Eastern and Southern Africa", Volume XXXIII, No. 5 (September 1994) pp.1072-1124; and United Nations Economic Commission for Africa (1981). *Treaty for the Establishment of the Preferential Trade Area for Eastern and Southern African States*, (Addis Ababa: United Nations Economic Commission for Africa) [Note added by the editor].

(c)   improve the competitiveness of the industrial sector thereby enhancing the expansion of intra-regional trade in manufactures in order to achieve structural transformation of the economy that would foster the overall socio-economic development in Member States; and

(d)   develop industrialists that would acquire ownership and management of the industries.

Article 100
Strategy and Priority Areas

For the purposes of Article 99 of this Treaty, the Member States undertake to formulate an industrial strategy aimed at:

(a)   the promotion of linkages among industries through specialisation and complementarity, paying due regard to comparative advantage in order to enhance the spread effects of industrial growth and to facilitate the transfer of technology;

(b)   the facilitation of the development of:

(i)   small-and-medium scale industries including sub-contracting and other relations between larger and smaller firms;

(ii)   basic capital and intermediate goods industries for the purposes of obtaining the advantages of economies of scale;

(iii)   food and agro industries;

(c)   the rational and full use of established industries so as to promote efficiency in production;

(d)   the promotion of industrial research and development, the transfer, adaptation and development of technology, training, management and consultancy services through the establishment of joint industrial support institutions and other infrastructural facilities;

(e)   the promotion of the linkage between the industrial sector and other sectors of the economies such as agriculture, transport, communications and other sectors;

(f)   the granting of investment incentives to industries particularly those that use local materials and labour;

(g)   the dissemination and exchange of industrial and technological information;

(h)   the improvement in the investment climate for both national and foreign investors and the encouragement of national savings and the re-investment of surpluses;

(i)   the development of human resources including training and the development of indigenous entrepreneurs and industrialists for sustained industrial growth;

(j)   the increased participation of the private sector in project development, promotion and implementation;

(k)   the rehabilitation, maintenance and upgrading of agro-industries and the metallurgical, engineering, chemical and building materials industries;

(l)   the development and promotion of integrated inter-State resource-based core and basic industries;

(m)   the promotion of multinational projects with the aim of increasing added value to raw materials in the Member States for export; and

(n)   the joint exploitation and utilisation of shared resources.

Article 101
Multinational Industrial Enterprises

1.   The Member States shall promote and encourage the establishment of multinational industrial enterprises in accordance with the laws in force in the Member States in which such enterprises shall be established, having due regard to the economic conditions and priorities of the particular Member States concerned.

2.   The Member States concerned shall determine:

(a)   the conditions and priorities that shall govern multinational industrial enterprises that:

(i)   require the combined markets of more than one Member State to be profitable and which require for their consumption large quantities of the natural resources or raw materials of the Member States which are either exported to third countries or are unused;

(ii)   require for their establishment and operation, large sums of money;

(iii)   lead to the earning or saving of substantial amounts of foreign exchange;

(iv)   through their activities, enhance the development or acquisition of modern technology, managerial and marketing experience; and

(v) through their activities, provide substantial employment or reduce unemployment within the territories of the Member States;

(b) the guidelines relating to the establishment and operation of multinational industrial enterprises which shall include:

(i) the location of multinational industrial enterprises and the criteria to be applied in that respect;

(ii) the repatriation of funds;

(iii) regulations regarding ownership and management by the Member States in a multinational industrial enterprise; and

(iv) any other matter designed to ensure the attainment of the objectives of this Chapter.

3. For the purposes of paragraph 2 of this Article, the Member States may take into account any recommendations that the Sectoral Ministerial Meeting on Industry, may make for the purpose of assisting in the co-ordination of and the provision of advice on the process of establishing multinational industrial enterprises in the Member States.

4. The Member States agree that in order to provide a comprehensive inventory of raw materials required by multinational industrial enterprises, they shall give consideration to the desirability of making an inventory of their potential natural resources.

Article 102
Industrial Manpower Development, Training, Management and Consultancy Services

1. The Member States shall take appropriate measures to establish, where necessary, joint training institutions and programmes, to share available national institutions and use African training institutions to meet the requirements for the training of skilled manpower for their industrial and technological development.

2. The Member States shall diligently endeavour to develop and make maximum use of their national entrepreneurs and technical managerial and marketing manpower and other human resources to promote and accelerate the process of their industrialization.

3. The Member States undertake to encourage the development and the use, as much as possible, of national industrial management and consultancy services in their industrial development and shall also use as much as practicable the services of any appropriate African institution for industrial management and consultancy services.

Article 103
Industrial Research and Development and the Acquisition of Modern Technology

1.   The Member States shall share and make the best use of existing and future industrial and scientific research institutions, facilities and technical know-how.   The institutions referred to herein include the Leather and Leather Products Institute and the Metallurgical Technology Centre.

2.   The Member States shall endeavour to adopt a common approach to and determine the terms and conditions governing the transfer or adaptation and development of technology.

3.   The Member States shall endeavour to co-ordinate their efforts and consult each other in matters relating to industrial property.

Article 104
Exchange of Industrial and Technological Information

1.   The Member States shall exchange information on:

    (a)   the production of and requirements for capital, intermediate and consumer goods;

    (c)   legislation and regulations concerning investment from third countries and related incentives;**

    (d)   legislation on patents, trade marks and designs; and

    (e)   industrial investment opportunities, processes, technology and related information.

2.   The Member States undertake to communicate to each other and exchange any information acquired as a result of industrial research, engineering and technological adaptation or innovation and managerial and marketing experience.

3.   The Member States shall disseminate and exchange any other information or documents deemed necessary by the Sectoral Ministerial Meeting on Industry.

4.   Notwithstanding the provisions of paragraphs 1, 2 and 3 of this Article, a Member State may withhold classified documents.

5.   The Member States undertake to strengthen their capability to compile, disseminate and absorb industrial information.

**Article 104.1 contains no part (b). This omission is also noted in the International Legal Materials reproduction of this text [Note added by the editor]

6.   The Member States agree that the provisions of this Article shall not apply where the communication of the information in question is prohibited under an agreement concluded before the entry into force of this Treaty, between a Member State and another party.

Article 105
Mechanism for the Promotion of Industrial Development

1.   The Member States shall establish a centre for the promotion of industrial development, referred to in this Chapter as "the Centre", as an institution of the Common Market whose constitution shall be determined by the Council.

2.   The objectives of the Centre shall be to:

(a)   promote co-operation in industrial development among the Member States;

(b)   assist the Member States to establish or strengthen national industrial development institutions;

(c)   assist in the training and development of various categories of industrial skills including management and marketing;

(d)   organize and maintain a data bank for industrial information;

(e)   assist in the development of common standards and quality control in accordance with the provisions of Chapter Fifteen of this Treaty; and

(f)   co-operate with the national industrial development institutions of the Member States and with African regional institutions for industrial development.

3.   The functions of the Centre shall include:

(a)   the undertaking of industrial surveys, project identification and prefeasibility studies.

(b)   the provision of advisory services for industrial development with particular reference to multinational enterprises;

(c)   working closely and exchanging information with the trade and investment promotion centers in the Member States; and

(d)   any other function that the Council, on the recommendation of the Sectoral Ministerial Meeting on Industry, may assign to it.

CHAPTER TWENTY SIX
INVESTMENT PROMOTION AND PROTECTION

Article 158
Scope of Co-operation in Investment Promotion and Protection

The member States recognise the need for effective resource mobilisation, investment and the importance of encouraging increased flow of private sector investment into the Common Market for development. To this end, the Member States agree to adopt harmonised macroeconomic policies that shall attract private sector investment into the Common Market.

Article 159
Investment Promotion and Protection

1. In order to encourage and facilitate private investment flows into the Common market, Member States shall:

   (a) accord fair and equitable treatment to private investors;

   (b) adopt a programme for the promotion of cross-border investment;

   (c) create and maintain a predictable, transparent and secure investment climate in the Member States;

   (d) remove administrative, fiscal and legal restrictions to intra-Common Market investment, and

   (e) accelerate the deregulation of the investment process.

2. For the purposes of investment protection, the following activities shall be considered as investment:

   (a) movable and immovable property and other property rights such as mortgages, loans and pledges;

   (b) shares and any other rights of participation in the management or economic results of a company or a firm, whether incorporated or not, including minority shares, corporate rights and any other kind of shareholding;

   (c) stocks, bonds, debentures, guarantees or other financial instruments of a company or a firm, government or other public authority or international organisation;

   (d) claims to money, goods, services or other performance having economic value;

(e) intellectual and industrial property rights, technical processes, know-how, goodwill and other benefits or advantages associated with a business; and

(f) such other activities that may be declared by the Council as investments.

3. The member States agree that part of the conducive climate to investment are measures aimed at protecting and guaranteeing such investment. To this end, the Member States shall:

(a) subject to the accepted principle of public interest, refrain from nationalising or expropriating private investment; and

(b) in the event private investment is nationalised or expropriated, pay adequate compensation.

4. For the purposes of paragraph 3 of this Article, expropriation shall include any measures attributable to the government of a Member State which have the effect of depriving an investor of his ownership or control of, or a substantial benefit from his investment and shall be interpreted to include all forms of expropriation such as nationalisation and attachment as well as creeping expropriation in the form of imposition of excessive and discriminatory taxes, restrictions in the procurement of raw materials, administrative action or omission where there is a legal obligation to act or measures that frustrate the exercise of the investor's rights to dividends, profits and proceeds of the right to dispose of the investment.

5. The benefits to private investors include the right to:

(a) repatriate investment returns including dividends and interest or other equivalent charges;

(b) repatriate royalties and other payments deriving from licences, franchises, concessions and other similar rights;

(c) repatriate funds for repayment of loans;

(d) repatriate proceeds from the liquidation or sale of the whole or part of the investment including an appreciation or increase of the value of the investment capital;

(e) payments for maintaining or developing the investment project, such as funds for acquiring raw or auxiliary materials, semi-finished products as well as replacing capital assets;

(f) remit the earnings of expatriate staff of the investment project; and

(g)   the right to enjoy exemption from customs duties and other fiscal exemptions for the period provided for in the investment package of a Member State and depending on the area of investment.

6.   The Member States agree that a reasonable period of stability of investment climate is the period required to refinance the investment.

Article 160
Information on Investment Incentives and Opportunities

The member States undertake to increase awareness of their investment incentives, opportunities, legislation, practices, major events affecting investments and other relevant information through regular dissemination and other awareness-promoting activities.

Article 161
Double Taxation Agreements

The Member States undertake to conclude between themselves agreements on the avoidance of double taxation.

Article 162
Multilateral Investment Agreements

The Member States agree to take necessary measures to accede to multilateral agreements on investment dispute resolution and guarantee arrangements as a means of creating a conducive climate for investment promotion. To this end, the Member States undertake to accede to:

(a)   the International Convention on Settlement of Investment Disputes Between States and Nationals of Other States, 1965;

(b)   the Convention Establishing the Multilateral Investment Guarantee Agency; and

(c)   any other multilateral agreements designed to promote or protect investment.

*   *   *

TREATY FOR THE ESTABLISHMENT OF THE PREFERENTIAL TRADE AREA FOR EASTERN AND SOUTHERN AFRICAN STATES
[excerpts]

CHAPTER SEVEN
ECONOMIC COMMUNITY FOR EASTERN AND SOUTHERN AFRICAN STATES

Article 29
Gradual establishment of a Common Market and an Economic Community for Eastern and Southern African States

Two years before the expiry of ten years from the definitive entry into force of this Treaty, the Commission shall propose to the Council for its consideration and recommendation to the Authority for its approval, measures which in addition to the provisions of this Treaty would be required to be implemented as from the end of the said period of ten years, in order to assist in the development of the Preferential Trade Area into a Common Market and eventually into an Economic Community for Eastern and Southern African States.

ANNEX VIII

Article 24

PROTOCOL ON CO-OPERATION IN THE FIELD OF INDUSTRIAL DEVELOPMENT

PREAMBLE

THE HIGH CONTRACTING PARTIES

CONVINCED that co-operation in industrial development offers favourable and good prospects not only for a more rapid and self-sustained industrialization but also for the expansion of trade between the Member States;

MINDFULL that such co-operation in industrial development can only be achieved on the basis of full recognition and understanding of the prevailing situation of industrial and overall economic development in each Member State;

CONSCIOUS of the fact that meaningful Preferential Trade Area arrangements between countries at different levels of economic development and pursuing economic and political policies cannot be realised without the restructuring of their economies through co-operation in industrial development; and

RECALLING the provisions of item (v) of subparagraph (a) of paragraph 4 of Article 3 of the Treaty requiring that a Protocol on co-operation in the field of industrial development within the Preferential Trade Area shall be annexed to the Treaty;

HEREBY AGREE AS FOLLOWS:

Article 4
Multinational industrial enterprises

1. The Member States agree to promote and encourage the establishment of multinational industrial enterprises in accordance with the laws in force in the Member States in which such enterprises shall be established, and having due regard to the economic conditions and priorities of the particular Member States concerned.

2. The Member States concerned shall determine:

(a) the conditions and priorities that shall govern multinational industrial enterprises that would:

    (i) require the combined markets of more than one Member State to be profitable and which require for their consumption large quantities of the natural resources or raw materials of the Member States which are either exported to third countries or are unused;

    (ii) require for their establishment and operation large sums of money;

    (iii) lead to the earning or saving of substantial amounts of foreign exchange;

    (iv) through their activities enhance the development or acquisition of modern technology, managerial and marketing experience; and

    (v) through their activities provide substantial employment or reduce unemployment within the territories of the Member States; and

(b) the guidelines relating to the establishment and operation of multinational industrial enterprises which shall include:

    (i) the location of multinational industrial enterprises and the criteria to be applied in that respect;

    (ii) the minimum capacity or size of multinational industrial enterprises and the conditions under which such industrial enterprises may be established;

    (iii) the quality and standard of the products of multinational industrial enterprises and any other requirements that may be deemed necessary for the protection of the consumer;

    (iv) regulations regarding ownership and management by the Member States in a multinational industrial enterprise; and

> (v)   any other matter designed to ensure the attainment of the objectives of this Protocol.

3.   In order to achieve the objectives set out in paragraph 2 of this Article, the Member States may take into account any recommendations that the Committee through the Council may make for the purpose of assisting in the co-ordination of and the provision of advice on the process of establishing multinational industrial enterprises in the Member States.

4.   Notwithstanding the provisions of this Protocol, the Member States agree that products of multinational industrial enterprises shall enjoy preferential tariff and non-tariff treatment in accordance with the provisions of the Treaty.

5.   The Member States agree that in order to provide a comprehensive inventory of raw materials required by multinational industrial enterprises, they shall give consideration to the desirability of making an inventory of their potential natural resources.

*   *   *

Annex B
Prototype Bilateral Investment Treaties
and list of Bilateral Investment Treaties (1959-1995)

ASIAN-AFRICAN LEGAL CONSULTATIVE COMMITTEE REVISED DRAFT OF MODEL AGREEMENTS FOR PROMOTION AND PROTECTION OF INVESTMENTS*a/

Model A

AGREEMENT between the Government of _____

and

the Government of _____

for the Promotion, Encouragement and Reciprocal Protection of Investments.

The Government of _____ and the Government of

_____

Recognizing in particular the need to promote wider co-operation between the countries of the Asian-African region to accelerate their economic growth and to encourage investments by developing countries in other developing countries of the region;

Also recognizing that reciprocal protection of such investments will be conducive to the attainment of desired objectives in a spirit of partnership;

Desirous to create conditions in which the investments by each other and their nationals would be facilitated and thus stimulate the flow of capital and technology within the region;

Have agreed as follows:

Article 1
Definitions

For the purpose of this Agreement

(a) 'Investment'

(Alternative A)

'Investment' means every kind of asset and in particular, though not exclusively, includes:

---

*Source: Asian-African Legal Consultative Committee (1985). *Models for Bilateral Agreements on Promotion and Protection of Investments: Report of the Committee* (Dehli: Asian-African Legal Consultative Committee) [Note added by the editor].

(i)   movable and immovable property and any other property rights such as mortgages, liens or pledges;

(ii)   shares, stocks and debentures of companies or interests in the property of such companies;

(iii)   claims to money or to any performance under contract having a financial value, and loans;

(iv)   copyrights, know-how (goodwill) and industrial property rights such as patents for inventions, trade marks, industrial designs and trade names;

(v)   rights conferred by law or under contract, including licence to search for, cultivate, extract or exploit natural resources.

(Alternative B)

'Investment' includes every kind of asset such as:

(i)   shares and other types of holdings of companies;

(ii)   claims to any performance under contract having a financial value, claims to money, and loans;

(iii)   rights with respect to movable and immovable property;

(iv)   rights with regard to patents, trade marks and any other industrial property; and

(v)   contractual rights relating to exploration and exploitation of natural resources.

(Alternative C)

'Investment' means:

(i)   in respect of investment in the territory of
        (First Party) _____

(ii)   in respect of investment in the territory of
        (Second Party) _____

(b)   'National'

(Alternative A)

'National' in respect of each Contracting Party means a natural person who is a national or deemed to be a national of the Party under its Constitution or relevant law.

(Alternative B)

'National' in respect of (First Party) means _____ and in respect of (Second Party) means _____.

(c) 'Companies'

(Alternative A)

'Companies' means corporations, partnerships or associations incorporated, constituted or registered in a Contracting Party in accordance with its laws [and includes such entities in which nationals of a Contracting Party have substantial interest and majority shareholding].

(Alternative B)

'Companies' means in respect of the (First Party) _____ and in respect of the (Second Party) _____.

(d) 'State Entity' means a department of government, corporation, institution or undertaking wholly owned or controlled by government and engaged in activities of a commercial nature.

(e) 'Returns' includes profits, interests, capital gains, dividends, royalties or fees.

(f) 'Host State' means the country in whose territory the investment is made.

(g) 'Territory' means:

(i) In respect of the (First Party) _____;

(ii) In respect of the (Second Party) _____.

Article 2
Promotion and encouragement of investments

(i) Each Contracting Party shall take steps to promote investments in the territory of the other Contracting Party and encourage its nationals, companies and State entities to make such investments through offer of appropriate incentives, wherever possible, which may include such modalities as tax concessions and investment guarantees.

(ii)   Each Contracting Party shall create favorable conditions to encourage the nationals, companies or State entities of the other Contracting Party to promote investment in its territory.

(iii)   The Contracting Parties shall periodically consult among themselves concerning investment opportunities within the territory of each other in various sectors such as industry, mining, communications, agriculture and forestry to determine where investments from one Contracting Party into the other may be most beneficial in the interest of both the parties.

(iv)   [Each Contracting Party shall duly honour all commitments made and obligations undertaken by it with regard to investments of nationals, companies or State entities of the other Contracting Party]. b/

Article 3
Reception of investments

(i)   Each Contracting Party shall determine the mode and manner in which investments are to be received in its territory.

(ii)   The Contracting Parties may determine that in a specified class of investments, a national, company or State entity of a Contracting Party intending to make investment in the territory of the other Contracting Party including collaboration arrangements on specific projects, shall submit its or his proposal to a designated authority of the Party where the investment is sought to be made. Such proposals shall be processed expeditiously and soon after the proposal is approved, a letter of authorization shall be issued and the investment shall be registered, where appropriate, with the designated authority of the host State. The investment shall be received subject to the terms and conditions specified in the letter of authorization.

(iii)   The host State shall facilitate the implementation and operation of the investment projects through suitable administrative measures and in particular in the matter of expeditious clearance of authorizations or permits for importation of goods, employment of consultants and technicians of foreign nationality in accordance with its laws and regulations.

Article 4
Most-favoured-nation treatment

(i)   Each Contracting Party shall accord in its territory to the investments or returns of nationals, companies or State entities of the other Contracting Party treatment that is not less favourable than that it accords to the investments or returns of nationals, companies or State entities of any third State.

(ii)   Each Contracting Party shall also ensure that the nationals, companies or State entities of the other Contracting Party are accorded treatment not less favourable than that it accords to the nationals or companies or State entities of any third State in regard to the management, use, enjoyment or disposal of their investments including management and control over business activities and other ancillary functions in respect of the investments.

Article 5 c/
National treatment

(i)   Each Contracting Party shall accord in its territory to the investments or returns of nationals, companies or State entities of the other Contracting Party treatment that is not less favourable than that it accords to the investments or returns of its own nationals, companies or State entities.

(ii)   Each of the Contracting Parties shall extend to the nationals, companies or State entities of the other Contracting Party, treatment that is not less favourable than it accords to its own nationals, companies or State entities in regard to management, control, use, enjoyment and disposal in relation to investments which have been received in its territory.

Article 6
Repatriation of capital and returns

(i)   Each Contracting Party shall ensure that the nationals, companies or State entities of the other Contracting Party are allowed full facilities in the matter of the right to repatriation of capital and returns on his or its investments subject, however, to any condition for re-investment and subject also to the right of the host State to impose reasonable restrictions for temporary periods in accordance with its laws to meet exceptional financial and economic situations [as determined in the light of guidelines generally applied by the IMF or such other criteria as may be agreed upon by the parties]. The capital and returns allowed to be repatriated shall include emoluments and earnings accruing from or in relation to the investment as also the proceeds arising out of sale of the assets in the event of liquidation or transfer.

(ii)   In the event of exceptional financial or economic situations as envisaged in paragraph (1) of this article, the host State shall exercise its powers to impose reasonable restrictions equitably and in good faith. Such restrictions shall not extend ordinarily beyond a period of _____. As any restriction in operation thereafter shall not impede the transfer of profits, interests, dividends, royalties, fees, emoluments or earnings; as regards the capital invested or any other form of returns, transfer of a minimum of 20 per cent in each year shall be guaranteed.

(iii)   Repatriation shall be permitted ordinarily to the country from which the investment originated and in the same currency in which the capital was originally invested or in any other currency agreed upon by the investor and the host State at the rate of exchange applicable on the date of transfer upon such repatriation, unless otherwise agreed by the investor and the host State.

Article 7
Nationalization, expropriation and payment of compensation in respect thereof

(i)   Investments of nationals, companies or State entities of either Contracting Party shall not be nationalized, expropriated or subjected to measures having effect equivalent to nationalization or expropriation in the territory of the other Contracting Party except [for a public purpose] [in national interest] of that Party and against prompt, adequate and effective compensation, provided that such measures are taken on a non-discriminatory basis and in accordance with its laws.

(ii)   Such compensation shall be computed on the basis of the value of the investment immediately prior to the point of time when the proposal for expropriation had become public knowledge to be determined in accordance with recognized principles of valuation such as market value. Where the market value cannot be readily ascertained, the compensation shall be determined on equitable principles taking into account, *inter alia*, the capital invested, depreciation, capital already repatriated and other relevant factors. The compensation shall include interest at a normal commercial rate from the date of expropriation until the date of payment. The determination of the compensation, in the absence of agreement being reached between the investor and the host State, shall be referred to an independent judicial or administrative tribunal or authority competent under the laws of the expropriating State or to arbitration in accordance with the provisions of any agreement between the investor and the host State. The compensation as finally determined shall be promptly paid and allowed to be repatriated.

(iii)   Where a Contracting Party nationalizes or expropriates the assets of a company which is incorporated or constituted under the laws in force in its territory and in which nationals or companies or State entities of the other Contracting Party own shares, it shall ensure that prompt, adequate and effective compensation is received and allowed to be repatriated by the owners of the shares in the other contracting Party. Such compensation shall be determined on the basis of the recognized principles of valuation such as the market value of the shares immediately prior to the point of time when the proposal for nationalization or expropriation had become public knowledge. The compensation shall include interest at a normal commercial rate from the date of nationalization or expropriation until the date of payment. If any question arises regarding the determination of the compensation or its payment, such questions shall be referred to an independent judicial or administrative tribunal or authority competent under the laws of the expropriating State or to arbitration in accordance with the provisions of any agreement between the investor and the host State.

Article 8
Compensation for losses

[(i)   Nationals, companies or State entities of one Contracting Party whose material assets in the investments in the territory of the other Contracting Party suffer losses owing to war or other armed conflict, revolution, a state of national emergency, revolt, insurrection or riot in the territory of the latter Contracting Party, shall be accorded by that Contracting Party treatment regarding restitution, indemnification, compensation or other settlement, no less favourable than that it accords to (its own nationals, companies or State entities or to) nationals, companies or State entities of any third State]. d/

(ii)   Nationals, companies or State entities of one Contracting Party who suffer losses in the territory of the other contracting Party resulting from:

(a)   requisitioning of their property by its forces or authorities; or

(b)   destruction of their property by its forces or authorities which was not caused in combat action or was not required by the necessity of the situation;

shall be accorded restitution or adequate compensation and the resulting payments shall be allowed to be repatriated.

Article 9
Access to courts and tribunals

The nationals, companies or State entities of one Contracting Party shall have the right of access to the courts, tribunals both judicial and administrative, and other authorities competent under the laws of the other Contracting Party for redress of his or its grievances in relation to any matter concerning any investment including judicial review of measures relating to expropriation or nationalization, determination of compensation in the event of expropriation or nationalization, or losses suffered and any restrictions imposed on repatriation of capital or returns.

Article 10
Settlement of investment disputes

(i)   Each Contracting Party consents to submit any dispute or difference that may arise out of or in relation to investments made in its territory by a national, company or State entity of the other contracting Party for settlement through conciliation or arbitration in accordance with the provisions of this Article.

(ii)   If any dispute or difference should arise between a Contracting Party and a national, company or State entity of the other Contracting Party, which cannot be resolved within a period of _____ through negotiations, either party to the dispute may initiate proceedings for conciliation or arbitration unless the investor has chosen to avail himself or itself of local remedies.

(iii)   Unless the parties have reached agreement to refer the disputes to conciliation under the provisions of the International Convention for the Settlement of Investment Disputes between States and Nationals of other States 1965, conciliation shall take place under the

UNCITRAL Conciliation Rules 1980 and the assistance of _____ may be enlisted in connection with the appointment of Conciliator(s).

(iv)   Where the conciliation proceedings have failed to resolve the dispute as also in the event of agreement having been reached to resort to arbitration, the dispute shall be referred to arbitration at the instance of either party to the dispute within a period of three months.

(v)   Any reference to arbitration shall be initiated under the provisions of the International Convention on the Settlement of Investment Disputes between States and Nationals of other States 1965 or "The Additional Facility Rules" of ICSID, whichever may be appropriate. In the event of neither of these procedures being applicable, the arbitration shall take place in accordance with the UNCITRAL Arbitration Rules 1976, and the appointing authority for the purposes of such rules shall be _____.

(vi)   Neither Contracting Party shall pursue through diplomatic channels any matter referred to arbitration until the proceedings have terminated and a Contracting Party has failed to abide by or to comply with the award rendered by the arbitral tribunal.

Article 11
Settlement of disputes between Contracting Parties

(i)   Disputes or differences between the Contracting Parties concerning interpretation or application of this agreement shall be settled through negotiations.

(ii)   If such disputes and differences cannot thus be settled, the same shall, upon the request of either Contracting Party be submitted to an arbitral tribunal.

(iii)   An arbitral tribunal shall be composed of three members. Each Contracting Party shall nominate one member on the tribunal within a period of two months of the receipt of the request for arbitration. The third member, who shall be the chairman of the tribunal, shall be appointed by agreement of the Contracting Parties. If a Contracting Party has failed to nominate its arbitrator or where agreement has not been reached in regard to appointment of the chairman of the tribunal within a period of three months, either Contracting Party may approach the President of the International Court of Justice to make the appointment. The chairman so appointed shall not be a national of either Contracting Party.

(iv)   The arbitral tribunal shall reach its decision by majority of votes. Such decision shall be binding on both the Contracting Parties. The tribunal shall determine its own procedure and give directions in regard to the costs of the proceedings.

Article 12
Subrogation

If either Contracting Party makes payment under an indemnity it has given in respect of an investment or any part thereof in the territory of the other Contracting Party, the latter Contracting Party shall recognize:

(a) The assignment of any right or claim from the party indemnified to the former Contracting Party or its designated Agency; and

(b) That the former Contracting Party or its designated Agency is entitled by virtue of subrogation to exercise the rights and enforce the claims of such a party.

Article 13
Exceptions

Neither Contracting Party shall be obliged to extend to the nationals or companies or State entities of the other, the benefit of any treatment, preference or privilege which may be accorded to any other State or its nationals by virtue of the formation of a customs union, a free trade area or any other regional arrangement on economic co-operation to which such a State may be a party.

Article 14
Application of the Agreement

The provisions of this Agreement shall apply to investments made after the coming into force of this Agreement [and the investments previously made which are approved and registered by the host State (in accordance with its laws) within a period of _____ from the date of entry into force of this Agreement]. e/

Article 15
Entry into force

[This Agreement shall enter into force on signature.]

or

[This Agreement shall enter into force as from _____.]

or

[This Agreement shall be ratified and shall enter into force on the exchange of instruments of ratification.] f/

Article 16
Duration and termination

This Agreement shall remain in force for a period of _____. Thereafter it shall continue in force until the expiration of twelve months from any date on which either

Contracting Party shall have given written notice of termination to the other. [Provided that in respect of investments made whilst the Agreement is in force, its provisions shall continue in effect with respect to such investments for a period of _____ years after the date of termination.] g/

In WITNESS WHEREOF the undersigned, duly authorized thereto by their respective Governments, have signed this Agreement.

DONE in duplicate at _____, this _____ day of _____ 1980. (In the _____ and _____ languages, both texts being equally authoritative.)

For the Government of   For the Government of

_____   _____

*   *   *

Addendum to Model "A"

ASIAN-AFRICAN LEGAL CONSULTATIVE COMMITTEE (AALCC)

Models for Bilateral Agreements on Promotion and Protection of Investments

as finally adopted at AALCC's Kathmandu session in February 1985.

SUGGESTIONS OF THE DELEGATION OF KUWAIT

1.   Article 2 (Promotion and encouragement of investments)

Paragraph (iv) should be expanded to read as follows (additions underlined):

"Each Contracting Party shall at all times ensure fair and equitable treatment to the investments of nationals, companies or State entities of the other Contracting Party. Each Contracting Party shall ensure that the management, maintenance, use, enjoyment or disposal of investments in its territory of nationals, companies or State entities of the other Contracting Party is not in any way impaired by unreasonable or discriminatory measures.

Each Contracting Party shall duly honour all commitments made and obligations undertaken by it with regard to investments of nationals, companies or State entities of the other Contracting Party."

2.   Article 6 (Repatriation of capital and returns)

It is proposed that the following paragraph be added to Article 6:

"(iv) The Contracting Parties undertake to accord to transfers referred to in paragraphs (i), (ii) and (iii) of this Article a treatment as favourable as that accorded to transfers originating from investments made by nationals, companies and State entities of any third Party."

3.   Article 11 (Settlement of disputes between Contracting Parties)

Paragraph (iii) of Article 11 should be expanded to read as follows:

... either Contracting Party may approach the President of the International Court of Justice to make the appointments. If the President is a national of either Contracting Party or if he is otherwise prevented from discharging the said function, the Vice-President shall be invited to make the necessary appointments. If the Vice-President is a national of either Contracting Party or if he too is prevented from discharging the said function, the member of the International Court of Justice next in seniority who is not a national of either Contracting Party shall be invited to make the necessary appointments.

4.   Suggested additional articles

There are two additional articles that should be incorporated into the agreement. They are related to the relations between governments and to the application of other rules.

Article
Relations between Governments

"The provisions of the present Agreement shall apply irrespective of the existence of diplomatic or consular relations between the Contracting Parties."

Article
Applications of other rules

"Notwithstanding the provisions of this Agreement, the relevant international agreements which bind both contracting parties may be applied with the consent of both parties."

*   *   *

Model B**

AGREEMENT between the Government of _____

and

the Government of _____ for Promotion, Encouragement and Reciprocal Protection of Investments.

The Government of _____ and the Government of _____,

Recognizing in particular the need to promote wider co-operation between the countries of the Asian-African region to accelerate their economic growth and to encourage investments by developing countries in other developing countries of the region;

Also recognizing that reciprocal protection of such investments will be conducive to the attainment of desired objectives in a spirit of partnership;

Desirous to create conditions in which investments by each other and their nationals would be facilitated and thus stimulate the flow of capital and technology within the region;

Have agreed as follows:

Article 1
Definitions

For the purpose of this Agreement

**The model agreement is intended to provide a possible negotiating text for consideration of Governments. It is merely a model and not an adhesive text. The possibility that the text would be modified or altered in the course of bilateral negotiations to suit the needs of the parties is clearly contemplated.

(a)   'Investment'

(Alternative A)

'Investment' means every kind of asset and in particular, though not exclusively, includes:

(i)   movable and immovable property and any other property rights such as mortgages, liens or pledges;

(ii)   shares, stocks and debentures of companies or interests in the property of such companies;

(iii)   claims to money or to any performance under contract having a financial value and loans;

(iv)   copyrights, know-how, [goodwill] and industrial property rights such as patents for inventions, trademarks, industrial designs and trade names;

(v)   rights conferred by law or under contract, including licence to search for, cultivate, extract or exploit natural resources.

(Alternative B)

'Investment' includes every kind of asset such as:

(i)   shares and other types of holdings of companies,

(ii)   claims to any performance under contract having a financial value, claims to money and loans;

(iii)   rights with respect to movable and immovable property,

(iv)   rights with regard to patents, trade marks, and any other industrial property; and

(v)   contractual rights relating to exploration and exploitation of natural resources.

(Alternative C)

'Investment' means:

(i)   in respect of investment in the territory of (First Party) _____;

(ii)   in respect of investment in the territory of (Second Party)_____ .

(b)   'National'

(Alternative A)

'National' in respect of each Contracting Party means a natural person who is national or deemed to be a national of the Party under its Constitution or relevant law.

(Alternative B)

'National' in respect _____(First Party)_____
means _____ and in respect of (Second Party)
means _____.

(c)   'Companies'

(Alternative A)

'Companies' means corporations, partnerships or associations incorporated, constituted or registered in a Contracting Party in accordance with its laws [and includes such entities in which nationals of a Contracting Party have substantial interest and majority shareholding.]

(Alternative B)

'Companies' means in respect of the (First Party) _____ and in respect of the (Second Party) _____.

(d)   'State Entity' means a department of government, corporation, institution or undertaking wholly owned or controlled by government and engaged in activities of a commercial nature.

(e)   'Returns' includes profits, interest, capital gains, dividends, royalties or fees.

(f)   'Host State' means the country in whose territory the investment is made.

(g)   'Territory' means:

(i)   in respect of the (First Party) _____;

(ii)   in respect of the (Second Party) _____.

Article 2
Promotion and encouragement of investments

(i)   Each Contracting Party shall take steps to promote investments in the territory of the other Contracting Party and encourage its nationals, companies and State entities to make such investments, through offer of appropriate incentives, wherever possible, which may include such modalities as tax concessions and investment guarantees.

(ii)   Each Contracting Party shall create favourable conditions for the nationals, companies or State entities of the other Contracting Party to promote investment in its territory.

(iii)   The Contracting Parties shall periodically consult among themselves concerning investment opportunities within the territory of each other in various sectors such as industry, mining, communications, agriculture and forestry to determine where investments from one Contracting Party into the other may be most beneficial in the interest of both the parties.

(iv)   *[Each Contracting Party shall duly honour all commitments made and obligations undertaken by it with regard to investments of nationals, companies or State entities of the other Contracting Party.]

Article 3
Reception of investments

(i)   A national, company or State entity of a Contracting Party intending to make investment in the territory of the other Contracting Party including collaboration arrangements on specific projects, shall submit his or its proposal to a designated authority of the Party where the investment is sought to be made. Such proposals shall be examined expeditiously and so soon after the proposal is approved, a letter of authorization shall be issued and the investment shall be registered, where appropriate, with the designated authority of the host State.

(ii)   The investment shall be received subject to the terms and conditions specified in the letter of authorization. Such terms and conditions may include the obligation or requirement concerning employment of local personnel and labour in the investment projects, organisation of training programmes, transfer of technology and marketing arrangements for the products.

(iii)   The host State shall facilitate the performance of the contracts relatable to the investments through suitable administrative measures and in particular in the matter of expeditious clearance of authorization or permits for importation of goods, employment of consultants and technicians of foreign nationality in accordance with its laws and regulations.

(iv)   The Contracting Parties shall make every endeavour through appropriate means at their disposal to ensure that their nationals, companies or State entities comply with the laws and regulations of the host State and also carry out in good faith the obligations undertaken in respect of the investments made in accordance with the terms and conditions specified by the host State.

---

*There were some differences of view on the needs for inclusion of this clause.

Article 4
Most-favoured-nation treatment

(i)   Each Contracting Party shall accord in its territory to the investments or returns of nationals, companies or State entities of the other Contracting Party treatment that is not less favourable than that it accords to the investments or returns of nationals, companies or State entities of any third State.

(ii)   Each Contracting Party shall also ensure that the nationals, companies or State entities of the other Contracting Party are accorded treatment not less favourable than that it accords to the nationals or companies or State entities of any third State in regard to the management, use, enjoyment or disposal of their investments including management and control over business activities and other ancilliary functions in respect of the investments.

Article 5
*National treatment

(i)   Each Contracting Party shall accord in its territory to the investments or returns of nationals, companies or State entities of the other Contracting Party treatment that is not less favourable than that it accords to the investments or returns of its own nationals, companies or State entities.

(ii)   Each of the Contracting Parties shall extend to the nationals, companies or State entities of the other Contracting Party, treatment that is not less favourable than that it accords to its own nationals, companies or State entities in regard to management, control, use, enjoyment and disposal in relation to investments which have been received in its territory.

Article 6
Repatriation of capital and returns

(i)   Each Contracting Party shall ensure that the nationals, companies or State entities of the other Contracting Party are allowed facilities in the matter of repatriation of capital and returns on his or its investments in accordance with the terms and conditions stipulated by the host State at the time of the reception of the investment.

(ii)   Such terms and conditions may specify:

(a)   the mode and manner of repatriation of profits and returns as also the requirement, if any, concerning re-investment;

(b)   the extent to which the capital invested may be allowed to be repatriated in each particular year;

---

*Some countries do not favour "national treatment" for foreign investments.

(c)   any requirement concerning the currency in which repatriation is to be made and the place or places of such repatriation;

(d)   the nature of restrictions that may be imposed by the host State on repatriation of capital and returns in its national interest during any period of exceptional financial or economic situations.

(iii)   The stipulations concerning repatriation of capital and returns shall be set out in the letter of authorization referred to in Article 3. The terms and conditions so specified shall remain operative throughout the period of the investment and shall not be altered without the agreement of the parties.

Article 7
Nationalization, expropriation and payment of compensation in respect thereof

(i)   (Alternative 1)

A Contracting Party may exercise its sovereign rights in the matter of nationalization or expropriation in respect of investments made in its territory by nationals, companies or State entities of the other Contracting Party upon payment of appropriate compensation, subject however, to the provisions of its laws. The host State shall abide by and honour any commitments made or assurances given both in regard to nationalization or expropriation and the principles for determination of appropriate compensation including the mode and manner of payment thereof.

(Alternative 2)

Investments of nationals, companies or State entities of either Contracting Party shall not be nationalized, expropriated or subjected to measures having effect equivalent to nationalization or expropriation in the territory of the other Contracting Party except [for a public purpose] [in national interest] of that party and against prompt payment of appropriate compensation.

(ii)   (Alternative 1)

*[Unless stipulations are made to the contrary at the time of the reception of the investment, the expression "appropriate compensation" shall mean compensation calculated on the basis of recognized principles of valuation.]

(Alternative 2)

Unless stipulations are made to the contrary at the time of the reception of the investment, the expression "appropriate compensation" shall mean compensation determined in accordance

---

*Some delegations had reservations on this provision.

with equitable principles taking into account the capital invested, depreciation, capital already repatriated and other relevant factors.

Article 8
Compensation for losses

The nationals, companies or State entities of one Contracting Party who suffer losses in the territory of the other Contracting Party resulting from:

(a)   Requisitioning of their property by its forces or authorities; or

(b)   Destruction of their property by its forces or authorities which was not caused in combat actions or was not required by the necessity of the situation;

shall be accorded restitution or adequate compensation [and the resulting payments shall be allowed to be repatriated.]

Article 9
Access to courts and tribunals

(Alternative 1)

The nationals, companies or State entities of one Contracting Party shall have the right of access to the courts, tribunals, both judicial and administrative, and other authorities competent under the laws of the other Contracting Party for redress of his or its grievances in relation to any matter concerning an investment including judicial review of measures relating to nationalization or expropriation, determination of compensation in the event of nationalization or expropriation or losses suffered and any restrictions imposed on repatriation of capital or returns. The local remedies shall be exhausted before any other step or proceeding is contemplated.

*[(Alternative 2)

Any difference or dispute between the investor and the host State in relation to any matter concerning an investment including those relating to nationalization or expropriation, determination of compensation in the event of nationalization or expropriation or losses suffered and any restrictions imposed on repatriation of capital and returns shall be settled through recourse to appropriate courts and tribunals, judicial or administrative and other authorities competent under the local laws of the host State. Neither Contracting Party shall pursue through diplomatic channel any such matter until the local remedies have been exhausted.]

---

*Several participants considered this provision to be inappropriate.

Article 10
Settlement of investment disputes

(i)   Each Contracting Party consents to submit any dispute or difference that may arise out of or in relation to investments made in its territory by a national, company or State entity of the other Contracting Party for settlement through conciliation or arbitration in accordance with the provisions of this Article.

(ii)   If any dispute or difference should arise between a Contracting Party and a national, company or State entity of the other Contracting Party, which cannot be resolved within a period of _____through negotiations, either party to the dispute may initiate proceedings for conciliation or arbitration after the local remedies have been exhausted.

(iii)   Conciliation shall take place under the UNCITRAL Conciliation Rules 1980 unless the parties have reached agreement to refer the dispute to conciliation under the provisions of the International Convention for the Settlement of Investment Disputes between States and Nationals of other States 1965.

(iv)   Where the conciliation proceedings have failed to resolve the dispute, it shall be referred to arbitration at the instance of either party to the dispute within a period of three months.

(v)   Any reference to arbitration shall be initiated under the provisions of the International Convention for the Settlement of Investment Disputes between States and Nationals of other States 1965 or "The Additional Facility Rules" of ICSID, whichever may be appropriate. In the event of neither of these procedures being applicable, the arbitration shall take place in accordance with the UNCITRAL Arbitration Rules of 1976, and the appointing authority for the purposes of such rules shall be _____.

(vi)   Neither Contracting Party shall pursue through diplomatic channel any matter referred to arbitration until the proceedings have terminated and a Contracting Party has failed to abide by or to comply with the award rendered by the arbitral tribunal.

Article 11
Settlement of disputes between Contracting Parties

(i)   Disputes or differences between the Contracting Parties concerning interpretation or application of this agreement shall be settled through negotiations.

(ii)   If such disputes and differences cannot thus be settled, the same shall upon the request of either Contracting Party be submitted to an arbitral tribunal.

(iii)   An arbitral tribunal shall be composed of three members. Each Contracting Party shall nominate one member on the tribunal within a period of two months of the receipt of the request for arbitration. The third member, who shall be the chairman of the tribunal, shall be appointed by agreement of the Contracting Parties. If a Contracting Party has failed to nominate its arbitrator or where agreement has not been reached in regard to the appointment of the chairman of the tribunal, within a period of three months, either Contracting Party may approach the President of the International Court of Justice to make the appointment.

(iv)   The arbitral tribunal shall reach its decision by majority of votes. Such decision shall be binding on both the Contracting Parties. The tribunal shall determine its own procedure and give direction in regard to the costs of the proceedings.

Article 12
Subrogation

If either Contracting Party makes payment under an indemnity it has given in respect of an investment or any part thereof in the territory of the other Contracting Party, the latter Contracting Party shall recognize:

(a)   The assignment of any right or claim from the party indemnified to the former Contracting Party or its designated Agency; and

(b)   That the former Contracting Party or its designated Agency is entitled by virtue of subrogation to exercise the rights and enforce the claims of such a party.

Article 13
Exceptions

Neither Contracting Party shall be obliged to extend to the nationals or companies or State entities of the other, the benefit of any treatment, preference or privilege which may be accorded to any other State or its nationals by virtue of the formation of a customs union, a free trade area or any other regional arrangement on economic co-operation to which such a State may be a party.

Article 14
Application of the Agreement

The provisions of this Agreement shall apply to investments made after the coming into force of this Agreement.

Article 15
Entry into force

*[This Agreement shall enter into force on signature.]

---

*Alternative provisions.

---

or

*[This Agreement shall enter into force as from _____.]

or

*[This Agreement shall be ratified and shall enter into force on the exchange of instruments of ratification].

Article 16
Duration and termination

This agreement shall remain in force for a period of _____ years. Thereafter it shall continue in force until the expiration of twelve months from any date on which either Contracting Party shall have given written notice of termination to the other. [Provided that in respect of investments made whilst the agreement is in force, its provisions shall continue in effect with respect to such investments for a period of _____ years after the date of termination.]

In witness whereof the undersigned, duly authorized thereto by their respective Governments, have signed this Agreement.

Done in duplicate at _____ this _____ day of _____ 198__. [In the _____ and _____ languages, both texts being equally authoritative.]

For the Government of   For the Government of

_____   _____

* * *

Model C

Note: The provisions for incorporation in the text of this model draft would be identical

_____

*Alternative provisions.

with the provisions set out in Model A, with the exception of the definition of "Investment" in article 1 (a) and the text of article 14. The suggested texts for these provisions are as follows:

Article 1
Definitions

(a) "Investment" means:

Capital and technology employed in projects or industries in specified sectors of national importance as set out in the schedule to this Agreement and includes the following in relation thereto:

(i) shares and other types of holdings of companies;

(ii) claims to any performance under contract having a financial value, claims to money and loans;

(iii) rights with regard to patents, trademarks and any other industrial property; and

(iv) contractual rights relating to exploration and exploitation of natural resources.

Article 14
Application of the Agreement

The provisions of this Agreement shall apply to investments made after the coming into force of this Agreement where the investment has been made in specified sectors set out in the schedule to this Agreement.

Explanatory notes to the provisions of the model agreement (Model C)

This Model Agreement has been prepared with a view to serve as a possible negotiating text for those States which prefer to conclude investment protection treaties relatable only to investments in specific sectors of national interest of the host State. The practice followed by these States generally reveals the position that with regard to investments covered under a treaty they would be prepared to accord full freedom in the matter of repatriation of capital and return as also market value as compensation in the event of nationalization or expropriation of the investment.

Model C accordingly contemplates that all the provisions contained in Model A should be incorporated in the text subject to only two variations, namely the definition of "investment" and the provision on application of the Agreement. These provisions are so drafted as to conform to the position that the investments covered under the treaty are those investments which are of national importance and related to those specified sectors as set out in the Schedule to the Agreement.

* * *

Notes

a/   The model agreements are intended to provide possible negotiating texts for consideration of Governments.   They are merely models and not adhesive texts. The possibility that the texts would be modified or altered in the course of bilateral negotiations to suit the needs of the parties is clearly contemplated.

The AALCC has prepared three draft models which are described as follows: Model A: Draft of a bilateral agreement basically on similar pattern as the agreements entered into between some of the countries of the region with industrialized States with certain changes and improvements particularly in the matter of promotion of investments. Model B: draft of an agreement whose provisions are somewhat more restrictive in the matter of protection of investments and contemplate a degree of flexibility in regard to reception and protection of investments. Model C: draft of an agreement on the pattern of Model A but applicable to specific classes of investments only as determined by the host State.

b/   There were some differences of views on the need for inclusion of this clause.

c/   Some countries do not favour "National Treatment" for foreign investments.

d/   Several participants had reservations on the provisions of this paragraph.

e/   There were some differences of view about the past investments being covered.

f/   Alternative provisions.

g/   There were some differences of views whether past investments should be covered.

*   *   *

CARICOM GUIDELINES FOR USE IN THE NEGOTIATION OF BILATERAL TREATIES*

Contribution Expected by CARICOM States from BITs

(i)   BITs should provide real opportunities for the promotion of the economic and social development of CARICOM countries, individually and collectively, through the enhancement of their production base in accordance with each country's particular criteria, goals and development strategy;

(ii)   CARICOM States, in the conclusion and implementation of BITs, should ensure the preservation and strengthening of the CARICOM Integration Movement.

Type of Agreement Desired

The preamble of the BIT should include:

(i)   a provision which reflects the objective of increasing capital flows from the USA to the CARICOM States to build up their productive base and hence enhance their economic and social development;

(ii)   a provision which reflects the undertaking of the USA to establish incentives and institutional arrangements to encourage the flow of investments from the USA to CARICOM States.

Most Favoured Nation Treatment

Subject to exceptions, preferential treatment should be given to investments in the following order:

(i)   nationals of country;

(ii)   nationals of other CARICOM countries;

(iii)   nationals of developing countries with whom there are arrangements;

(iv)   nationals of developed countries with whom there are arrangements;

(v)   nationals of other countries.

---

*Source: Caribbean Community Secretariat (1984). "Guidelines for use in the Negotiation of Bilateral Treaties", mimeo. [Note added by the editor].

Performance Obligations

(i) CARICOM countries should not accept any restrictions on their freedom to impose performance obligations;

(ii) performance obligations, which should include but not limited to, export performance, employment, conformity with national laws and with trade union practices, and transfer of technology, should be linked to the benefits to be derived and in this context provision should be made for such obligations to be reviewed periodically.

Exclusion Areas

CARICOM countries should, as part of their development plans and strategies, determine the terms on which foreign investment may enter their economies; the areas of their economies from which foreign investment would be prohibited or in which it would be permitted only under special conditions and the circumstances and criteria which will occasion restriction of foreign investment from any sector or activity.

Where no determination of such areas, circumstances or criteria has been made in advance of the negotiations, the BIT should incorporate an elaboration of the policy and/or criteria governing foreign investment.

Nationalisation and Compensation

(i) CARICOM host countries should ensure that in any bilateral investment treaty they maintain the right to nationalise foreign-owned property, subject to fair and just compensation or other provisions as contained in national law;

(ii) CARICOM host countries should ensure that in any bilateral investment treaty they maintain the right to determine at the time of the nationalisation the quantum of compensation and the terms of payment;

(iii) in the event of any dispute, local remedies should be exhausted before recourse to any international remedy.

Dispute Settlement

(i) In the case of disputes between the investor and the host country, resort to arbitration would only be permitted after all national remedies have been exhausted;

(ii) In the case of disputes between the parties, or where there is resort to arbitration as provided for at (i) above, the following should be the proposed approach:

    (a) ad hoc arbitration tribunal;

(b)   arbitration takes place in the host country;

(c)   the dispute be determined by national law and, where appropriate, rules of international law;

(d)   to use the UNCITRAL Rules which are favoured by developing countries.

Retroactive Applicability and Duration of Treaty

The Treaty should apply to new investments. In this connection, Article IX, paragraph (i) of the US Draft Proposals should be amended by the deletion of 1(a) and (b) and the redrafting of (c) in such a way as to ensure that there was no automatic right of an existing investment to more favourable terms which might be in the Treaty.

Monitoring

(i)   The US Government should undertake to do all in its power to ensure that US-based investors be good corporate citizens in CARICOM host countries;

(ii)   The US Government should guarantee that machinery established under the CBI to promote capital transfer to CARICOM countries be effective.

Transfers

(i)   Transfers must be subject to the national law of the host country;

(ii)   A distinction should be made between the following types of transfers;

(a)   capital transfer, however realised; and

(b)   current transfer;

(iii)   In view of possible size of capital transfers and the possible impact on the balance of payments, integrity of the currency, etc. capital transfers should be restricted; (Several existing reciprocal and investment promotion and protection agreements provide for this);

(iv)   Free transfer of current account transactions is a desirable goal, subject to balance of payments and other economic considerations.

*   *   *

AGREEMENT

BETWEEN

THE GOVERNMENT OF THE REPUBLIC OF CHILE

AND

THE GOVERNMENT OF _____

ON THE RECIPROCAL PROMOTION AND PROTECTION

OF INVESTMENTS*

The Government of the Republic of Chile and the Government of _____, hereinafter the "Contracting Parties",

Desiring to intensify economic cooperation to the mutual benefit of both countries;

With the intention to create and maintain favourable conditions for investments by investors of one Contracting Party which implies the transfer of capital in the territory of the other Contracting Party;

Recognizing that the reciprocal promotion and protection of such foreign investments favour the economic prosperity of both countries;

Have agreed as follows:

Article 1
Definitions

For the purpose of this Agreement:

(1)   "investor" means the following subjects which have made an investment in the territory of the other Contracting Party in accordance with the present Agreement:

    (a)   natural persons who, according to the law of that Contracting Party, are considered to be its nationals;

_____

*Source: Government of the Republic of Chile (1994) [Note added by the editor].

(b)   a legal entity, including companies, corporations, business associations and other legally recognized entities, which are constituted or otherwise duly organised under the law of that Contracting Party and have their seat together with effective economic activities in the territory of that same Contracting Party.

(2)   "investment" means any kind of asset, provided that the investment has been admitted in accordance with the laws and regulations of the other Contracting Party, and shall include in particular, though not exclusively:

(a)   movable and immovable property and any other property rights such as mortgages, liens or pledges;

(b)   shares, debentures or any other kinds of participation in companies;

(c)   a loan or other claim to money or to any performance having an economic value;

(d)   intellectual and industrial property rights, including copyright, patents, trademarks, trade names, technical processes, know-how and goodwill;

(e)   concessions conferred by law or under contract, including concessions to search for, cultivate, extract or exploit natural resources.

(3)   "territory" means in respect of each Contracting Party the territory under its sovereignty, including the exclusive economic zone and the continental shelf where that Contracting Party exercises, in conformity with international law, sovereign rights or jurisdiction.

Article 2
Scope of application

This Agreement shall apply to investments in the territory of one Contracting Party made in accordance with its legislation, prior to or after the entry into force of the Agreement, by investors of the other Contacting Party. It shall however not be applicable to disputes which arose prior to its entry into force or to disputes directly related to events which occurred prior to its entry into force.

Article 3
Promotion and Protection of investments

(1)   Each Contracting Party shall, subject to its general policy in the field of foreign investments, promote investments by investors of the other Contracting Party.

(2)   Each Contracting Party shall protect within its territory investments made in accordance with its laws and regulations by investors of the other Contracting Party and shall not impair by unreasonable or discriminatory measures the management, maintenance, use,

enjoyment, extension, sale and liquidation of such investments.

Article 4
Treatment of investments

(1) Each Contracting Party shall extend fair and equitable treatment to investments made by investors of the other Contracting Party on its territory and shall ensure that the exercise of the right thus recognized shall not be hindered in practice.

(2) A Contracting Party shall accord investments of the investors of one Contracting Party in its territory a treatment which is no less favourable than that accorded to investments made by its own investors or by investors of any third country, whichever is the most favourable.

(3) If a Contracting Party accords special advantages to investors of any third country by virtue of an agreement establishing a free trade area, a customs union, a common market, an economic union or any other form of regional economic organization to which the Party belongs or through the provisions of an agreement relating wholly or mainly to taxation, it shall not be obliged to accord such advantages to investors of the other Contracting Party.

Article 5
Free transfer

(1) Each Contracting Party shall allow without delay the investors of the other Contracting Party the transfer of funds in connection with an investment in a freely convertible currency, particularly of:

 (a) interests, dividends, profits and other returns;

 (b) repayments of a loan agreement related to the investment;

 (c) any capital or proceeds from the sale or partial sale or liquidation of the investment; and

 (d) compensation for expropriation or loss described in Article 6 of this Agreement.

(2) Transfers shall be made at the exchange rate applying on the date of transfer in accordance with the law of the Contracting Party which has admitted the investment.

Article 6
Expropriation and compensation

(1) Neither Contracting party shall take any measures depriving, directly or indirectly, an

investor of the other Contracting Party of an investment unless the following conditions are complied with:

    (a)   the measures are taken in the public or national interest and in accordance with the law;

    (b)   the measures are not discriminatory;

    (c)   the measures are accompanied by provisions for the payment of prompt, adequate and effective compensation.

(2)   The compensation shall be based on the market value of the investments affected immediately before the measure became public knowledge. Where that value cannot be readily ascertained, the compensation may be determined in accordance with generally recognised equitable principles of valuation taking into account the capital invested, depreciation, capital already repatriated, replacement value and other relevant factors. This compensation shall carry an interest at the appropriate market rate of interest from the date of expropriation or loss until the date of payment.

(3)   The investor affected shall have a right to access, under the law of the Contracting Party making the expropriation, to the judicial authority of that Party, in order to review the amount of compensation and the legality of any such expropriation or comparable measure.

(4)   The investors of one Contracting Party whose investments have suffered losses due to a war or any other armed conflict, revolution, state of emergency or rebellion, which took place in the territory of the other Contracting Party shall be accorded by the latter Contracting Party treatment as regard restitution, indemnification, compensation or other valuable consideration, no less favourable than that which that Contracting Party accords to its domestic investors or to investors of any third country, whichever is more favourable to the investors concerned.

Article 7
Subrogation

(1)   Where one Contracting Party or an agency authorized by the Contracting Party has granted a contract of insurance or any form of financial guarantee against non-commercial risks with regard to an investment by one of its investors in the territory of the other Contracting Party, the latter shall recognize the rights of the first Contracting Party by virtue of the principle of subrogation to the rights of the investor when payment has been made under this contract or financial guarantee by the first Contracting Party.

(2)   Where a Contracting Party has made a payment to its investor and has taken over rights and claims of the investor, that investor shall not, unless authorized to act on behalf of

the Contracting Party making the payment, pursue those rights and claims against the other Contracting Party.

Article 8
Settlement of Disputes between a Contracting Party
and an investor of the other Contracting Party

(1)   With a view to an amicable solution of disputes, which arises within the terms of this Agreement, between a Contracting Party and an investor of the other Contracting Party consultations will take place between the parties concerned.

(2)   If these consultations do not result in a solution within three months from the date of request for settlement, the investor may submit the dispute either;

(a)   to the competent tribunal of the Contracting Party in whose territory the investment was made; or

(b)   to international arbitration of the International Centre for the Settlement of Investment Disputes (ICSID), created by the Convention for the Settlement of Disputes in respect of Investments occurring between States and Nationals of other States, signed in Washington on March 18, 1965.

(3)   Once the investor has submitted the dispute to the competent tribunal of the Contracting Party in whose territory the investment was made or to international arbitration, that election shall be final.

(4)   For the purpose of this Article, any legal person which is constituted in accordance with the legislation of one Contracting Party, and in which, before a dispute arises, the majority of shares are owned by investors of the other Contracting Party, shall be treated, in accordance with Article 25 (2) (b) of the said Washington Convention, as a legal person of the other Contracting Party.

(5)   The arbitration decisions shall be final and binding on both parties and shall be enforced in accordance with the laws of the Contracting Party in whose territory the investment was made.

(6)   Once a dispute has been submitted to the competent tribunal or international arbitration in accordance with this Article, neither Contracting Party shall pursue the dispute through diplomatic channels unless the other Contracting Party has failed to abide or comply with any judgement, award, order or other determination made by the competent international or local tribunal in question.

Article 9
Settlement of Disputes between Contracting Parties

(1)   The Contracting Parties shall endeavour to resolve any difference between them regarding the interpretation or application of the provisions of this Agreement by friendly negotiations.

(2)   If the difference cannot thus be settled within six months following the date of notification of the difference, either Contracting Party may submit it to an Ad-hoc Arbitral Tribunal in accordance with this Article.

(3)   The Arbitral Tribunal shall be formed by three members and shall be constituted as follows: within two months of the notification by a Contracting Party of its wish to settle the dispute by arbitration, each Contracting Party shall appoint one arbitrator. These two members shall then, within thirty days of the appointment of the last one, agree upon a third member who shall be a national of a third country and who shall act as the Chairman. The Contracting Parties shall appoint the Chairman within thirty days of that person's nomination.

(4)   If, within the time limits provided for in paragraph (2) and (3) of this Article the required appointment has not been made or the required approval has not been given, either Contracting Party may request the President of the International Court of Justice to make the necessary appointment. If the President of the International Court of Justice is prevented from carrying out the said function or if that person is a national of either Contracting Party, the appointment shall be made by the Vice-President, and if the latter is prevented or if that person is a national of either Contracting Party, the appointment shall be made by the most senior Judge of the Court who is not a national of either Contracting Party.

(5)   The Chairman of the Tribunal shall be a national of a third country which has diplomatic relations with both Contracting Parties.

(6)   The arbitral tribunal shall reach its decisions taking into account the provisions of this Agreement, the principles of international law on this subject and the generally recognized principles of international law. The Tribunal shall reach its decisions by a majority vote and shall determine its procedure.

(7)   Each Contracting Party shall bear the cost of the arbitrator it has appointed and of its representation in the arbitral proceedings. The cost of the Chairman and the remaining costs shall be borne in equal parts by the Contracting Parties unless agreed otherwise.

(8)   The decisions of the arbitral tribunal shall be final and binding on both Parties.

Article 10
Consultations between Contracting Parties

The Contracting Parties shall consult at the request of either of them on matters concerning the interpretation or application of this Agreement.

Article 11
Final provisions

(1) The Contracting Parties shall notify each other when the constitutional requirements for the entry into force of this Agreement have been fulfilled. The Agreement shall enter into force thirty days after the date of the latter notification.

(2) This Agreement shall remain in force for a period of fifteen years. Thereafter it shall remain in force indefinitely unless one of the Contracting Parties gives one year's written notice of termination through diplomatic channels.

(3) In respect of investments made prior to the date when the notice of termination of this Agreement becomes effective, the provisions of this Agreement shall remain in force a further period of fifteen years from that date.

(4) This Agreement shall be applicable irrespective of whether diplomatic or consular relations exist between the Contracting Parties.

Done at _____, this _____ day of _____ in duplicate in the Spanish and English languages, both texts being equally authentic.

For the Government of the Republic of Chile   For the Government of _____.

PROTOCOL

On signing the Agreement on the Reciprocal Promotion and Protection of Investments between the Government of the Republic of Chile and the Government of _____ have, in addition, agreed on the following provisions, which shall be regarded as an integral part of the said Agreement.

Ad Article 5

(1)   Transfers concerning investments made under the Chilean Program of Foreign Debt Equity Swaps are subject to special regulations.

(2)   Capital can only be tranferred one year after it has entered the territoery of the Contracting Party unless its legislation provides for a more favourable treatment.

(3)   A transfer shall be deemed to have been made without delay if carried out within such period as is normally required for the completion of transfer formalities. The said period shall start on the day on which the relevant request has been submitted in due form and may in no case exceed thirty days.

*   *   *

AGREEMENT BETWEEN

THE GOVERNMENT OF THE PEOPLE'S REPUBLIC OF CHINA

AND

THE GOVERNMENT OF _____

CONCERNING

THE ENCOURAGEMENT AND RECIPROCAL PROTECTION OF INVESTMENTS*

The Government of the People's Republic of China and the Government of the _____ (hereinafter referred to as the Contracting Parties),

Intending to create favorable conditions for investments by investors of one Contracting Party in the territory of the other Contracting Party;

Recognizing that the reciprocal encouragement, promotion and protection of such investments will be conducive to stimulating business initiative of the investors and will increase prosperity in both States;

Desiring to intensify the economic cooperation of both States on the basis of equality and mutual benefits;

Have agreed as follows:

Article 1

For the purpose of this Agreement,

1.   The term "investment" means every kind of asset invested by investors of one Contracting Party in accordance with the laws and regulations of the other Contracting Party in the territory of the Latter, and in particular, though not exclusively, includes:

   (a)   movable, immovable property and other property rights such as mortgages and pledges;

   (b)   shares, stock and any other kind of participation in companies;

---

*Source: Government of the People's Republic of China, Department of Treaty and Law, Ministry of Foreign Trade and Economic Cooperation [Note added by the editor].

151

(c)   claims to money or to any other performance having an economic value;

(d)   copyrights, industrial property, know-how and technological process;

(e)   concessions conferred by law, including concessions to search for or exploit natural resources.

2.   The term "investors" means:

in respect of the People's Republic of China:

(a)   natural persons who have nationality of the People's Republic of China in accordance with its laws;

(b)   economic entities established in accordance with the laws of the People's Republic of China and domiciled in the territory of the People's Republic of China;

in respect of the _____:

(a)

(b)

3.   The term "returns" means the amounts yielded by investments, such as profits, dividends, interests, royalties or other legitimate income.

Article 2

1.   Each Contracting Party shall encourage investors of the other Contracting Party to make investments in its territory and admit such investments in accordance with its laws and regulations.

2.   Each Contracting Party shall grant assistance in and provide facilities for obtaining visa and working permit to nationals of the other Contracting Party to or in the territory of the Former in connection with activities associated with such investments.

Article 3

1.   Investments and activities associated with investments of investors of either Contracting Party shall be accorded fair and equitable treatment and shall enjoy protection in the territory of the other Contracting Party.

2.   The treatment and protection referred to in Paragraph 1 of this Article shall not be less

favorable than that accorded to investments and activities associated with such investments of investors of a third State.

3.   The treatment and protection as mentioned in Paragraphs 1 and 2 of this Article shall not include any preferential treatment accorded by the other Contracting Party to investments of investors of a third State based on customs union, free trade zone, economic union, agreement relating to avoidance of double taxation or for facilitating frontier trade.

Article 4

1.   Neither Contracting Party shall expropriate, nationalize or take similar measures (hereinafter referred to as "expropriation") against investments of investors of the other Contracting Party in its territory, unless the following conditions are met:

(a) for the public interests;

(b) under domestic legal procedure;

(c) without discrimination;

(d) against compensation.

2.   The compensation mentioned in Paragraph 1, (d) of this Article shall be equivalent to the value of the expropriated investments at the time when expropriation is proclaimed, be convertible and freely transferable. The compensation shall be paid without unreasonable delay.

Article 5

Investors of one Contracting Party who suffer losses in respect of their investments in the territory of the other Contracting Party owing to war, a state of national emergency, insurrection, riot or other similar events, shall be accorded by the latter Contracting Party, if it takes relevant measures, treatment no less favorable than that accorded to investors of a third State.

Article 6

1.   Each Contracting Party shall, subject to its laws and regulations, guarantee investors of the other Contracting Party the transfer of their investments and returns held in the territory of the one Contracting Party, including:

(a)   profits, dividends, interests and other legitimate income;

(b)   amounts from total or partial liquidation of investments;

(c)   payment made pursuant to a loan agreement in connection with investment;

(d)   royalties in Paragraph 1, (d) of Article 1;

(e)   payments of technical assistance or technical service fee, management fee;

(f)   payments in connection with projects on contract associated with investment;

(g)   earnings of nationals of the other Contracting Party who work in connection with an investment in the territory of the one Contracting Party.

2.   The transfers mentioned above shall be made at the prevailing exchange rate of the Contracting Party accepting the investment on the date of transfer.

Article 7

If a Contracting Party or its Agency makes payment to an investor under a guarantee it has granted to an investment of such investor in the territory of the other Contracting Party, such other Contracting Party shall recognize the transfer of any right or claim of such investor to the former Contracting Party or its Agency and recognize the subrogation of the former Contracting Party or its Agency to such right or claim. The subrogated right or claim shall not be greater than the original right or claim of the said investor.

Article 8

1.   Any dispute between the Contracting Parties concerning the interpretation or application of this Agreement shall, as far as possible, be settled by consultation through diplomatic channel.

2.   If a dispute cannot thus be settled within six months, it shall, upon the request of either Contracting Party, be submitted to an ad hoc arbitral tribunal.

3.   Such tribunal comprises of three arbitrators. Within two months from the date on which either Contracting Party receives the written notice requesting for arbitration from the other Contracting Party, each Contracting Party shall appoint one arbitrator. Those two arbitrators shall, within further two months, together select a third arbitrator who is a national of a third State which has diplomatic relations with both Contracting Parties. The third arbitrator shall be appointed by the two Contracting Parties as Chairman of the arbitral tribunal.

4.   If the arbitral tribunal has not been constituted within four months from the date of the receipt of the written notice for arbitration, either Contracting Party may, in the absence of any other agreement, invite the President of the International Court of Justice to appoint the arbitrator(s) who has or have not yet been appointed. If the President is a national of either Contracting Party or is otherwise prevented from discharging the said function, the next most senior member of the International Court of Justice who is not a national of either Contracting Party shall be invited to make the necessary appointment(s).

5.   The arbitral tribunal shall determine its own procedure. The tribunal shall reach its award

in accordance with the provisions of this Agreement and the principles of international law recognized by both Contracting Parties.

6.   The tribunal shall reach its award by a majority of votes. Such award shall be final and binding on both Contracting Parties. The ad hoc arbitral tribunal shall, upon the request of either Contracting Party, explain the reasons of its award.

7.   Each Contracting Party shall bear the cost of its appointed arbitrator and of its representation in arbitral proceedings. The relevant costs of the Chairman and the tribunal shall be borne in equal parts by the Contracting Parties.

Article 9

1.   Any dispute between an investor of one Contracting Party and the other Contracting Party in connection with an investment in the territory of the other Contracting Party shall, as far as possible, be settled amicably through negotiations between the parties to the dispute.

2.   If the dispute cannot be settled through negotiations within six months, either party to the dispute shall be entitled to submit the dispute to the competent court of the Contracting Party accepting the investment.

3.   If a dispute involving the amount of compensation for expropriation cannot be settled within six months after resort to negotiations as specified in Paragraph 1 of this Article, it may be submitted at the request of either party to an ad hoc arbitral tribunal. The provisions of this Paragraph shall not apply if the investor concerned has resorted to the procedure specified in the Paragraph 2 of this Article.

4.   Such an arbitral tribunal shall be constituted for each individual case in the following way: each party to the dispute shall appoint an arbitrator, and these two shall select a national of a third State which has diplomatic relations with the two Contracting Parties as Chairman. The first two arbitrators shall be appointed within two months of the written notice for arbitration by either party to the dispute to the other, and the Chairman be selected within four months. If within the period specified above, the tribunal has not been constituted, either party to the dispute may invite the Secretary General of the International Centre for Settlement of Investment Disputes to make the necessary appointments.

5.   The tribunal shall determine its own procedure. However, the tribunal may, in the course of determination of procedure, take as guidance the Arbitration Rules of the International Centre for Settlement of Investment Disputes.

6.   The tribunal shall reach its decision by a majority of votes. Such decision shall be final and binding on both parties to the dispute. Both Contracting Parties shall commit themselves to the enforcement of the decision in accordance with their respective domestic law.

7.   The tribunal shall adjudicate in accordance with the law of the Contracting Party to the

dispute accepting the investment including its rules on the conflict of laws, the provisions of this Agreement as well as the generally recognized principles of international law accepted by both Contracting Parties.

8.   Each party to the dispute shall bear the cost of its appointed member of the tribunal and of its representation in the proceedings. The cost of the appointed Chairman and the remaining costs shall be borne in equal parts by the parties to the dispute.

Article 10

If the treatment to be accorded by one Contracting Party in accordance with its laws and regulations to investments or activities associated with such investments of investors of the other Contracting Party is more favorable than the treatment provided for in this Agreement, the more favorable treatment shall be applicable.

Article 11

This Agreement shall apply to investments which are made prior to or after its entry into force by investors of either Contracting Party in accordance with the laws and regulations of the other Contracting Party in the territory of the Latter.

Article 12

1.   The representatives of the two Contracting Parties shall hold meetings from time to time for the purpose of:

(a) reviewing the implementation of this Agreement;

(b) exchanging legal information and investment opportunities;

(c) resolving dispute arising out of investments;

(d) forwarding proposals on promotion of investment;

(e) studying other issues in connection with investments.

2.   Where either Contracting Party requests consultation on any matters of Paragraph 1 of this Article, the other Contracting Party shall give prompt response and the consultation be held alternately in Beijing and _____.

Article 13

1.   This Agreement shall enter into force on the first day of the following month after the date on which both Contracting Parties have notified each other in writing that their respective internal legal procedures have been fulfilled, and shall remain in force for a period of five years.

2.   This Agreement shall continue in force if either Contracting Party fails to give a written notice to the other Contracting Party to terminate this Agreement one year before the expiration specified in Paragraph 1 of this Article.

3.   After the expiration of the initial five years period, either Contracting Party may at any time thereafter terminate this Agreement by giving at least one year's written notice to the other Contracting Party.

4.   With respect to investments made prior to the date of termination of this Agreement, the provisions to Article 1 to 12 shall continue to be effective for a further period of ten years from such date of termination.

In witness whereof, the duly authorized representatives of their respective Governments have signed this Agreement.

Done in duplicate at _____ on _____, 1994 in the Chinese, _____ and English languages, all texts being equally authentic. In case of divergence of interpretation, the English text shall prevail.

For the Government of the
People's Republic of China   For the Government of _____.

*   *   *

Projet d'Accord entre

Le Gouvernement de la Republique Francaise

et

Le Gouvernement _____

sur l'Encouragement et la Protection Reciproques des Investissements*

Le Gouvernement de la République française et le Gouvernement _____, ci-après dénommés "les Parties contractantes",

Désireux de renforcer la coopération économique entre les deux Etats et de créer des conditions favorables pour les investissements français au _____ et _____ en France,

Persuadés que l'encouragement et la protection de ces investissements sont propres à stimuler les transferts de capitaux et de technologie entre les deux pays, dans l'intérêt de leur développement économique,

Sont convenus des dispositions suivantes:

Article 1

Pour l'application du présent accord:

1.   Le terme "investissement" désigne tous les avoirs, tels que les biens, droits et interêts de toutes natures et, plus particulièrement mais non exclusivement:

    a)   les biens meubles et immeubles, ainsi que tous autres droits réels tels que les hypothèques, privilèges, usufruits, cautionnements et droits analogues;

    b)   les actions, primes d'émission et autres formes de participation, même minoritaires ou indirectes, aux sociétés constituées sur le territoire de l'une des Parties contractantes;

    c)   les obligations, créances et droits à toutes prestations ayant valeur économique;

---

*Source: Government of France, Ministry of Foreign Affairs [Note added by the editor].

d) les droits de propriété intellectuelle, commerciale et industrielle tels que les droits d'auteur, les brevets d'invention, les licences, les marques déposées, les modèles et maquettes industrielles les procèdés techniques, le savoir-faire, les noms déposés et la clientèle;

e) les concessions accordées par la loi ou en vertu d'un contrat, notamment les concessions relatives à la prospection, la culture, l'extraction ou l'exploitation de richesses naturelles, y compris celles qui se situent dans la zone maritime des Parties contractantes.

Il est entendu que lesdits avoirs doivent être ou avoir été investis conformément à la législation de la Partie contractante sur le territoire ou dans la zone maritime de laquelle l'investissement est effectué avant ou après l'entrée en vigueur du présent accord.

Toute modification de la forme d'investissement des avoirs n'affecte pas leur qualification d'investissement, à condition que cette modification ne soit pas contraire à la législation de la Partie contractante sur le territoire ou dans la zone maritime de laquelle l'investissement est réalisé.

2. Le terme de "nationaux" désigne les personnes physiques possédant la nationalité de l'une des Parties contractantes.

3. Le terme de "sociétés" désigne toute personne morale constituée sur le territoire de l'une des Parties contractantes, conformément à la législation de celle-ci et y possédant son siège social, ou contrôlée directement ou indirectement par des nationaux de l'une des Parties contractantes, ou par des personnes morales possédant leur siège social sur le territoire de l'une des Parties contractantes et constituées conformément à la législation de celle-ci.

4. Le terme de "revenus" désigne toutes les sommes produites par un investissement, telles que bénéfices, redevances ou intérêts, durant une période donnée.

Les revenus de l'investissement et, en cas de réinvestissement, les revenus de leur réinvestissement jouissent de la même protection que l'investissement.

5. Le présent accord s'applique au territoire de chacune des Parties contractantes ainsi qu'à la zone maritime de chacune des Parties contractantes, ci-après définie comme la zone économique et le plateau continental qui s'étendent au-delà de la limite des eaux territoriales de chacune des Parties contractantes et sur lesquels elles ont, en conformité avec le Droit international, des droits souverains et une juridiction aux fins de prospection, d'exploitation et de préservation des ressources naturelles.

Article 2

Chacune des Parties contractantes admet et encourage, dans le cadre de sa législation et des dispositions du présent accord, les investissements effectués par les nationaux et sociétés de l'autre Partie sur son territoire et dans sa zone maritime.

Article 3

Chacune des Parties contractantes s'engage à assurer, sur son territoire et dans sa zone maritime, un traitement juste et équitable, conformément aux principes du Droit international, aux investissements des nationaux et sociétés de l'autre Partie et à faire en sorte que l'exercice du droit ainsi reconnu ne soit entravé ni en droit, ni en fait. En particulier, bien que non exclusivement, sont considérées comme des entraves de droit ou de fait au traitement juste et équitable, toute restriction à l'achat et au transport de matières premières et de matières auxiliaires, d'énergie et de combustibles, ainsi que de moyens de production et d'exploitation de tout genre, toute entrave à la vente et au transpot des produits à l'interieur du pays et à l'étranger, ainsi que toutes autres mesures ayant un effet analogue.

Les Parties contractentes examineront avec bienveillance, dans le cadre de leur législation interne, les demandes d'entrée et d'autorisation de séjour, de travail, et de circulation introduites par des nationaux d'une Partie contractante, au titre d'un investissement réalisé sur le territoire ou dans la zone maritime de l'autre Partie contractante.

Article 4

Chaque Partie contractante applique, sur son territoire et dans sa zone maritime, aux nationaux ou sociétés de l'autre Partie, en ce qui concerne leurs investissements et activités liées à ces investissements, un traitement non moins favorable que celui accordé à ses nationaux ou sociétés, ou le traitement accordé aux nationaux ou sociétés de la Nation la plus favorisée, si celui-ci est plus avantageux. A ce titre, les nationaux autorisés à travailler sur le territoire et dans la zone maritime de l'une des Parties contractantes doivent pouvoir bénéficier des facilités matérielles appropriées pour l'exercice de leurs activités professionnelles.

Ce traitement ne s'étend toutefois pas aux privilèges qu'une Partie contractante accorde aux nationaux ou sociétés d'un Etat tiers, en vertu de sa participation ou de son association à une zone de libre échange, une union douanière, un marché commun ou toute autre forme d'organisation économique régionale.

Les dispositions de cet Article ne s'appliquent pas aux questions fiscales.

Article 5

1. Les investissements effectués par des nationaux ou sociétés de l'une ou l'autre des Parties contractantes bénéficient, sur le territoire et dans la zone maritime de l'autre Partie contractante, d'une protection et d'une sécurité pleines et entières.

2. Les Parties contractantes ne prennent pas de mesures d'expropriation ou de nationalisation ou toutes autres mesures dont l'effet est de déposséder, directement ou indirectement, les nationaux et sociétés de l'autre Partie des investissements leur appartenant, sur leur territoire et dans leur zone maritime, si ce n'est pour cause d'utilité publique et à condition que ces mesures ne soient ni discriminatoires, ni contraires à un engagement particulier.

Toutes les mesures de dépossession qui pourraient être prises doivent donner lieu au paiement d'une indemnité prompte et adéquate dont le montant, égal à la valeur réelle des investissements concernés, doit être évalué par rapport à une situation économique normale et antérieure à toute menace de dépossession.

Cette indemnité, son montant et ses modalités de versement sont fixés au plus tard à la date de la dépossession. Cette indemnité est effectivement réalisable, versée sans retard et librement transférable. Elle produit, jusqu'à la date de versement, des intérêts calculés au taux d'intérêt de marché approprié.

3. Les nationaux ou sociétés de l'une des Parties contractantes dont les investissements auront subi des pertes dues à la guerre ou à tout autre conflit armé, révolution, état d'urgence national ou révolte survenu sur le territoire ou dans la zone maritime de l'autre Partie contractante, bénéficieront, de la part de cette dernière, d'un traitement non moins favorable que celui accordé à ses propres nationaux ou sociétés ou à ceux de la Nation la plus favorisée.

Article 6

Chaque Partie contractante, sur le territoire ou dans la zone maritime de laquelle des investissements ont été effectués par des nationaux ou sociétés de l'autre Partie contractante, accorde à ces nationaux ou sociétés le libre transfert:

a) des intérêts, dividendes, bénéfices et autres revenus courants;

b) des redevances découlant des droits incorporels désignés au paragraphe 1, lettres d) et e) de l'Article 1;

c) des versements effectués pour le remboursement des emprunts régulièrement contractés;

d) du produit de la cession ou de la liquidation totale ou partielle de l'investissement, y compris les plus-values du capital investi;

e) des indemnités de dépossession ou de perte prévues à l'Article 5, paragraphes 2 et 3 ci-dessus.

Les nationaux de chacune des Parties contractantes qui ont été autorisés à travailler sur le territoire ou dans la zone maritime de l'autre Partie contractante, au titre d'un investissement agréé sont également autorisés à transférer dans leur pays d'origine une quotité appropriée de leur rémunération.

Les transfers visés aux paragraphes précédents sont effectués sans retard au taux de change normal officiellement applicable à la date du transfert.

Article 7

Dans la mesure où la réglementation de l'une des Parties contractantes prévoit une garantie pour les investissements effectués à l'etranger, celle-ci peut être accordée, dans le cadre d'un examen cas par cas à des investissements effectués par des nationaux ou sociétés de cette Partie sur le territoire ou dans la zone maritime de l'autre Partie.

Les investissements des nationaux et sociétés de l'une des Parties contractantes sur le territoire ou dans la zone maritime de l'autre Partie ne pourront obtenir la garantie visée à l'alinéa ci-dessus que s'ils ont, au préalable, obtenu l'agrément de cette dernière Partie.

Article 8

Tout différend relatif aux investissements entre l'une des Parties contractantes et un national ou une société de l'autre Partie contractante est réglé à l'amiable entre les deux parties concernées.

Si un tel différend n'a pas pu être réglé dans un délai de six mois à partir du moment où il à été soulevé par l'une ou l'autre des parties au différend, il est soumis à la demande de l'une ou l'autre de ces parties à l'arbitrage du Centre international pour le réglement des différends relatifs aux investissements (C.I.R.D.I.), créé par la Convention pour le réglement des différends relatifs aux investissements entre Etats et ressortissants d'autres Etats, signée à Washington le 18 mars 1965.

Article 9

Si l'une des Parties contractantes, en vertu d'une garantie donnée pour un investissement réalisé sur le territoire ou dans la zone maritime de l'autre Partie, effectue des versements à l'un de ses nationaux ou à l'une de ses sociétés, elle est, de ce fait, subrogée dans les droits et actions de ce national ou de cette société.

Lesdits versements n'affectent pas les droits du bénéficiaire de la garantie à recourir au C.I.R.D.I. ou à poursuivre les actions introduites devant lui jusqu'à l'aboutissement de la procédure.

Article 10

Les investissements ayant fait l'objet d'un engagement particulier de l'une des Parties contractantes à l'égard des nationaux et sociétés de l'autre Partie contractante sont régis, sans préjudice des dispositions du présent accord, par les termes de cet engagement dans la mesure où celui-ci comporte des dispositions plus favorables que celles qui sont prévues par le présent accord.

Article 11

1. Les différends relatifs à l'interprétation ou à l'application du présent accord doivent être réglés, si possible, par la voie diplomatique.

2. Si dans un délai de six mois à partir du moment où il.a été soulevé par l'une ou l'autre des Parties contractantes, le différend n'est pas réglé, il est soumis, à la demande de l'une ou l'autre Partie contractante, à un tribunal d'arbitrage.

3. Ledit tribunal sera constitué pour chaque cas particulier de la manière suivante: chaque Partie contractante désigne un membre, et les deux membres désignent, d'un commun accord, un ressortissant d'un Etat tiers qui est nommé Président du tribunal par les deux Parties contractantes. Tous les membres doivent être nommés dans un délai de deux mois à compter de la date à laquelle une des Parties contractantes a fait part à l'autre Partie contractante de son intention de soumettre le différend à arbitrage.

4. Si les délais fixés au paragraphe 3 ci-dessus n'ont pas été observés, l'une ou l'autre Partie contractante, en l'absence de tout autre accord, invite le Secrétaire général de l'Organisation des Nations-Unies a procéder aux désignations nécessaires. Si le Secrétaire général est ressortissant de l'une ou l'autre Partie contractante ou si, pour une autre raison, il est empêché d'exercer cette fonction, le Secrétaire général adjoint le plus ancien et ne possédant pas la nationalité de l'une des Parties contractantes procéde aux désignations nécessaires.

5. Le tribunal d'arbitrage prend ses décisions à la majorité des voix. Ces décisions sont définitives et exécutoires de plein droit pour les Parties contractantes.

Le tribunal fixe lui-même son réglement. Il interprète la sentence à la demande de l'une ou l'autre Partie contractante. A moins que le tribunal n'en dispose autrement, compte tenu de circonstances particulières, les frais de la procédure arbitrale, y compris les vacations des arbitres, sont répartis également entre les Parties Contractantes.

Article 12

Chacune des Parties notifiera à l'autre l'accomplissement des procédures internes requises pour l'entrée en vigueur du present accord, qui prendra effet un mois après le jour de la réception de la dernière notification.

L'accord est conclu pour une durée initiale de dix ans. Il restera en vigueur après ce terme, à moins que l'une des Parties ne le dénonce par la voie diplomatique avec préavis d'un an.

A l'expiration de la période de validité du présent accord, les investissements effectués pendant qu'il était en vigueur continueront de bénéficier de la protection de ses dispositions pendant une période supplémentaire de vingt ans.

Fait à _____, le _____ en deux originaux, chacun en langue française et en langue _____ les deux textes faisant également foi.

Pour le Gouvernement   Pour le Gouvernement
de la République française   _____

*   *   *

MODEL TREATY   **February 1991 (2)**

TREATY BETWEEN

THE FEDERAL REPUBLIC OF GERMANY

AND

_____

CONCERNING

THE ENCOURAGEMENT AND RECIPROCAL PROTECTION OF INVESTMENTS*

Federal Ministry of Economics
Bonn

THE FEDERAL REPUBLIC OF GERMANY

AND

_____

desiring to intensify economic co-operation between both States,

intending to create favourable conditions for investments by nationals and companies of either State in the territory of the other State,

recognizing that the encouragement and contractual protection of such investments are apt to stimulate private business initiative and to increase the prosperity of both nations,

have agreed as follows:

Article 1

For the purpose of this Treaty

1.   the term "investments" comprises every kind of asset, in particular:

_____

*Source: Government of Germany, Federal Ministry of Economics [Note added by the editor].

(a)   movable and immovable property as well as any other rights in rem, such as mortgages, liens and pledges;

(b)   shares of companies and other kinds of interest in companies;

(c)   claims to money which has been used to create an economic value or claims to any performance having an economic value;

(d)   intellectual property rights, in particular copyrights, patents, utility-model patents, registered designs, trade-marks, trade-names, trade and business secrets, technical processes, know-how, and good will;

(e)   business concessions under public law, including concessions to search for, extract and exploit natural resources;

Any alteration of the form in which assets are invested shall not affect their classification as investment;

2.   the term "returns" means the amounts yielded by an investment for a definite period, such as profit, dividends, interest, royalties or fees;

3.   the term "nationals" means

(a)   in respect of the Federal Republic of Germany:

Germans within the meaning of the Basic Law of the Federal Republic of Germany,

(b)   in respect of _____:

_____;

4.   the term "companies" means

(a)   in respect of the Federal Republic of Germany:

any juridical person as well as any commercial or other company or association with or without legal personality having its seat in the territory of the Federal Republic of Germany, irrespective of whether or not its activities are directed at profit,

(b)   in respect of _____:

_____.

Article 2

(1)   Each Contracting Party shall in its territory promote as far as possible investments by nationals or companies of the other Contracting Party and admit such investments in accordance with its legislation. It shall in any case accord such investments fair and equitable treatment.

(2)   Neither Contracting Party shall in any way impair by arbitrary or discriminatory measures the management, maintenance, use or enjoyment of investments in its territory of nationals or companies of the other Contracting Party.

Article 3

(1)   Neither Contracting Party shall subject investments in its territory owned or controlled by nationals or companies of the other Contracting Party to treatment less favourable than it accords to investments of its own nationals or companies or to investments of nationals or companies of any third State.

(2)   Neither Contracting Party shall subject nationals or companies of the other Contracting Party, as regards their activity in connection with investments in its territory, to treatment less favourable than it accords to its own nationals or companies or to nationals or companies of any third state.

(3)   Such treatment shall not relate to privileges which either Contracting Party accords to nationals or companies of third States on account of its membership of, or association with, a customs or economic union, a common market or a free trade area.

(4)   The treatment granted under this Article shall not relate to advantages which either Contracting Party accords to nationals or companies of third States by virtue of a double taxation agreement or other agreements regarding matters of taxation.

Article 4

(1)   Investments by nationals or companies of either Contracting Party shall enjoy full protection and security in the territory of the other Contracting Party.

(2)   Investments by nationals or companies of either Contracting Party shall not be expropriated, nationalized or subjected to any other measure the effects of which would be tantamount to expropriation or nationalization in the territory of the other Contracting Party except for the public benefit and against compensation. Such compensation shall be equivalent to the value of the expropriated investment immediately before the date on which the actual or threatened expropriation, nationalization or comparable measure has become publicly known. The compensation shall be paid without delay and shall carry the usual bank interest until the time of payment; it shall be effectively realizable and freely transferable. Provision shall have been made in an appropriate manner at or prior to the time of expropriation, nationalization or comparable measure for the determination and payment of such compensation. The legality of

any such expropriation, nationalization or comparable measure and the amount of compensation shall be subject to review by due process of law.

(3)   Nationals or companies of either Contracting Party whose investments suffer losses in the territory of the other Contracting Party owing to war or other armed conflict, revolution, a state of national emergency, or revolt, shall be accorded treatment no less favourable by such other Contracting Party than that which the latter Contracting Party accords to its own nationals or companies as regards restitution, indemnification, compensation or other valuable consideration. Such payments shall be freely transferable.

(4)   Nationals or companies of either Contracting Party shall enjoy most-favoured-nation treatment in the territory of the other Contracting Party in respect of the matters provided for in this Article.

Article 5

Each Contracting Party shall guarantee to nationals or companies of the other Contracting Party the free transfer of payments in connection with an investment, in particular

(a)   of the principal and additional amounts to maintain or increase the investment;

(b)   of the returns;

(c)   in repayment of loans;

(d)   of the proceeds from the liquidation or the sale of the whole or any part of the investment.

(e)   of the compensation provided for in Article 4.

Article 6

If either Contracting Party makes a payment to any of its nationals or companies under a guarantee it has assumed in respect of an investment in the territory of the other Contracting Party, the latter Contracting Party shall, without prejudice to the rights of the former Contracting Party under Article 10, recognize the assignment, whether under a law or pursuant to a legal transaction, of any right or claim of such national or company to the former Contracting Party. The latter Contracting Party shall also recognize the subrogation of the former Contracting Party to any such right or claim (assigned claims) which that Contracting Party shall be entitled to assert to the same extent as its predecessor in title. As regards the transfer of payments made by virtue of such assigned claims, Article 4 (2) and (3) as well as Article 5 shall apply mutatis mutandis.

Article 7

(1)   Transfers under Article 4 (2) or (3), under Article 5 or article 6 shall be made without delay at the applicable rate of exchange.

(2)   This rate of exchange shall correspond to the cross rate obtained from those rates which would be applied by the International Monetary Fund on the date of payment for conversions of the currencies concerned into Special Drawing Rights.

Article 8

(1)   If the legislation of either Contracting Party or obligations under international law existing at present or established hereafter between the Contracting Parties in addition to this Treaty contain a regulation, whether general or specific, entitling investments by nationals or companies of the other Contracting Party to a treatment more favourable than is provided for by this Treaty, such regulation shall to the extent that it is more favourable prevail over this Treaty.

(2)   Each contracting Party shall observe any other obligation it has assumed with regard to investments in its territory by nationals or companies of the other Contracting Party.

Article 9

This Treaty shall also apply to investments made prior to its entry into force by nationals or companies of either Contracting Party in the territory of the other Contracting Party consistent with the latter's legislation.

Article 10

(1)   Divergencies between the Contracting Parties concerning the interpretation or application of this Treaty should as far as possible be settled by the governments of the two Contracting Parties.

(2)   If a divergency cannot thus be settled, it shall upon the request of either Contracting Party be submitted to an arbitration tribunal.

(3)   Such arbitration tribunal shall be constituted ad hoc as follows: each Contracting Party shall appoint one member, and these two members shall agree upon a national of a third State as their chairman to be appointed by the governments of the two Contracting Parties. Such members shall be appointed within two months, and such chairman within three months from the date on which either Contracting Party has informed the other Contracting Party that it intends to submit the dispute to an arbitration tribunal.

(4)   If the periods specified in paragraph 3 above have not been observed, either Contracting Party may, in the absence of any other arrangement, invite the President of the International Court of Justice to make the necessary appointments. If the President is a national of either

Contracting Party or if he is otherwise prevented from discharging the said function, the Vice-President should make the necessary appointments. If the Vice-President is a national of either Contracting Party or if he, too, is prevented from discharging the said function, the member of the Court next in seniority who is not a national of either Contracting Party should make the necessary appointments.

(5)   The arbitration tribunal shall reach its decisions by a majority of votes. Such decisions shall be binding. Each Contracting Party shall bear the cost of its own member and of its representatives in the arbitration proceedings; the cost of the chairman and the remaining costs shall be borne in equal parts by the Contracting Parties. The arbitration tribunal may make a different regulation concerning costs. In all other respects, the arbitration tribunal shall determine its own procedure.

(6)   If both Contracting Parties are Contracting States of the Convention of 18 March 1965 on the Settlement of Investment Disputes between States and Nationals of Other States the arbitration tribunal provided for above may in consideration of the provisions of Article 27 (1) of the said Convention not be appealed to insofar as agreement has been reached between the national or company of one Contracting Party and the other Contracting Party under Article 25 of the Convention. This shall not affect the possibility of appealing to such arbitration tribunal in the event that a decision of the Arbitration Tribunal established under the said Convention is not complied with (Article 27) or in the case of an assignment under a law or pursuant to a legal transaction as provided for in Article 6 of this Treaty.

Model I
Article 11

(1)   Divergencies concerning investments between a Contracting Party and a national or company of the other Contracting Party should as far as possible be settled amicably between the parties in dispute.

(2)   If the divergency cannot be settled within six months of the date when it has been raised by one of the parties in dispute, it shall, at the request of the national or company of the other Contracting Party, be submitted for arbitration. Unless the parties in dispute agree otherwise, the divergency shall be submitted for arbitration under the Convention of 18 March 1965 on the Settlement of Investment Disputes between States and Nationals of Other States.

(3)   The award shall be binding and shall not be subject to any appeal or remedy other than those provided for in the said Convention. The award shall be enforced in accordance with domestic law.

(4)   During arbitration proceedings or the enforcement of an award, the Contracting Party involved in the dispute shall not raise the objection that the national or company of the other Contracting Party has received compensation under an insurance contract in respect of all or part of the damage.

Model II
Article 11

(1)   Divergencies concerning investments between a Contracting Party and a national or company of the other Contracting Party shall as far as possible be settled amicably between the parties in dispute.

(2)   If the divergency cannot be settled within six months of the date when it has been raised by one of the parties in dispute, it shall, at the request of the national or company of the other Contracting Party, be submitted for arbitration. Each Contracting Party herewith declares its acceptance of such an arbitration procedure. Unless the parties in dispute have agreed otherwise, the provisions of Article 10 (3) to (5) shall be applied mutatis mutandis on condition that the appointment of the members of the arbitration tribunal in accordance with Article 10 (3) is effected by the parties in dispute and that, insofar as the periods specified in Article 10 (3) are not observed, either party in dispute may, in the absence of other arrangements, invite the President of the Court of International Arbitration of the International Chamber of Commerce in Paris to make the required appointments. The award shall be enforced in accordance with domestic law.

(3)   During arbitration proceedings or the enforcement of an award, the Contracting Party involved in the dispute shall not raise the objection that the national or company of the other Contracting Party has received compensation under an insurance contract in respect of all or part of the damage.

(4)   In the event of both Contracting Parties having become Contracting States of the Convention of 18 March 1965 on the Settlement of Investment Disputes between States and Nationals of Other States, divergencies under this Article between the parties in dispute shall be submitted for arbitration under the aforementioned Convention, unless the parties in dispute agree otherwise; each Contracting Party herewith declares its acceptance of such a procedure.

Article 12

This Treaty shall be in force irrespective of whether or not diplomatic or consular relations exist between the Contracting Parties.

Article 13

(1)   This Treaty shall be ratified; the instruments of ratification shall be exchanged as soon as possible in_____.

(2)   This Treaty shall enter into force one month after the date of exchange of the instruments of ratification. It shall remain in force for a period of ten years and shall be extended thereafter for an unlimited period unless denounced in writing by either Contracting Party twelve months before its expiration. After the expiry of the period of ten years this Treaty may be denounced at any time by either Contracting Party giving twelve months' notice.

(3)   In respect of investments made prior to the date of termination of this Treaty, the provisions of Articles 1 to 12 shall continue to be effective for a further period of twenty years from the date of termination of this Treaty.

Done at _____ on_____

in duplicate in the German and English languages, both texts being equally authentic.

For the Federal Republic of Germany   For _____.

Protocol

On signing the Treaty between the Federal Republic of Germany and _____ concerning the Encouragement and Reciprocal Protection of Investments, the undersigned plenipotentiaries have, in addition, agreed on the following provisions, which shall be regarded as an integral part of the said Treaty;

(1)   Ad Article 1

(a)   Returns from the investment and, in the event of their re-investment, the returns therefrom shall enjoy the same protection as the investment.

(b)   Without prejudice to any other method of determining nationality, in particular any person in possession of a national passport issued by the competent authorities of the Contracting Party concerned shall be deemed to be a national of that Party.

(2)   Ad Article 2

(a)   Investments made, in accordance with the legislation of either Contracting Party, within the area of application of the law of that Contracting Party by nationals or companies of the other Contracting Party shall enjoy the full protection of the Treaty.

(b)   The Treaty shall also apply to the areas of the exclusive economic zone and the continental shelf insofar as international law permits the Contracting Party concerned to exercise sovereign rights or jurisdiction in these areas.

(3)   Ad Article 3

(a)   The following shall more particularly, though not exclusively, be deemed "activity" within the meaning of Article 3 (2): the management, maintenance, use and enjoyment of an investment. The following shall, in particular, be deemed "treatment less favourable" within the meaning of Article 3: unequal treatment in the case of restrictions on the purchase of raw or auxiliary materials, of energy or fuel or of means of production or operation of any kind, unequal treatment in the case of impeding the marketing of products inside or outside the country, as well as any other measures having similar effects. Measures that have to be taken for reasons of public security and order, public health or morality shall not be deemed "treatment less favourable" within the meaning of Article 3.

(b)   The provisions of Article 3 do not oblige a Contracting Party to extend to natural persons or companies resident in the territory of the other Contracting Party tax privileges, tax exemptions and tax reductions which according to its tax laws are granted only to natural persons and companies resident in its territory.

(c)   The Contracting Parties shall within the framework of their national legislation give sympathetic consideration to applications for the entry and sojourn of persons of either Contracting Party who wish to enter the territory of the other Contracting Party in connection with an investment; the same shall apply to employed persons of either Contracting Party who in connection with an investment wish to enter the territory of the other Contracting Party and sojourn there to take up employment. Applications for work permits shall also be given sympathetic consideration.

(4)   Ad Article 4

A claim to compensation shall also exist when, as a result of State intervention in the company in which the investment is made, its economic substance is severely impaired.

(5)   Ad Article 7

A transfer shall be deemed to have been made "without delay" within the meaning of Article 7 (1) if effected within such period as is normally required for the completion of transfer formalities. The said period shall commence on the day on which the relevant request has been submitted and may on no account exceed two months.

(6)   Whenever goods or persons connected with an investment are to be transported, each Contracting Party shall neither exclude nor hinder transport enterprises of the other Contracting Party and shall issue permits as required to carry out such transport. This shall include the transport of

(a)   goods directly intended for an investment within the meaning of the Treaty or acquired in the territory of either Contracting Party or of any third State by or on behalf of an enterprise in which assets within the meaning of the Treaty are invested;

    (b)   persons travelling in connection with an investment.

Done at_____on_____
in duplicate in the German and English languages, both texts being equally authentic.

For the Federal Republic of Germany   For _____.

* * *

AGREEMENT BETWEEN

THE SWISS CONFEDERATION

AND

ON THE PROMOTION AND RECIPROCAL PROTECTION OF INVESTMENTS*

Preamble

The Swiss Federal Council and the Government of _____,

Desiring to intensify economic cooperation to the mutual benefit of both States,

Intending to create and maintain favourable conditions for investments by investors of oneContracting Party in the territory of the other Contracting Party,

Recognizing the need to promote and protect foreign investments with the aim to foster the economic prosperity of both States,

Have agreed as follows:

Article 1
Definitions

For the purpose of this Agreement:

(1)   The term "investor" refers with regard to either Contracting Party to

    (a)   natural persons who, according to the law of that Contracting Party, are considered to be its nationals;

    (b)   legal entities, including companies, corporations, business associations and other organisations, which are constituted or otherwise duly organised under the law of that Contracting Party and have their seat, together with real economic activities, in the territory of that same Contracting Party;

*Source: Government of the Swiss Confederation, Swiss Draft (1986/1995) [Note added by the editor].

(c)   legal entities established under the law of any country which are, directly or indirectly, controlled by nationals of that Contracting Party or by legal entities having their seat, together with real economic activities, in the territory of that Contracting Party.

(2)   The term "investments" shall include every kind of assets in particular:

(a)   movable and immovable property as well as any other rights in rem, such as servitudes, mortgages, liens, pledges and usufructs;

(b)   shares, parts or any other kinds of participation in companies;

(c)   claims to money or to any performance having an economic value;

(d)   copyrights, industrial property rights (such as patents, utility models, industrial designs or models, trade or service marks, trade names, indications of origin), know-how and goodwill;

(e)   concessions under public law, including concessions to search for, extract or exploit natural resources as well as all other rights given by law, by contract or by decision of the authority in accordance with the law.

(3)   The term "returns" means the amounts yielded by an investment and includes in particular, profits, interest, capital gains, dividends, royalties and fees.

(4)   The term "territory" includes the maritime areas adjacent to the coast of the State concerned, to the extent to which that State may exercise sovereign rights or jurisdiction in those areas according to international law.

Article 2
Scope of application

The present Agreement shall apply to investments in the territory of one Contracting Party made in accordance with its laws and regulations by investors of the other Contracting Party, whether prior to or after the entry into force of the Agreement.

Article 3
Promotion, admission

(1)   Each Contracting Party shall in its territory promote as far as possible investments by investors of the other Contracting Party and admit such investments in accordance with its laws and regulations.

(2)   When a Contracting Party shall have admitted an investment on its territory, it shall grant the necessary permits in connection with such an investment and with the carrying out

of licensing agreements and contracts for technical, commercial or administrative assistance. Each Contracting Party shall, whenever needed, endeavour to issue the necessary authorizations concerning the activities of consultants and other qualified persons of foreign nationality.

Article 4
Protection, treatment

(1)   Investments and returns of investors of each Contracting Party shall at all times be accorded fair and equitable treatment and shall enjoy full protection and security in the territory of the other Contracting Party. Neither Contracting Party shall in any way impair by unreasonable or discriminatory measures the management, maintenance, use, enjoyment, extension, or disposal of such investments.

(2)   Each Contracting Party shall in its territory accord investments or returns of investors of the other Contracting Party treatment not less favourable than that which it accords to investments or returns of its own investors or to investments or returns of investors of any third State, whichever is more favourable to the investor concerned.

(3)   Each Contracting Party shall in its territory accord investors of the other Contracting Party, as regards the management, maintenance, use, enjoyment or disposal of their investments, treatment not less favourable than that which it accords to its own investors or investors of any third State, whichever is more favourable to the investor concerned.

(4)   If a Contracting Party accords special advantages to investors of any third State by virtue of an agreement establishing a free trade area, a customs union or a common market or by virtue of an agreement on the avoidance of double taxation, it shall not be obliged to accord such advantages to investors of the other Contracting Party.

Article 5
Free transfer

Each Contracting Party in whose territory investments have been made by investors of the other Contracting Party shall grant those investors the free transfer of the amounts relating to these investments, in particular of:

(a)   returns;

(b)   repayments of loans;

(c)   amounts assigned to cover expenses relating to the management of the investment;

(d)   royalties and other payments deriving from rights enumerated in Article 1, paragraph (2), letters (c), (d) and (e) of this Agreement;

(e)   additional contributions of capital necessary for the maintenance or development of the investment;

(f)   the proceeds of the partial or total sale or liquidation of the investment, including possible increment values.

Article 6
Dispossession, compensation

(1)   Neither of the Contracting Parties shall take, either directly or indirectly, measures of expropriation, nationalization or any other measures having the same nature or the same effect against investments of investors of the other Contracting Party, unless the measures are taken in the public interest, on a non discriminatory basis, and under due process of law, and provided that provisions be made for effective and adequate compensation. Such compensation shall amount to the market value of the investment expropriated immediately before the expropriatory action was taken or became public knowledge, whichever is earlier. The amount of compensation, interest included, shall be settled in the currency of the country of origin of the investment and paid without delay to the person entitled thereto without regard to its residence or domicile.

(2)   The investors of one Contracting Party whose investments have suffered losses due to a war or any other armed conflict, revolution, state of emergency or rebellion, which took place in the territory of the other Contracting Party shall benefit, on the part of this latter, from a treatment in accordance with Article 4 of this Agreement as regards restitution, indemnification, compensation or other settlement.

Article 7
Principle of subrogation

Where one Contracting Party has granted any financial guarantee against non-commercial risks in regard to an investment by one of its investors in the territory of the other Contracting Party, the latter shall recognize the rights of the first Contracting Party by virtue of the principle of subrogation to the rights of the investor when payment has been made under this guarantee by the first Contracting Party.

Article 8
Disputes between a Contracting Party
and an investor of the other Contracting Party

(1)   For the purpose of solving disputes with respect to investments between a Contracting Party and an investor of the other Contracting Party and without prejudice to Article 9 of this Agreement (Disputes between Contracting Parties), consultations will take place between the parties concerned.

(2)   If these consultations do not result in a solution within six months from the date of request for consultations and if the investor concerned gives a written consent, the dispute shall be submitted to the International Centre for Settlement of Investment Disputes, instituted by the Convention of Washington of March 18, 1965, for the settlement of disputes regarding investments between States and nationals of other States.

Each party may start the procedure by addressing a request to that effect to the Secretary-General of the Centre as foreseen by Article 28 and 36 of the above-mentioned Convention. Should the parties disagree on whether the conciliation or arbitration is the most appropriate procedure, the investor concerned shall have the choice. The Contracting Party which is party to the dispute can, at no time whatsoever during the settlement procedure or the execution of the sentence, allege the fact that the investor has received, by virtue of an insurance contract, a compensation covering the whole or part of the incurred damage.

(3)   A company which has been incorporated or constituted according to the laws in force on the territory of the Contracting Party and which, prior to the origin of the dispute, was under the control of nationals or companies of the other Contracting Party, is considered, in the sense of the Convention of Washington and according to its Article 25 (2) (b), as a company of the latter.

(4)   Neither Contracting Party shall pursue through diplomatic channels a dispute submitted to the Centre, unless

(a)   the Secretary-General of the Centre or a commission of conciliation or an arbitral tribunal decides that the dispute is beyond the jurisdiction of the Centre, or

(b)   the other Contracting Party does not abide by and comply with the award rendered by an arbitral tribunal.

Article 9
Disputes between Contracting Parties

(1)   Disputes between Contracting Parties regarding the interpretation or application of the provisions of this Agreement shall be settled through diplomatic channels.

(2)   If both Contracting Parties cannot reach an agreement within six months after the beginning of the dispute between themselves, the latter shall, upon request of either Contracting Party, be submitted to an arbitral tribunal of three members. Each Contracting Party shall appoint one arbitrator, and these two arbitrators shall nominate a chairman who shall be a national of a third State.

(3)   If one of the Contracting Parties has not appointed its arbitrator and has not followed the invitation of the other Contracting Party to make that appointment within two months,

the arbitrator shall be appointed upon the request of that Contracting Party by the President of the International Court of Justice.

(4)   If both arbitrators cannot reach an agreement about the choice of the chairman within two months after their appointment, the latter shall be appointed upon the request of either Contracting Party by the President of the International Court of Justice.

(5)   If, in the cases specified under paragraphs (3) and (4) of this Article, the President of the International Court of Justice is prevented from carrying out the said function or if he is a national of either Contracting Party, the appointment shall be made by the Vice-President, and if the latter is prevented or if he is a national of either Contracting Party, the appointment shall be made by the most senior Judge of the Court who is not a national of either Contracting Party.

(6)   Subject to other provisions made by the Contracting Parties, the tribunal shall determine its procedure.

(7)   The decisions of the tribunal are final and binding for each Contracting Party.

Article 10
Other commitments

(1)   If provisions in the legislation of either Contracting Party or rules of international law entitle investments by investors of the other Contracting Party to treatment more favourable than is provided for by this Agreement, such provisions shall to the extent that they are more favourable prevail over this Agreement.

(2)   Each Contracting Party shall observe any obligation it has assumed with regard to investments in its territory by investors of the other Contracting Party.

Article 11
Final provisions

(1)   This Agreement shall enter into force on the day when both Governments have notified each other that they have complied with the constitutional requirements for the conclusion and entry into force of international agreements, and shall remain binding for a period of ten years. Unless written notice of termination is given six months before the expiration of this period, the Agreement shall be considered as renewed on the same terms for a period of two years, and so forth.

(2)   In case of official notice as to the termination of the present Agreement, the provisions of Articles 1 to 10 shall continue to be effective for a further period of ten years for investments made before official notice was given.

Done in duplicate, at _____, on _____, each in [French], _____ and [English], each text being equally authentic. [In case of any divergence of interpretation, the English text shall prevail.]

For the Swiss Federal Council   For the Government of _____

*   *   *

AGREEMENT BETWEEN THE GOVERNMENT OF THE UNITED KINGDOM OF GREAT BRITAIN AND NORTHERN IRELAND

AND

THE GOVERNMENT OF

_____

FOR THE PROMOTION AND PROTECTION OF INVESTMENTS*

The Government of the United Kingdom of Great Britain and Northern Ireland and the Government of _____,

Desiring to create favourable conditions for greater investment by nationals and companies of one State in the territory of the other State;

Recognising that the encouragement and reciprocal protection under international agreement of such investments will be conducive to the stimulation of individual business initiative and will increase prosperity in both States;

Have agreed as follows:

Article 1
Definitions

For the purposes of this Agreement:

(a)   "investment" means every kind of asset and in particular, though not exclusively, includes:

(i)   movable and immovable property and any other property rights such as mortgages, liens or pledges;

(ii)   shares in and stock and debentures of a company and any other form of participation in a company;

---

*Source: Government of the United Kingdom, Department of Trade and Industry [Note added by the editor].

> (iii) claims to money or to any performance under contract having a financial value;
>
> (iv) intellectual property rights, goodwill, technical processes and know-how;
>
> v) business concessions conferred by law or under contract, including concessions to search for, cultivate, extract or exploit natural resources.

A change in the form in which assets are invested does not affect their character as investments and the term "investment" includes all investments, whether made before or after the date of entry into force of this Agreement;

(b) "returns" means the amounts yielded by an investment and in particular, though not exclusively, includes profit, interest, capital gains, dividends, royalties and fees;

(c) "nationals" means:

> (i) in respect of the United Kingdom: physical persons deriving their status as United Kingdom nationals from the law in force in the United Kingdom;
>
> (ii) in respect of _____;

(d) "companies" means:

> (i) in respect of the United Kingdom: corporations, firms and associations incorporated or constituted under the law in force in any part of the United Kingdom or in any territory to which this Agreement is extended in accordance with the provisions of Article 12;
>
> (ii) in respect of _____: corporations, firms and associations incorporated or constituted under the law in force in any part of _____;

(e) "territory" means:

> (i) in respect of the United Kingdom: Great Britain and Northern Ireland, including the territorial sea and any maritime area situated beyond the territorial sea of the United Kingdom which has been or might in the future be designated under the national law of the United Kingdom in accordance with international law as an area within which the United Kingdom may exercise rights with regard to the sea-bed and subsoil and the natural resources and any territory to which this Agreement is extended in accordance with the provisions of Article 12;

(ii)   in respect of _____:

Article 2
Promotion and Protection of Investment

(1)   Each Contracting Party shall encourage and create favourable conditions for nationals or companies of the other Contracting Party to invest capital in its territory, and, subject to its right to exercise powers conferred by its laws, shall admit such capital.

(2)   Investments of nationals or companies of each Contracting Party shall at all times be accorded fair and equitable treatment and shall enjoy full protection and security in the territory of the other Contracting Party. Neither Contracting Party shall in any way impair by unreasonable or discriminatory measures the management, maintenance, use, enjoyment or disposal of investments in its territory of nationals or companies of the other Contracting Party. Each Contracting Party shall observe any obligation it may have entered into with regard to investments of nationals or companies of the other Contracting Party.

Article 3
National Treatment and Most-favoured-nation Provisions

(1)   Neither Contracting Party shall in its territory subject investments or returns of nationals or companies of the other Contracting Party to treatment less favourable than that which it accords to investments or returns of its own nationals or companies or to investments or returns of nationals or companies of any third State.

(2)   Neither Contracting Party shall in its territory subject nationals or companies of the other Contracting Party, as regards their management, maintenance, use, enjoyment or disposal of their investments, to treatment less favourable than that which it accords to its own nationals or companies or to nationals or companies of any third State.

(3)   For the avoidance of doubt it is confirmed that the treatment provided for in paragraphs (1) and (2) above shall apply to the provisions of Articles 1 to 11 of this Agreement.

Article 4
Compensation for Losses

(1)   Nationals or companies of one Contracting Party whose investments in the territory of the other Contracting Party suffer losses owing to war or other armed conflict, revolution, a state of national emergency, revolt, insurrection or riot in the territory of the latter Contracting Party shall be accorded by the latter Contracting Party treatment, as regards restitution, indemnification, compensation or other settlement, no less favourable than that which the latter Contracting Party accords to its own nationals or companies or to nationals or companies of any third State. Resulting payments shall be freely transferable.

(2)   Without prejudice to paragraph (1) of this Article, nationals and companies of one

Contracting Party who in any of the situations referred to in that paragraph suffer losses in the territory of the other Contracting Party resulting from

(a)   requisitioning of their property by its forces or authorities, or

(b)   destruction of their property by its forces or authorities, which was not caused in combat action or was not required by the necessity of the situation,

shall be accorded restitution or adequate compensation. Resulting payments shall be freely transferable.

Article 5
Expropriation

(1)   Investments of nationals or companies of either Contracting Party shall not be nationalised, expropriated or subjected to measures having effect equivalent to nationalisation or expropriation (hereinafter referred to as "expropriation") in the territory of the other Contracting Party except for a public purpose related to the internal needs of that Party on a non-discriminatory basis and against prompt, adequate and effective compensation.   Such compensation shall amount to the genuine value of the investment expropriated immediately before the expropriation or before the impending expropriation became public knowledge, whichever is the earlier, shall include interest at a normal commercial rate until the date of payment, shall be made without delay, be effectively realizable and be freely transferable. The national or company affected shall have a right, under the law of the Contracting Party making the expropriation, to prompt review, by a judicial or other independent authority of that Party, of his or its case and of the valuation of his or its investment in accordance with the principles set out in this paragraph.

(2)   Where a Contracting Party expropriates the assets of a company which is incorporated or constituted under the law in force in any part of its own territory, and in which nationals or companies of the other Contracting Party own shares, it shall ensure that the provisions of paragraph (1) of this Article are applied to the extent necessary to guarantee prompt, adequate and effective compensation in respect of their investment to such nationals or companies of the other Contracting Party who are owners of those shares.

Article 6
Repatriation of Investment and Returns

Each Contracting Party shall in respect of investments guarantee to nationals or companies of the other Contracting Party the unrestricted transfer of their investments and returns.   Transfers shall be effected without delay in the convertible currency in which the capital was originally invested or in any other convertible currency agreed by the investor and the Contracting Party concerned. Unless otherwise agreed by the investor transfers shall be made at the rate of exchange applicable on the date of transfer pursuant to the exchange regulations in force.

Article 7
Exceptions

The provisions of this Agreement relative to the grant of treatment not less favourable than that accorded to the nationals or companies of either Contracting Party or of any third State shall not be construed so as to oblige one Contracting Party to extend to the nationals or companies of the other the benefit of any treatment, preference or privilege resulting from

(a) any existing or future customs union or similar international agreement to which either of the Contracting Parties is or may become a party, or

(b) any international agreement or arrangement relating wholly or mainly to taxation or any domestic legislation relating wholly or mainly to taxation.

[Preferred]

Article 8
Reference to International Centre for Settlement of Investment Disputes

(1)   Each Contracting Party hereby consents to submit to the International Centre for the Settlement of Investment Disputes (hereinafter referred to as "the Centre") for settlement by conciliation or arbitration under the Convention on the Settlement of Investment Disputes between States and Nationals of Other States opened for signature at Washington on 18 March 1965 any legal dispute arising between that Contracting Party and a national or company of the other Contracting Party concerning an investment of the latter in the territory of the former.

(2)   A company which is incorporated or constituted under the law in force in the territory of one Contracting Party and in which before such a dispute arises the majority of shares are owned by nationals or companies of the other Contracting Party shall in accordance with Article 25(2)(b) of the Convention be treated for the purposes of the Convention as a company of the other Contracting Party.

(3)   If any such dispute should arise and agreement cannot be reached within three months between the parties to this dispute through pursuit of local remedies or otherwise, then, if the national or company affected also consents in writing to submit the dispute to the Centre for settlement by conciliation or arbitration under the Convention, either party may institute proceedings by addressing a request to that effect to the Secretary-General of the Centre as provided in Articles 28 and 36 of the Convention.   In the event of disagreement as to whether conciliation or arbitration is the more appropriate procedure the national or company affected shall have the right to choose.   The Contracting Party which is a party to the dispute shall not raise as an objection at any stage of the proceedings or enforcement of an award the fact that the national or company which is the other party to the dispute has received in pursuance of an insurance contract an indemnity in respect of some or all of his or its losses.

(4)   Neither Contracting Party shall pursue through the diplomatic channel any dispute referred

to the Centre unless

(a)   the Secretary-General of the Centre, or a conciliation commission or an arbitral tribunal constituted by it, decides that the dispute is not within the jurisdiction of the Centre, or

(b)   the other Contracting Party should fail to abide by or to comply with any award rendered by an arbitral tribunal.

[Alternative]

Article 8
Settlement of Disputes between an Investor and a Host State

(1)   Disputes between a national or company of one Contracting Party and the other Contracting Party concerning an obligation of the latter under this Agreement in relation to an investment of the former which have not been amicably settled shall, after a period of three months from written notification of a claim, be submitted to international arbitration if the national or company concerned so wishes.

(2)   Where the dispute is referred to international arbitration, the national or company and the Contracting Party concerned in the dispute may agree to refer the dispute either to:

(a)   the International Centre for the Settlement of Investment Disputes (having regard to the provisions, where applicable, of the Convention on the Settlement of Investment Disputes between States and Nationals of other States, opened for signature at Washington DC on 18 March 1965 and the Additional Facility for the Administration of Conciliation, Arbitration and Fact-Finding Proceedings); or

(b)   the Court of Arbitration of the International Chamber of Commerce or;

(c)   an international arbitrator or ad hoc arbitration tribunal to be appointed by a special agreement or establishment under the Arbitration Rules of the United Nations Commission on International Trade Law.

If after a period of three months from written notification of the claim there is no agreement to one of the above alternative procedures, the dispute shall at the request in writing of the national or company concerned be submitted to arbitration under the Arbitration Rules of the United Nations Commission on International Trade Law as then in force. The parties to the dispute may agree in writing to modify these Rules.

Article 9
Disputes between the Contracting Parties

(1)   Disputes between the Contracting Parties concerning the interpretation or application of

this Agreement should, if possible, be settled through the diplomatic channel.

(2)   If a dispute between the Contracting Parties cannot thus be settled, it shall upon the request of either Contracting Party be submitted to an arbitral tribunal.

(3)   Such an arbitral tribunal shall be constituted for each individual case in the following way. Within two months of the receipt of the request for arbitration, each Contracting Party shall appoint one member of the tribunal. Those two members shall then select a national of a third State who on approval by the two Contracting Parties shall be appointed Chairman of the tribunal. The Chairman shall be appointed within two months from the date of appointment of the other two members.

(4)   If within the periods specified in paragraph (3) of this Article the necessary appointments have not been made, either Contracting Party may, in the absence of any other agreement, invite the President of the International Court of Justice to make any necessary appointments. If the President is a national of either Contracting Party or if he is otherwise prevented from discharging the said function, the Vice-President shall be invited to make the necessary appointments. If the Vice-President is a national of either Contracting Party or if he too is prevented from discharging the said function, the Member of the International Court of Justice next in seniority who is not a national of either Contracting Party shall be invited to make the necessary appointments.

(5)   The arbitral tribunal shall reach its decision by a majority of votes. Such decision shall be binding on both Contracting Parties. Each Contracting Party shall bear the cost of its own member of the tribunal and of representation in the arbitral proceedings; the cost of the Chairman and the remaining costs shall be borne in equal parts by the Contracting Parties. The tribunal may, however, in its decision direct that a higher proportion of costs shall be borne by one of the two Contracting Parties, and this award shall be binding on both Contracting Parties. The tribunal shall determine its own procedure.

Article 10
Subrogation

(1)   If one Contracting Party or its designated Agency ("the first Contracting Party") makes a payment under an indemnity given in respect of an investment in the territory of the other Contracting Party, ("the second Contracting Party"), the second Contracting Party shall recognise

(a)   the assignment to the first Contracting Party by law or by legal transaction of all the rights and claims of the party indemnified, and

(b)   that the first Contracting Party is entitled to exercise such rights and enforce such claims by virtue of subrogation, to the same extent as the party indemnified.

(2)   The first Contracting Party shall be entitled in all circumstances to

(a)   the same treatment in respect of the rights and claims acquired by it by virtue of the assignment, and

(b)   any payments received in pursuance of those rights and claims,

as the party indemnified was entitled to receive by virtue of this Agreement in respect of the investment concerned and its related returns.

(3)   Any payments received in non-convertible currency by the first Contracting Party in pursuance of the rights and claims acquired shall be freely available to the first Contracting Party for the purpose of meeting any expenditure incurred in the territory of the second Contracting Party.

Article 11
Application of other Rules

If the provisions of law of either Contracting Party or obligations under international law existing at present or established hereafter between the Contracting Parties in addition to the present Agreement contain rules, whether general or specific, entitling investments by investors of the other Contracting Party to a treatment more favourable than is provided for by the present Agreement, such rules shall to the extent that they are more favourable prevail over the present Agreement.

Article 12
Territorial Extension

At the time of [signature] [ratification] of this Agreement, or at any time thereafter, the provisions of this Agreement may be extended to such territories for whose international relations the Government of the United Kingdom are responsible as may be agreed between the Contracting Parties in an Exchange of Notes.

Article 13
Entry into Force

[This Agreement shall enter into force on the day of signature]

or

[Each Contracting Party shall notify the other in writing of the completion of the constitutional formalities required in its territory for the entry into force of this Agreement. This Agreement shall enter into force on the date of the latter of the two notifications]

or

[This Agreement shall be ratified and shall enter into force on the exchange of Instruments of Ratification]

Article 14
Duration and Termination

This Agreement shall remain in force for a period of ten years.   Thereafter it shall continue in force until the expiration of twelve months from the date on which either Contracting Party shall have given written notice of termination to the other.   Provided that in respect of investments made whilst the Agreement is in force, its provisions shall continue in effect with respect to such investments for a period of twenty years after the date of termination and without prejudice to the application thereafter of the rules of general international law.

In witness whereof the undersigned, duly authorised thereto by their respective Governments, have signed this Agreement.

Done in duplicate at _____ this _____ day of _____ 19__ [in the English and _____ languages, both texts being equally authoritative].

For the Government of   For the Government of
the United Kingdom of   _____
Great Britain and Northern Ireland

*   *   *

April 1994

TREATY BETWEEN

THE GOVERNMENT OF THE UNITED STATES OF AMERICA

AND

THE GOVERNMENT OF_____

CONCERNING THE ENCOURAGEMENT
AND RECIPROCAL PROTECTION OF INVESTMENT*

The Government of the United States of America and the Government of_____ (hereinafter the "Parties");

Desiring to promote greater economic cooperation between them, with respect to investment by nationals and companies of one Party in the territory of the other Party;

Recognizing that agreement upon the treatment to be accorded such investment will stimulate the flow of private capital and the economic development of the Parties;

Agreeing that a stable framework for investment will maximize effective utilization of economic resources and improve living standards;

Recognizing that the development of economic and business ties can promote respect for internationally recognized worker rights;

Agreeing that these objectives can be achieved without relaxing health, safety and environmental measures of general application; and

Having resolved to conclude a Treaty concerning the encouragement and reciprocal protection of investment;

Have agreed as follows:

Article I

For the purposes of this Treaty,

---

* Source: Government of the United States of America, Department of State [Note added by the editor].

(a)   "company" means any entity constituted or organized under applicable law, whether or not for profit, and whether privately or governmentally owned or controlled, and includes a corporation, trust, partnership, sole proprietorship, branch, joint venture, association, or other organization;

(b)   "company of a Party" means a company constituted or organized under the laws of that Party;

(c)   "national" of a Party means a natural person who is a national of that Party under its applicable law;

(d)   "investment" of a national or company means every kind of investment owned or controlled directly or indirectly by that national or company, and includes investment consisting or taking the form of:

   (i)   a company;

   (ii)   shares, stock, and other forms of equity participation, and bonds, debentures, and other forms of debt interests, in a company;

   (iii)   contractual rights, such as under turnkey, construction or management contracts, production or revenue-sharing contracts, concessions, or other similar contracts;

   (iv)   tangible property, including real property; and intangible property, including rights, such as leases, mortgages, liens and pledges;

   (v)   intellectual property, including:

           copyrights and related rights,
           patents,
           rights in plant varieties,
           industrial designs,
           rights in semiconductor layout designs,
           trade secrets, including know-how and confidential business information,
           trade and service marks, and
           trade names; and

   (vi)   rights conferred pursuant to law, such as licenses and permits;

(e)   "covered investment" means an investment of a national or company of a Party in the territory of the other Party;

(f)   "state enterprise" means a company owned, or controlled through ownership interests, by a Party;

(g)   "investment authorization" means an authorization granted by the foreign investment authority of a Party to a covered investment or a national or company of the other Party;

(h)   "investment agreement" means a written agreement between the national authorities of a Party and a covered investment or a national or company of the other Party that (i) grants rights with respect to natural resources or other assets controlled by the national authorities and (ii) the investment, national or company relies upon in establishing or acquiring a covered investment.

(i)   "ICSID Convention" means the Convention on the Settlement of Investment Disputes between States and Nationals of Other States, done at Washington, March 18, 1965;

(j)   "Centre" means the International Centre for Settlement of Investment Disputes Established by the ICSID Convention; and

(k)   "UNCITRAL Arbitration Rules" means the arbitration rules of the United Nations Commission on International Trade Law.

Article II

1.   With respect to the establishment, acquisition, expansion, management, conduct, operation and sale or other disposition of covered investments, each Party shall accord treatment no less favorable than that it accords, in like situations, to investments in its territory of its own nationals or companies (hereinafter "national treatment") or to investments in its territory of nationals or companies of a third country (hereinafter "most favored nation treatment"), whichever is most favorable (hereinafter "national and most favored nation treatment"). Each Party shall ensure that its state enterprises, in the provision of their goods or services, accord national and most favored nation treatment to covered investments.

2.   (a)   A Party may adopt or maintain exceptions to the obligations of paragraph 1 in the sectors or with respect to the matters specified in the Annex to this Treaty. In adopting such an exception, a Party may not require the divestment, in whole or in part, of covered investments existing at the time the exception becomes effective.

(b)   The obligations of paragraph 1 do not apply to procedures provided in multilateral agreements concluded under the auspices of the World Intellectual Property Organization relating to the acquisition or maintenance of intellectual property rights.

3.   (a)   Each Party shall at all times accord to covered investments fair and equitable treatment and full protection and security, and shall in no case accord treatment less favorable than that required by international law.

(b)   Neither Party shall in any way impair by unreasonable and discriminatory measures the management, conduct, operation, and sale or other disposition of covered investments.

4.   Each Party shall provide effective means of asserting claims and enforcing rights with respect to covered investments.

5.   Each Party shall ensure that its laws, regulations, administrative practices and procedures of general application, and adjudicatory decisions, that pertain to or affect covered investments are promptly published or otherwise made publicly available.

Article III

1.   Neither Party shall expropriate or nationalize a covered investment either directly or indirectly through measures tantamount to expropriation or nationalization ("expropriation") except for a public purpose; in a non-discriminatory manner; upon payment of prompt, adequate and effective compensation; and in accordance with due process of law and the general principles of treatment provided for in Article II(3).

2.   Compensation shall be paid without delay; be equivalent to the fair market value of the expropriated investment immediately before the expropriatory action was taken ("the date of expropriation"); and be fully realizable and freely transferable. The fair market value shall not reflect any change in value occurring because the expropriatory action had become known before the date of expropriation.

3.   If the fair market value is denominated in a freely usable currency, the compensation paid shall be no less than the fair market value on the date of expropriation, plus interest at a commercially reasonable rate for that currency, accrued from the date of expropriation until the date of payment.

4.   If the fair market value is denominated in a currency that is not freely usable, the compensation paid -- converted into the currency of payment at the market rate of exchange prevailing on the date of payment -- shall be no less than:

(a)   the fair market value on the date of expropriation, converted into a freely usable currency at the market rate of exchange prevailing on that date, plus

(b)   interest, at a commercially reasonable rate for that freely usable currency, accrued from the date of expropriation until the date of payment.

Article IV

1. Each Party shall accord national and most favored nation treatment to covered investments as regards any measure relating to losses that investments suffer in its territory owing to war or other armed conflict, revolution, state of national emergency, insurrection, civil disturbance, or similar events.

2. Each Party shall accord restitution, or pay compensation in accordance with paragraphs 2 through 4 of Article III, in the event that covered investments suffer losses in its territory, owing to war or other armed conflict, revolution, state of national emergency, insurrection, civil disturbance, or similar events, that result from:

    (a) requisitioning of all or part of such investments by the Party's forces or authorities, or

    (b) destruction of all or part of such investments by the Party's forces or authorities that was not required by the necessity of the situation.

Article V

1. Each Party shall permit all transfers relating to a covered investment to be made freely and without delay into and out of its territory. Such transfers include:

    (a) contributions to capital;

    (b) profits, dividends, capital gains, and proceeds from the sale of all or any part of the investment or from the partial or complete liquidation of the investment;

    (c) interest, royalty payments, management fees, and technical assistance and other fees;

    (d) payments made under a contract, including a loan agreement; and

    (e) compensation pursuant to Articles III and IV, and payments arising out of an investment dispute.

2. Each Party shall permit transfers to be made in a freely usable currency at the market rate of exchange prevailing on the date of transfer.

3. Each Party shall permit returns in kind to be made as authorized or specified in an investment authorization, investment agreement, or other written agreement between the Party and a covered investment or a national or company of the other Party.

4. Notwithstanding paragraphs 1 through 3, a Party may prevent a transfer through the equitable, non-discriminatory and good faith application of its laws relating to:

(a)   bankruptcy, insolvency or the protection of the rights of creditors;

(b)   issuing, trading or dealing in securities;

(c)   criminal or penal offenses; or

(d)   ensuring compliance with orders or judgments in adjudicatory proceedings.

Article VI

Neither Party shall mandate or enforce, as a condition for the establishment, acquisition, expansion, management, conduct or operation of a covered investment, any requirement (including any commitment or undertaking in connection with the receipt of a governmental permission or authorization):

(a)   to achieve a particular level or percentage of local content, or to purchase, use or otherwise give a preference to products or services of domestic origin or from any domestic source;

(b)   to limit imports by the investment of products or services in relation to a particular volume or value of production, exports or foreign exchange earnings;

(c)   to export a particular type, level or percentage of products or services, either generally or to a specific market region;

(d)   to limit sales by the investment of products or services in the Party's territory in relation to a particular volume or value of production, exports or foreign exchange earnings;

(e)   to transfer technology, a production process or other proprietary knowledge to a national or company in the Party's territory, except pursuant to an order, commitment or undertaking that is enforced by a court, administrative tribunal or competition authority to remedy an alleged or adjudicated violation of competition laws; or

(f)   to carry out a particular type, level or percentage of research and development in the Party's territory.

Such requirements do not include conditions for the receipt or continued receipt of an advantage.

Article VII

1.   (a)   Subject to its laws relating to the entry and sojourn of aliens, each Party shall permit to enter and to remain in its territory nationals of the other Party for the purpose of establishing, developing, administering or advising on the operation of

an investment to which they, or a company of the other Party that employs them, have committed or are in the process of committing a substantial amount of capital or other resources.

    (b)   Neither Party shall, in granting entry under paragraph l(a), require a labor certification test or other procedures of similar effect, or apply any numerical restriction.

2.   Each Party shall permit covered investments to engage top managerial personnel of their choice, regardless of nationality.

Article VIII

The Parties agree to consult promptly, on the request of either, to resolve any disputes in connection with the Treaty, or to discuss any matter relating to the interpretation or application of the Treaty or to the realization of the objectives of the Treaty.

Article IX

1.   For purposes of this Treaty, an investment dispute is a dispute between a Party and a national or company of the other Party arising out of or relating to an investment authorization, an investment agreement or an alleged breach of any right conferred, created or recognized by this Treaty with respect to a covered investment.

2.   A national or company that is a party to an investment dispute may submit the dispute for resolution under one of the following alternatives:

    (a)   to the courts or administrative tribunals of the Party that is a party to the dispute; or

    (b)   in accordance with any applicable, previously agreed dispute-settlement procedures; or

    (c)   in accordance with the terms of paragraph 3.

3.   (a)   Provided that the national or company concerned has not submitted the dispute for resolution under paragraph 2 (a) or (b), and that three months have elapsed from the date on which the dispute arose, the national or company concerned may submit the dispute for settlement by binding arbitration:

        (i)   to the Centre, if the Centre is available; or

        (ii)   to the Additional Facility of the Centre, if the Centre is not available; or

        (iii)   in accordance with the UNCITRAL Arbitration Rules; or

(iv)   if agreed by both parties to the dispute, to any other arbitration institution or in accordance with any other arbitration rules.

(b)   a national or company, notwithstanding that it may have submitted a dispute to binding arbitration under paragraph 3(a), may seek interim injunctive relief, not involving the payment of damages, before the judicial or administrative tribunals of the Party that is a party to the dispute, prior to the institution of the arbitral proceeding or during the proceeding, for the preservation of its rights and interests.

4.   Each Party hereby consents to the submission of any investment dispute for settlement by binding arbitration in accordance with the choice of the national or company under paragraph 3(a)(i), (ii), and (iii) or the mutual agreement of both parties to the dispute under paragraph 3(a)(iv). This consent and the submission of the dispute by a national or company under paragraph 3(a) shall satisfy the requirement of:

(a)   Chapter II of the ICSID Convention (Jurisdiction of the Centre) and the Additional Facility Rules for written consent of the parties to the dispute; and

(b)   Article II of the United Nations Convention on the Recognition and Enforcement of Foreign Arbitral Awards, done at New York, June 10, 1958, for an "agreement in writing".

5.   Any arbitration under paragraph 3(a)(ii), (iii) or (iv) shall be held in a state that is a party to the United Nations Convention on the Recognition and Enforcement of Foreign Arbitral Awards, done at New York, June 10, 1958.

6.   Any arbitral award rendered pursuant to this Article shall be final and binding on the parties to the dispute. Each Party shall carry out without delay the provisions of any such award and provide in its territory for the enforcement of such award.

7.   In any proceeding involving an investment dispute, a Party shall not assert, as a defense, counterclaim, right of set-off or for any other reason, that indemnification or other compensation for all or part of the alleged damages has been received or will be received pursuant to an insurance or guarantee contract.

8.   For purposes of Article 25(2)(b) of the ICSID Convention and this Article, a company of a Party that, immediately before the occurrence of the event or events giving rise to an investment dispute, was a covered investment, shall be treated as a company of the other Party.

Article X

1.   Any dispute between the Parties concerning the interpretation or application of the Treaty, that is not resolved through consultations or other diplomatic channels, shall be submitted

upon the request of either Party to an arbitral tribunal for binding decision in accordance with the applicable rules of international law. In the absence of an agreement by the Parties to the contrary, the UNCITRAL Arbitration Rules shall govern, except to the extent these rules are (a) modified by the Parties or (b) modified by the arbitrators unless either Party objects to the proposed modification.

2. Within two months of receipt of a request, each Party shall appoint an arbitrator. The two arbitrators shall select a third arbitrator as chairman, who shall be a national of a third state. The UNCITRAL Arbitration Rules applicable to appointing members of three-member panels shall apply <u>mutatis mutandis</u> to the appointment of the arbitral panel except that the appointing authority referenced in those rules shall be the Secretary General of the Centre.

3. Unless otherwise agreed, all submissions shall be made and all hearings shall be completed within six months of the date of selection of the third arbitrator, and the arbitral panel shall render its decisions within two months of the date of the final submissions or the date of the closing of the hearings, whichever is later.

4. Expenses incurred by the Chairman and other arbitrators, and other costs of the proceedings, shall be paid for equally by the Parties. However, the arbitral panel may, at its discretion, direct that a higher proportion of the costs be paid by one of the Parties.

Article XI

This Treaty shall not derogate from any of the following that entitle covered investments to treatment more favorable than that accorded by this Treaty:

(a) laws and regulations, administrative practices or procedures, or administrative or adjudicatory decisions of a Party;

(b) international legal obligations; or

(c) obligations assumed by a Party, including those contained in an investment authorization or an investment agreement.

Article XII

Each Party reserves the right to deny to a company of the other Party the benefits of this Treaty if nationals of a third country own or control the company and

(a) the denying Party does not maintain normal economic relations with the third country; or

(b) the company has no substantial business activities in the territory of the Party under whose laws it is constituted or organized.

Article XIII

1. No provision of this Treaty shall impose obligations with respect to tax matters, except that:

    (a) Articles III, IX and X will apply with respect to expropriation; and

    (b) Article IX will apply with respect to an investment agreement or an investment authorization.

2. A national or company, that asserts in an investment dispute that a tax matter involves an expropriation, may submit that dispute to arbitration pursuant to Article IX(3) only if:

    (a) the national or company concerned has first referred to the competent tax authorities of both Parties the issue of whether the tax matter involves an expropriation; and

    (b) the competent tax authorities have not both determined, within nine months from the time the national or company referred the issue, that the matter does not involve an expropriation.

Article XIV

1. This Treaty shall not preclude a Party from applying measures necessary for the fulfillment of its obligations with respect to the maintenance or restoration of international peace or security, or the protection of its own essential security interests.

2. This Treaty shall not preclude a Party from prescribing special formalities in connection with covered investments, such as a requirement that such investments be legally constituted under the laws and regulations of that Party, or a requirement that transfers of currency or other monetary instruments be reported, provided that such formalities shall not impair the substance of any of the rights set forth in this Treaty.

Article XV

1. (a) The obligations of this Treaty shall apply to the political subdivisions of the Parties.

    (b) With respect to the treatment accorded by a State, Territory or possession of the United States of America, national treatment means treatment no less favorable than the treatment accorded thereby, in like situations, to investments of nationals of the United States of America resident in, and companies legally constituted under the laws and regulations of, other States, Territories or possessions of the United States of America.

2.   A Party's obligations under this Treaty shall apply to a state enterprise in the exercise of any regulatory, administrative or other governmental authority delegated to it by that Party.

Article XVI

1.   This Treaty shall enter into force thirty days after the date of exchange of instruments of ratification. It shall remain in force for a period of ten years and shall continue in force unless terminated in accordance with paragraph 2. It shall apply to covered investments existing at the time of entry into force as well as to those established or acquired thereafter.

2.   A Party may terminate this treaty at the end of the initial ten year period or at any time thereafter by giving one year's written notice to the other Party.

3.   For ten years from the date of termination, all other Articles shall continue to apply to covered investments established or acquired prior to the date of termination, except insofar as those Articles extend to the establishment or acquisition of covered investments.

4.   The Annex [and Protocol (if any)] shall form an integral part of the Treaty.

IN WITNESS WHEREOF, the respective plenipotentiaries have signed this Treaty.

DONE in duplicate at [city] this [number] day of [month], [year], in the english and _____ languages, each text being equally authentic.

FOR THE GOVERNMENT OF THE UNITED STATES OF AMERICA:

FOR THE GOVERNMENT OF _____:

ANNEX

1. The Government of the United States of America may adopt or maintain exceptions to the obligation to accord national treatment to covered investments in the sectors or with respect to the matters specified below:

   atomic energy; customhouse brokers; licenses for broadcast, common carrier, or aeronautical radio stations; COMSAT; subsidies or grants, including government-supported loans, guarantees and insurance; state and local measures exempt from Article 1102 of the North American Free Trade Agreement pursuant to Article 1108 thereof; and landing of submarine cables.

   Most favored nation treatment shall be accorded in the sectors and matters indicated above.

2. The Government of the United States of America may adopt or maintain exceptions to the obligation to accord national and most favored nation treatment to covered investments in the sectors or with respect to the matters specified below:

   fisheries; air and maritime transport, and related activities; banking* insurance* securities* and other financial services*.

   *Note: if the Treaty Partner undertakes acceptable commitments with respect to all or certain financial services, the Government of the United States of America will consider limiting these exceptions accordingly, so that, for example, particular obligations as to treatment would apply on no less favorable terms than in the North American Free Trade Agreement.

3. The Government of _____ may adopt or maintain exceptions...

4. Notwithstanding paragraph 3, each Party agrees to accord national treatment to covered investments in the following sectors:

   leasing of minerals or pipeline rights-of-way on government lands.

* * *

INVESTMENT INCENTIVE AGREEMENT

BETWEEN

THE GOVERNMENT OF THE UNITED STATES OF AMERICA

AND

[NAME OF COUNTRY]*

THE GOVERNMENT OF THE UNITED STATES OF AMERICA AND THE GOVERNMENT OF [NAME OF COUNTRY];

AFFIRMING their common desire to encourage economic activities in [Name of Country] that promote the development of the economic resources and productive capacities of [Name of Country]; and

RECOGNIZING that this objective can be promoted through investment support provided by the Overseas Private Investment Corporation ("OPIC"), a development institution and an agency of the United States of America, in the form of investment insurance and reinsurance, debt and equity investments and investment guaranties;

HAVE AGREED as follows:

Article I

As used in this Agreement, the following terms have the meanings herein provided. The term "Investment Support" refers to any debt or equity investment, any investment guaranty and any investment insurance or reinsurance which is provided by the Issuer in connection with a project in the territory of [Name of Country]. The term "Issuer" refers to OPIC and any successor agency of the United States of America, and any agent of either. The term "Taxes" means all present and future taxes, levies, imposts, stamps, duties and charges imposed by the Government of [Name of Country] and all liabilities with respect thereto.

---

* Source: The Overseas Private Investment Corporation (New York) [Note added by the editor].

Article 2

(a)   The Issuer shall not be subject to regulation under the laws of [Name of Country] applicable to insurance or financial organizations.

(b)   All operations and activities undertaken by the Issuer in connection with any Investment Support, and all payments, whether of interest, principal, fees, dividends, premiums or the proceeds from the liquidation of assets or of any other nature, that are made, received or guaranteed by the Issuer in connection with any Investment Support shall be exempt from Taxes. The Issuer shall not be subject to any Taxes in connection with any transfer, succession or other acquisition which occurs pursuant to paragraph [c] of this Article or Article 3[a] hereof. Any project in connection with which Investment Support has been provided shall be accorded tax treatment no less favourable than that accorded to projects benefiting from the investment support programs of any other national or multilateral development institution which operates in [Name of Country].

(c)   If the Issuer makes a payment of any person or entity, or exercises its rights as a creditor or subrogee, in connection with any Investment Support, the Government of [Name of Country] shall recognize the transfer to, or acquisition by, the Issuer of any cash, accounts, credits, instruments or other assets in connection with such payment or the exercise of such rights, as well as the succession of the Issuer to any right, title, claim, privilege or cause of action existing or which may arise, in connection therewith.

(d)   With respect to any interests transferred to the Issuer or any interests to which the Issuer succeeds under this Article, the Issuer shall assert no greater rights than those of the person or entity from whom such interests were received, provided that nothing in this Agreement shall limit the right of the Government of the United States of America to assert a claim under international law in its sovereign capacity, as distinct from any rights it may have as the Issuer pursuant to paragraph [c] of this Article.

Article 3

(a)   Amounts in the currency of [Name of Country], including cash, accounts, credits, instruments or otherwise, acquired by the Issuer upon making a payment, or upon the exercise of its rights as a creditor, in connection with any Investment Support provided by the Issuer for a project in [Name of Country], shall be accorded treatment in the territory of [Name of Country] no less favorable as to use and conversion than the treatment to which such funds would have been entitled in the hands of the person or entity from which the Issuer acquired such amounts.

(b)   Such currency and credits may be transferred by the Issuer to any person or entity and upon such transfer shall be freely available for use by such person or entity in the territory of [Name of Country] in accordance with its laws.

Article 4

(a)   Any dispute between the Government of the United States of America and the Government of [Name of Country] regarding the interpretation of this Agreement or which, in the opinion of either party hereto, presents a question of international law arising out of any project or activity for which Investment Support has been provided shall be resolved, insofar as possible, through negotiations between the two Governments. If, six months following a request for negotiations hereunder, the two Governments have not resolved the dispute, the dispute, including the question of whether such dispute presents a question of international law, shall be submitted, at the initiative of either Government, to an arbitral tribunal for resolution in accordance with paragraph [b] of this Article.

(b)   The arbitral tribunal referred to in paragraph [a] of this Article shall be established and shall function as follows:

(i)   Each Government shall appoint one arbitrator. These two arbitrators shall by agreement designate a president of the tribunal who shall be a citizen of a third state and whose appointment shall be subject to acceptance by the two Governments. The arbitrators shall be appointed within three months, and the president within six months, of the date of receipt of either Government's request for arbitration. If the appointments are not made within the foregoing time limits, either Government may, in the absence of any other agreement, request the Secretary-General of the International Centre for the Settlement of Investment Disputes to make the necessary appointment or appointments. Both Governments hereby agree to accept such appointment or appointments.

(ii)   Decisions of the arbitral shall be made by majority vote and shall be based on the applicable principles and rules of international law. Its decision shall be final and binding.

(iii)   During the proceedings, each Government shall bear the expense of its arbitrator and of its representation in the proceedings before the tribunal, whereas the expenses of the president and other costs of the arbitration shall be paid in equal parts by the two Governments. In its award, the arbitral tribunal may reallocate expenses and costs between the two Governments.

(iv)   In all other matters, the arbitral tribunal shall regulate its own procedures.

Article 5

(a)   This Agreement shall enter into force on the date on which the Government of [Name of Country] notifies the Government of the United States of America that all legal requirements for entry into force of this Agreement have been fulfilled.

(b)   This Agreement shall continue in force until six months from the date of a receipt of a note by which one Government informs the other of an intent to terminate this Agreement. In such event, the provisions of this Agreement shall, with respect to Investment Support provided while this Agreement was in force, remain in force so long as such Investment Support remains outstanding, but in no case longer than twenty years after the termination of this Agreement.

IN WITNESS WHEREOF, the undersigned, duly authorized by their respective Governments, have signed this Agreement.

DONE at Washington, District of Columbia, United States of America, on the [_____] day of _____, 199___, in duplicate, in the English and _____ languages, both texts being equally authentic.

FOR THE GOVERNMENT OF	**FOR THE GOVERNMENT OF**
THE UNITED STATES OF AMERICA	**[NAME OF COUNTRY]**
_____	_____

* * *

Appendix
Bilateral Investment Treaties Concluded
up to July 1995

BILATERAL INVESTMENT TREATIES CONCLUDED UP TO JULY 1995

Country	Date of signature	Date of entry into force
Albania		
Greece	1 August 1991	--
Italy	12 September 1991	--
Germany	31 October 1991	Provisional application
Turkey	1 June 1992	--
Switzerland	22 September 1992	30 April 1993
Poland	5 March 1993	9 August 1993
China	13 February 1993	--
Austria	18 March 1993	--
Egypt	22 May 1993	6 April 1994
Tunisia	30 October 1993	--
United Kingdom	30 March 1994	--
Czech Republic	27 June 1994	--
Netherlands	15 April 1994	--
Bulgaria	27 April 1994	--
United States	10 January 1995	--
Algeria		
Belgium/Luxembourg	24 April 1991	--
Italy	18 May 1991	--
France	13 February 1993	--
Italy	18 May 1991	--
Antigua and Barbuda		
United Kingdom	12 June 1987	12 June 1987
Argentina		
Italy	22 May 1990	14 October 1993
Belgium/Luxembourg	28 June 1990	20 May 1994
United Kingdom	11 December 1990	19 February 1993
Germany	9 April 1991	8 November 1993
Switzerland	12 April 1991	6 November 1992
France	3 July 1991	3 March 1993
Poland	31 July 1991	1 September 1992
Spain	3 October 1991	28 September 1992
Canada	5 November 1991	29 April 1993
United States	14 November 1991	20 October 1994
Sweden	22 November 1991	28 September 1992
Turkey	8 May 1992	--
Egypt	11 May 1992	3 December 1993
Tunisia	17 June 1992	23 January 1995
Chile	2 August 1991	1 January 1995
Austria	7 August 1992	1 January 1995
Netherlands	20 October 1992	1 October 1994
China	5 November 1992	1 August 1994
Denmark	6 November 1992	2 February 1995
Hungary	5 February 1993	--
Senegal	6 April 1993	--
Armenia	16 April 1993	20 December 1994
Romania	29 July 1993	--

Country	Date of signature	Date of entry into force
Bulgaria	21 September 1993	--
Finland	5 November 1993	--
Venezuela	16 November 1993	--
Jamaica	8 February 1994	--
Ecuador	20 February 1994	--
Bolivia	17 March 1994	--
Republic of Korea	17 May 1994	--
Malaysia	6 September 1994	--
Portugal	6 October 1994	--
Peru	10 November 1994	--
Croatia	2 December 1994	--
Armenia [a]		
China	4 July 1992	--
United States	23 September 1992	--
Argentina	16 April 1993	20 December 1994
United Kingdom	22 May 1993	--
Greece	24 May 1993	--
Cyprus	18 January 1995	--
Bulgaria	10 April 1995	--
Australia		
China	11 July 1988	11 July 1988
Papua New Guinea	3 September 1990	20 October 1991
Viet Nam	5 March 1991	11 September 1991
Poland	7 May 1991	27 March 1992
Czechoslovakia	29 July 1991	--
Hungary	15 August 1991	10 May 1992
Indonesia	17 November 1992	29 July 1993
Romania	21 June 1993	22 April 1994
Hong Kong	15 September 1993	15 October 1993
Czech Republic	30 September 1993	29 June 1994
Lao People's Democratic Republic	6 April 1994	--
Philippines	25 January 1995	--
Austria		
Romania	30 September 1976	8 November 1977
Bulgaria	15 May 1981	--
Malaysia	12 April 1985	1 January 1987
China	12 September 1985	11 October 1986
Hungary	26 May 1988	1 September 1989
Turkey	16 September 1988	1 January 1992
Poland	14 November 1988	1 November 1989
Yugoslavia	25 October 1989	1 June 1991
Soviet Union	8 February 1990	1 September 1991
Czechoslovakia	15 October 1990	1 October 1991
Republic of Korea	14 March 1991	1 November 1991
Cape Verde	3 September 1991	1 April 1993
Argentina	7 August 1992	1 January 1995
Morocco	2 November 1992	--
Paraguay	13 August 1993	--
Albania	18 March 1993	--

Country	Date of signature	Date of entry into force
Estonia	16 May 1994	--
Latvia	17 November 1994	--
Azerbaijan [a]		
Turkey	9 February 1994	--
China	8 March 1994	1 April 1995
Bahrain		
United Kingdom	30 October 1991	30 October 1991
Bangladesh		
United Kingdom	19 June 1980	19 June 1980
Germany	6 May 1981	14 September 1986
Belgium/Luxembourg	27 February 1986	14 September 1987
France	10 September 1985	3 October 1986
United States	12 March 1986	25 July 1989
Republic of Korea	18 June 1986	6 October 1988
Romania	13 March 1987	--
Turkey	12 November 1987	21 June 1990
Thailand	13 March 1988	--
Italy	20 March 1990	13 August 1994
Netherlands	1 November 1994	--
Malaysia	12 October 1994	--
Barbados		
United Kingdom	7 April 1993	7 April 1993
Venezuela	15 July 1994	--
Germany	2 December 1994	2 December 1994
Switzerland	29 March 1995	--
Belarus [a]		
Poland	24 April 1992	18 January 1993
Finland	20 May 1992	21 March 1993
China	13 January 1993	14 January 1995
Germany	2 April 1993	--
Switzerland	28 May 1993	13 July 1994
France	28 October 1993	--
United States	15 January 1994	--
United Kingdom	1 March 1994	--
Sweden	20 December 1994	--
Netherlands	11 April 1995	--
Belgium/Luxembourg		
Tunisia	15 July 1964	9 March 1966
Morocco	28 April 1965	18 October 1967
Indonesia [b]	15 January 1970	17 June 1972
Republic of Korea	20 December 1974	3 September 1976
Zaire	28 March 1976	1 January 1977
Egypt	28 February 1977	20 September 1978
Romania	8 May 1978	1 May 1980

215

Country	Date of signature	Date of entry into force
Singapore	17 November 1978	27 November 1980
Malaysia	22 November 1979	8 February 1982
Cameroon	27 March 1980	1 November 1981
Sri Lanka	5 April 1982	26 April 1984
Rwanda	2 November 1983	1 August 1985
Mauritania	23 November 1983	--
China	4 June 1984	5 October 1986
Liberia	5 June 1985	--
Bangladesh	27 February 1986	14 September 1987
Thailand	19 March 1986	--
Hungary	14 May 1986	23 September 1988
Turkey	27 August 1986	4 May 1990
Malta	5 March 1987	--
Poland c	19 April 1987	2 August 1991
Bulgaria	25 October 1988	29 May 1991
Soviet Union c	9 February 1989	13 October 1991
Burundi	13 April 1989	--
Czechoslovakia	24 April 1989	13 February 1992
Bolivia	25 April 1990	--
Argentina	28 June 1990	20 May 1994
Viet Nam	24 January 1991	--
Cyprus	26 February 1991	--
Algeria	24 April 1991	13 February 1992
Uruguay	4 November 1991	--
Mongolia	3 March 1992	--
Chile	15 July 1992	--
Paraguay	6 October 1992	--
Georgia	23 June 1993	--
Belize		
United Kingdom	30 April 1982	30 April 1982
Benin		
Switzerland	20 April 1966	6 October 1973
Germany	29 June 1978	18 July 1985
United Kingdom	27 November 1987	27 November 1987
Bolivia		
Germany	23 March 1987	9 November 1990
Switzerland	6 November 1987	13 May 1991
United Kingdom	24 May 1988	16 February 1990
France	25 October 1989	--
Spain	24 April 1990	12 May 1992
Belgium/Luxembourg	25 April 1990	
Italy	30 April 1990	22 February 1992
Sweden	20 September 1990	3 July 1992
Netherlands	10 March 1992	1 November 1994
China	8 May 1992	--
Peru	30 July 1993	--
Argentina	17 March 1994	--
Chile	20 September 1994	--
Denmark	13 March 1995	--

Country	Date of signature	Date of entry into force
Brazil		
Chile	22 March 1994	--
Switzerland	11 November 1994	--
Portugal	9 February 1994	--
United Kingdom	19 July 1994	--
Bulgaria		
Austria	15 May 1981	--
Finland	16 February 1984	16 July 1985
Malta	12 June 1984	4 December 1984
Germany	12 April 1986	10 March 1988
Cyprus	12 November 1987	18 May 1988
Netherlands	8 March 1988	24 May 1990
Belgium/Luxembourg	25 October 1988	29 May 1991
Italy	5 December 1988	27 December 1990
France	5 April 1989	1 May 1990
China	27 June 1989	21 August 1994
Ghana	20 October 1989	--
Switzerland	28 October 1991	26 October 1993
United States	23 September 1992	2 June 1994
Greece	12 March 1993	29 April 1995
Denmark	14 April 1993	--
Portugal	27 May 1993	--
Russian Federation	8 June 1993	--
Argentina	21 September 1993	--
Israel	6 December 1993	--
Ukraine	1 January 1994	--
Poland	11 April 1994	9 March 1995
Sweden	19 April 1994	1 April 1995
Albania	27 April 1994	--
Romania	1 June 1994	--
Hungary	8 June 1994	--
Turkey	6 July 1994	--
Slovakia	21 July 1994	9 March 1995
Georgia	19 January 1995	--
Armenia	10 April 1995	--
Burkina Faso		
Switzerland	6 May 1969	15 September 1969
Tunisia	7 January 1993	--
Burundi		
Germany	10 September 1984	9 December 1987
Belgium/Luxembourg	13 April 1989	--
United Kingdom	13 September 1990	13 September 1990
Cameroon		
Germany	29 June 1962	21 November 1963
Switzerland	28 January 1963	6 April 1964
Netherlands	6 July 1965	7 May 1966
Belgium/Luxembourg	27 March 1980	1 November 1981
Romania	30 August 1980	16 December 1981

Country	Date of signature	Date of entry into force
United Kingdom	4 June 1982	7 June 1985
United States	26 February 1986	6 April 1989
Canada [d]		
Soviet Union	20 November 1989	27 June 1991
Poland	6 April 1990	22 November 1990
Czechoslovakia	15 November 1990	9 March 1992
Uruguay	16 May 1991	--
Hungary	3 October 1991	21 November 1993
Argentina	5 November 1991	29 April 1993
Ukraine	24 October 1994	--
Cape Verde		
Germany	18 January 1990	15 December 1993
Portugal	26 October 1990	4 October 1991
Austria	3 September 1991	1 April 1993
Switzerland	28 October 1991	6 May 1992
Netherlands	11 November 1991	25 November 1992
Central African Republic		
France	13 August 1960	--
Germany	23 August 1965	21 January 1968
Switzerland	28 February 1973	4 July 1973
Chad		
France	13 August 1960	--
Switzerland	21 February 1967	31 October 1967
Germany	11 April 1967	23 November 1968
Italy	11 June 1969	11 June 1969
Chile		
Switzerland	11 November 1991	--
Spain	2 October 1991	28 March 1994
Germany	19 October 1991	--
Belgium/Luxembourg	15 July 1992	--
France	14 July 1992	13 July 1993
Argentina	2 August 1991	1 January 1995
Malaysia	11 November 1992	--
Italy	8 March 1993	--
Venezuela	2 April 1993	11 January 1994
Sweden	24 May 1993	--
Finland	27 May 1993	--
Denmark	28 May 1993	--
Norway	1 June 1993	7 September 1994
Ecuador	27 October 1993	--
Brazil	22 March 1994	--
China	23 March 1994	--
Bolivia	22 September 1994	--
Croatia	28 November 1994	--

Country	Date of signature	Date of entry into force
China		
Sweden	29 March 1982	29 March 1982
Romania	10 February 1983	12 January 1984
Germany	7 October 1983	18 March 1985
France	30 May 1984	19 March 1985
Belgium/Luxembourg	4 June 1984	5 October 1986
Finland	4 September 1984	26 January 1986
Norway	21 November 1984	10 July 1985
Italy	28 January 1985	28 August 1987
Thailand	12 March 1985	13 December 1985
Denmark	29 April 1985	29 April 1985
Netherlands	17 June 1985	1 February 1987
Austria	12 September 1985	11 October 1986
Singapore	21 November 1985	7 February 1986
Kuwait	23 November 1985	24 December 1986
Sri Lanka	13 March 1986	25 March 1987
United Kingdom	15 May 1986	15 May 1986
Switzerland	12 November 1986	18 March 1987
Poland	7 June 1988	8 January 1989
Australia	11 July 1988	11 July 1988
Japan	27 August 1988	14 May 1989
Malaysia	21 November 1988	31 March 1990
New Zealand	22 November 1988	25 March 1989
Pakistan	12 February 1989	30 September 1990
Bulgaria	27 June 1989	21 August 1994
Ghana	12 October 1989	--
Soviet Union	21 July 1990	--
Turkey	13 November 1990	19 August 1994
Papua New Guinea	12 April 1991	12 February 1993
Hungary	29 May 1991	1 April 1993
Mongolia	26 August 1991	1 November 1993
Czechoslovakia	4 December 1991	1 December 1992
Portugal	3 February 1992	1 December 1992
Spain	6 February 1992	1 May 1993
Uzbekistan	13 March 1992	--
Panama	26 March 1992	14 July 1992
Bolivia	8 May 1992	--
Kyrgyzstan	14 May 1992	--
Greece	25 June 1992	21 December 1993
Armenia	4 July 1992	--
Philippines	20 July 1992	--
Kazakhstan	10 August 1992	13 August 1994
Republic of Korea	30 September 1992	4 December 1992
Ukraine	31 October 1992	29 May 1993
Argentina	5 November 1992	1 August 1994
Republic of Moldova	7 November 1992	1 March 1995
Turkmenistan	21 November 1992	6 June 1995
Viet Nam	2 December 1992	1 September 1993
Belarus	13 January 1993	14 January 1995
Lao People's Democratic Republic	31 January 1993	1 June 1993
Albania	13 February 1993	--
Tajikistan	9 March 1993	20 January 1994
Georgia	3 June 1993	1 March 1995
Croatia	7 June 1993	1 July 1994

Country	Date of signature	Date of entry into force
United Arab Emirates	1 July 1993	--
Estonia	2 September 1993	1 June 1994
Slovenia	13 September 1993	1 January 1995
Lithuania	8 November 1993	1 June 1994
Uruguay	2 December 1993	--
Azerbaijan	8 March 1994	1 April 1995
Ecuador	21 March 1994	--
Chile	23 March 1994	--
Iceland	31 March 1994	--
Egypt	21 April 1994	--
Peru	9 June 1994	1 February 1995
Romania	12 July 1994	--
Jamaica	26 October 1994	--
Indonesia	18 November 1994	21 April 1995
Israel	10 April 1995	--
Cuba	24 April 1995	--
Oman	18 March 1995	--
Morocco	27 March 1995	--
Colombia		
United Kingdom	9 March 1994	--
Peru	26 April 1994	--
Cuba	16 July 1994	--
Congo		
France	15 August 1960	--
Switzerland	18 October 1962	11 July 1964
Germany	13 September 1965	14 October 1967
United Kingdom	25 May 1989	9 November 1990
United States	12 February 1990	--
Italy	17 March 1994	--
Costa Rica		
Switzerland	1 September 1965	18 August 1966
United Kingdom	7 September 1982	--
France	8 March 1984	--
Germany	13 September 1994	--
Côte d'Ivoire		
Switzerland	26 June 1962	18 November 1962
Netherlands	26 April 1965	8 September 1966
Sweden	27 August 1965	3 November 1966
Germany	27 October 1966	10 June 1968
Denmark	23 November 1966	10 January 1968
Italy	23 July 1969	--
Croatia		
China	7 June 1993	1 July 1994
Poland	15 April 1994	--
Chile	28 November 1994	--
Argentina	2 December 1994	--

Country	Date of signature	Date of entry into force
Cuba		
Italy	7 May 1993	--
Russian Federation	7 May 1993	--
Colombia	16 July 1994	--
Spain	27 May 1994	--
United Kingdom	30 January 1995	--
China	24 April 1995	--
Cyprus		
Bulgaria	12 November 1987	18 May 1988
Hungary	24 May 1989	25 May 1990
Belgium/Luxembourg	26 February 1991	--
Romania	26 July 1991	10 July 1993
Greece	30 March 1992	26 February 1993
Poland	4 June 1992	1 July 1993
Armenia	18 January 1995	--
Czechoslovakia [e]		
Belgium/Luxembourg	24 April 1989	13 February 1992
United Kingdom	10 July 1990	26 October 1992
Italy	1 August 1990	--
France	13 September 1990	27 September 1991
Germany	2 October 1990	2 August 1992
Austria	15 October 1990	1 October 1991
Finland	6 November 1990	23 October 1991
Sweden	13 November 1990	23 September 1991
Canada	15 November 1990	9 March 1992
Spain	12 December 1990	28 November 1991
Denmark	6 March 1991	19 September 1992
Netherlands	29 April 1991	1 October 1992
Norway	21 May 1991	6 August 1992
Greece	3 June 1991	31 December 1992
Australia	29 July 1991	--
United States	22 October 1991	19 December 1992
China	4 December 1991	1 December 1992
Republic of Korea	27 April 1992	--
Turkey	30 April 1992	--
Czech Republic [e]		
Slovakia	23 November 1992	--
Hungary	14 January 1993	--
Slovenia	4 May 1993	21 May 1994
Egypt	29 May 1993	4 June 1994
Poland	16 July 1993	29 June 1994
Australia	30 September 1993	29 June 1994
Romania	8 November 1993	28 July 1994
Portugal	11 November 1993	3 August 1994
Tajikistan	11 February 1994	--
Thailand	12 February 1994	--
Peru	16 March 1994	--
Ukraine	17 March 1994	--
Russian Federation	5 April 1994	--

Country	Date of signature	Date of entry into force
Albania	27 June 1994	--
Estonia	24 October 1994	--
Latvia	25 October 1994	--
Lithuania	27 October 1994	--
United Arab Emirates	23 November 1994	--
Denmark [f]		
Madagascar	10 December 1965	26 July 1967
Malawi	1 August 1966	1 August 1966
Côte d'Ivoire	23 November 1966	10 January 1968
Indonesia	30 January 1968	2 July 1968
Romania	12 November 1980	9 April 1981
China	29 April 1985	29 April 1985
Sri Lanka	4 June 1985	4 June 1985
Hungary	2 May 1988	1 October 1988
Republic of Korea	2 June 1988	2 June 1988
Turkey	7 February 1990	1 August 1992
Poland	1 May 1990	13 October 1990
Soviet Union	1 May 1990	--
Czechoslovakia	6 March 1991	19 September 1992
Malaysia	6 January 1992	18 September 1992
Ghana	13 January 1992	6 January 1995
Latvia	30 March 1992	18 November 1994
Lithuania	30 March 1992	9 December 1992
Ukraine	23 October 1992	29 April 1994
Argentina	6 November 1992	2 February 1995
Estonia	6 November 1991	24 February 1993
Bulgaria	14 April 1993	--
Paraguay	22 April 1993	--
Chile	28 May 1993	--
Viet Nam	23 July 1993	7 August 1994
Uzbekistan	23 September 1993	--
Russian Federation	4 November 1993	--
Hong Kong	2 February 1994	4 March 1994
Romania	13 June 1994	--
Peru	23 November 1994	--
Venezuela	28 November 1994	--
Nicaragua	13 March 1995	--
Mongolia	13 March 1995	--
Bolivia	13 March 1995	--
Dominica		
Germany	1 October 1984	11 May 1986
United Kingdom	23 January 1987	23 January 1987
Dominican Republic		
Germany	16 December 1959	3 June 1960
Ecuador		
Germany	28 June 1965	30 November 1966
Switzerland	2 May 1968	11 September 1969
Egypt	19 April 1992	--

Country	Date of signature	Date of entry into force
United States	27 August 1993	--
Chile	27 October 1993	--
Venezuela	16 November 1993	1 February 1995
Paraguay	28 January 1994	--
Argentina	20 February 1994	--
China	21 March 1994	--
United Kingdom	10 May 1994	--
El Salvador	16 May 1994	--
France	7 September 1994	--

Egypt

Country	Date of signature	Date of entry into force
Kuwait	2 May 1966	9 August 1966
Switzerland	25 July 1973	4 June 1974
Germany	5 July 1974	22 July 1978
France	22 December 1974	1 October 1975
United Kingdom	11 June 1975	24 February 1976
Romania	10 May 1976	22 January 1977
Morocco	3 June 1976	7 September 1978
Netherlands	30 October 1976	1 January 1978
Japan	28 January 1977	14 January 1978
Belgium/Luxembourg	28 February 1977	20 September 1978
Sudan	28 May 1977	14 March 1978
Yugoslavia	3 June 1977	--
Sweden	15 July 1978	29 January 1979
Finland	5 May 1980	22 January 1982
Oman	28 April 1985	9 October 1985
United States	11 March 1986	27 June 1992
United Arab Emirates	19 June 1988	--
Yemen	19 October 1988	3 March 1990
Italy	2 March 1989	--
Tunisia	8 December 1989	2 January 1991
Saudi Arabia	13 March 1990	15 September 1992
Libyan Arab Jamahiriya	3 December 1990	4 July 1991
Ecuador	19 April 1992	--
Argentina	11 May 1992	3 December 1993
Spain	3 November 1992	26 April 1994
Uzbekistan	16 December 1992	--
Ukraine	21 December 1992	10 October 1993
Kazakhstan	24 December 1992	--
Czech Republic	29 May 1993	5 June 1994
Albania	22 May 1993	6 April 1994
Greece	16 July 1993	--
Indonesia	19 January 1994	5 August 1994
China	21 April 1994	--

El Salvador

Country	Date of signature	Date of entry into force
France	20 September 1978	12 December 1992
Switzerland	8 December 1994	--
Ecuador	16 May 1994	--
Spain	14 February 1995	--

Equatorial Guinea

Country	Date of signature	Date of entry into force
France	3 March 1982	23 September 1983

Country	Date of signature	Date of entry into force
Estonia [a]		
Finland	13 February 1992	2 December 1992
Sweden	31 March 1992	20 May 1992
France	14 May 1992	17 February 1995
Norway	15 June 1992	15 June 1992
Netherlands	27 October 1992	1 September 1993
Denmark	6 November 1991	24 February 1993
Germany	12 November 1992	Provisional application
Switzerland	21 December 1992	18 August 1993
Poland	6 May 1993	6 August 1993
China	2 September 1993	1 June 1994
Israel	14 March 1994	--
Austria	16 May 1994	--
United States	19 April 1994	--
United Kingdom	12 May 1994	--
Czech Republic	24 October 1994	--
Ethiopia		
Germany	21 April 1964	--
Italy	23 December 1994	--
Finland		
Egypt	5 May 1980	22 January 1982
Bulgaria	16 February 1984	16 July 1985
China	4 September 1984	26 January 1986
Malaysia	15 April 1985	3 January 1988
Sri Lanka	27 April 1985	25 October 1987
Hungary	6 June 1988	12 May 1989
Soviet Union	8 February 1989	15 August 1991
Poland	5 April 1990	21 February 1991
Czechoslovakia	6 November 1990	23 October 1991
Indonesia	7 February 1992	--
Estonia	13 February 1992	2 December 1992
Latvia	5 March 1992	7 December 1992
Romania	26 March 1992	6 January 1993
Ukraine	14 May 1992	30 January 1993
Belarus	20 May 1992	21 March 1993
Lithuania	12 June 1992	8 January 1993
Kazakhstan	29 September 1992	--
Uzbekistan	1 October 1992	22 October 1993
Turkey	13 May 1993	--
Chile	27 May 1993	--
Viet Nam	13 September 1993	--
Republic of Korea	21 October 1993	--
Argentina	5 November 1993	--
Thailand	18 March 1994	--
France		
Chad	11 August 1960	--
Central Africa	13 August 1960	--
Congo	15 August 1960	--
Tunisia	30 June 1972	30 June 1972

Country	Date of signature	Date of entry into force
Zaire	5 October 1972	1 March 1975
Mauritius	22 March 1973	1 April 1974
Indonesia	14 June 1973	29 April 1975
Gabon	12 February 1974	--
Yugoslavia	28 March 1974	3 March 1975
Senegal	29 March 1974	--
Egypt	22 December 1974	1 October 1975
Malaysia	24 April 1975	1 September 1976
Morocco	15 July 1975	13 December 1976
Singapore	8 September 1975	18 October 1976
Philippines	14 June 1976	1 July 1976
Malta	11 August 1976	1 January 1978
Romania	16 December 1976	1 August 1978
Syrian Arab Republic	28 November 1977	1 March 1979
Republic of Korea	28 December 1977	1 February 1979
Jordan	23 February 1978	18 October 1979
Sudan	31 July 1978	5 July 1980
El Salvador	20 September 1978	12 December 1992
Paraguay	30 November 1978	11 December 1980
Liberia	23 March 1979	22 January 1982
Sri Lanka	10 April 1980	19 April 1982
Equatorial Guinea	3 March 1982	23 September 1983
Panama	5 November 1982	9 October 1985
Nepal	2 May 1983	13 June 1985
Pakistan	1 June 1983	14 December 1984
Israel	9 June 1983	11 January 1985
Costa Rica	8 March 1984	--
Yemen	27 April 1984	1 October 1991
Haiti	23 May 1984	25 March 1985
China	30 May 1984	19 March 1985
Bangladesh	10 September 1985	3 October 1986
Hungary	6 November 1986	30 September 1987
Poland	14 February 1989	10 February 1990
Bulgaria	5 April 1989	1 May 1990
Soviet Union	4 July 1989	18 July 1991
Kuwait	27 September 1989	16 May 1991
Bolivia	25 October 1989	--
Lao People's Democratic Republic	12 December 1989	8 March 1991
Nigeria	27 February 1990	19 August 1991
Czechoslovakia	13 September 1990	27 September 1991
Argentina	3 July 1991	3 March 1993
United Arab Emirates	9 September 1991	18 December 1992
Mongolia	8 November 1991	22 December 1993
Lithuania	14 May 1992	17 February 1995
Estonia	14 May 1992	17 February 1995
Latvia	15 May 1992	1 October 1994
Viet Nam	26 May 1992	10 August 1994
Chile	14 July 1992	13 July 1993
Kazakhstan	25 September 1992	--
Jamaica	25 January 1993	15 September 1994
Algeria	13 February 1993	--
Peru	6 October 1993	--
Uruguay	14 October 1993	--
Uzbekistan	27 October 1993	--
Trinidad and Tobago	28 October 1993	--

Country	Date of signature	Date of entry into force
Belarus	28 October 1993	--
Turkmenistan	28 April 1994	--
Ukraine	3 May 1994	--
Kyrgyzstan	2 June 1994	--
Ecuador	7 September 1994	--
Philippines	13 September 1994	--
Oman	17 October 1994	--
Gabon		
Italy	18 November 1968	--
Germany	16 May 1969	29 March 1971
Switzerland	28 January 1972	18 October 1972
France	12 February 1974	--
Morocco	13 January 1979	7 November 1979
Romania	11 April 1979	18 September 1982
Gambia		
Switzerland	22 November 1993	--
Georgia		
Turkey	31 July 1992	--
China	3 June 1993	1 March 1995
Belgium/Luxembourg	23 June 1993	--
Germany	25 June 1993	--
United States	7 March 1994	--
Bulgaria	19 January 1995	--
United Kingdom	15 February 1995	15 February 1995
Germany		
Pakistan	25 November 1959	28 April 1962
Dominican Republic	16 December 1959	3 June 1960
Malaysia	22 December 1960	6 July 1963
Greece	27 March 1961	15 July 1963
Togo	16 May 1961	21 December 1964
Morocco	31 August 1961	21 January 1968
Liberia	12 December 1961	22 October 1967
Thailand	13 December 1961	10 April 1965
Guinea	19 April 1962	13 March 1965
Turkey	20 June 1962	16 December 1965
Cameroon	29 June 1962	21 November 1963
Madagascar	21 September 1962	21 March 1966
Sudan	7 February 1963	24 November 1967
Sri Lanka	8 November 1963	7 December 1966
Tunisia	20 December 1963	6 February 1966
Senegal	24 January 1964	16 January 1966
Republic of Korea	4 February 1964	15 January 1967
Chile	30 March 1964	--
Ethiopia	21 April 1964	--
India	15 October 1964	15 October 1964
Niger	29 October 1964	10 January 1966
United Republic of Tanzania	30 January 1965	12 July 1968

Country	Date of signature	Date of entry into force
Sierra Leone	8 April 1965	10 December 1966
Ecuador	28 June 1965	30 November 1966
Central African Republic	23 August 1965	21 January 1968
Congo	13 September 1965	14 October 1967
Islamic Republic of Iran	11 November 1965	6 April 1968
Côte d'Ivoire	27 October 1966	10 June 1968
Uganda	29 November 1966	19 August 1968
Zambia	10 December 1966	25 August 1972
Chad	11 April 1967	23 November 1968
Rwanda	18 May 1967	28 February 1969
Indonesia	8 November 1968	19 April 1971
Zaire	18 March 1969	22 July 1971
Gabon	16 May 1969	29 March 1971
Mauritius	25 May 1971	27 August 1973
Haiti	14 August 1973	1 December 1975
Singapore	3 October 1973	1 October 1975
Yemen	21 June 1974	19 December 1978
Jordan	15 July 1974	10 October 1977
Egypt	5 July 1974	22 July 1978
Malta	17 September 1974	14 December 1975
Israel	24 June 1976	Provisional application
Mali	28 July 1977	16 May 1980
Syria	2 August 1977	20 April 1980
Benin	29 June 1978	18 July 1985
Saudi Arabia	2 February 1979	15 March 1980
Oman	25 June 1979	4 February 1986
Romania	12 October 1979	10 January 1981
Portugal	16 September 1980	23 April 1982
Papua New Guinea	12 November 1980	3 November 1983
Bangladesh	6 May 1981	14 September 1986
Somalia	27 November 1981	15 February 1985
Lesotho	11 November 1982	17 August 1985
Mauritania	8 December 1982	26 April 1986
China	7 October 1983	18 March 1985
Panama	2 November 1983	10 March 1989
Burundi	10 September 1984	9 December 1987
Dominica	1 October 1984	11 May 1986
Saint Lucia	16 March 1985	22 July 1987
Saint Vincent and the Grenadines	25 March 1986	8 January 1989
Bulgaria	12 April 1986	10 March 1988
Hungary	30 April 1986	7 November 1987
Nepal	20 October 1986	7 July 1988
Bolivia	23 March 1987	9 November 1990
Uruguay	4 May 1987	29 June 1990
Soviet Union	13 June 1989	5 August 1991
Yugoslavia	10 July 1989	26 October 1990
Poland	10 November 1989	24 February 1991
Guyana	6 December 1989	8 March 1994
Cape Verde	18 January 1990	15 December 1993
Swaziland	5 April 1990	--
Czechoslovakia	2 October 1990	2 August 1992
Argentina	9 April 1991	8 November 1993
Mongolia	26 June 1991	--
Chile	19 October 1991	--
Albania	31 October 1991	Provisional application

Country	Date of signature	Date of entry into force
Lithuania	28 February 1992	Provisional application
Kazakhstan	22 September 1992	--
Jamaica	24 September 1992	--
Estonia	12 November 1992	--
Ukraine	15 February 1993	Provisional application
Belarus	2 April 1993	--
Viet Nam	3 April 1993	Provisional application
Latvia	20 April 1993	Provisional application
Uzbekistan	28 April 1993	Provisional application
Georgia	25 June 1993	Provisional application
Paraguay	11 August 1993	--
Slovenia	28 October 1993	--
Namibia	21 January 1994	--
Republic of Moldova	28 February 1994	Provisional application
Kuwait	30 March 1994	--
Costa Rica	13 September 1994	--
Barbados	2 December 1994	2 December 1994
Peru	30 January 1995	--
Ghana	24 February 1995	--

Ghana

United Kingdom	22 March 1989	25 October 1991
Netherlands	31 March 1989	1 July 1991
Romania	14 September 1989	--
China	12 October 1989	--
Bulgaria	20 October 1989	--
Switzerland	8 October 1991	16 June 1993
Denmark	13 January 1992	6 January 1995
Germany	24 February 1995	--

Greece

Germany	27 March 1961	15 July 1963
Hungary	29 May 1989	1 February 1992
Czechoslovakia	3 June 1991	31 December 1992
Albania	1 August 1991	--
Romania	16 September 1991	21 October 1992
Cyprus	30 March 1992	26 February 1993
China	25 June 1992	21 December 1993
Poland	14 October 1992	--
Tunisia	31 October 1992	--
Bulgaria	12 March 1993	29 April 1995
Armenia	24 May 1993	--
Russian Federation	30 June 1993	--
Egypt	16 July 1993	--
Morocco	16 February 1994	--

Grenada

United States	2 May 1986	3 March 1989
United Kingdom	25 February 1988	25 February 1988

Guinea

Germany	19 April 1962	13 March 1965

Country	Date of signature	Date of entry into force
Switzerland	26 April 1962	29 July 1963
Italy	20 February 1964	20 February 1964
Tunisia	18 November 1990	--
Guinea Bissau		
Portugal	24 June 1991	--
Guyana		
Germany	6 December 1989	8 March 1994
United Kingdom	27 October 1989	11 April 1990
Haiti		
Germany	14 August 1973	1 December 1975
United States	13 December 1983	--
France	23 May 1984	25 March 1985
United Kingdom	18 March 1985	--
Honduras		
Switzerland	14 October 1993	--
United Kingdom	7 December 1993	--
Spain	18 March 1994	--
Hong Kong		
Netherlands	19 November 1992	1 September 1993
Australia	15 September 1993	15 October 1993
Denmark	2 February 1994	4 March 1994
Sweden	27 May 1994	26 June 1994
Switzerland	22 September 1994	22 October 1994
Hungary		
Germany	30 April 1986	7 November 1987
Belgium/Luxembourg	14 May 1986	23 September 1988
France	6 November 1986	30 September 1987
Italy	17 February 1987	23 February 1990
United Kingdom	9 March 1987	28 August 1987
Sweden	21 April 1987	21 April 1987
Netherlands	2 September 1987	1 June 1988
Denmark	2 May 1988	1 October 1988
Austria	26 May 1988	1 September 1989
Finland	6 June 1988	12 May 1989
Switzerland	5 October 1988	16 May 1989
Republic of Korea	28 December 1988	1 January 1989
Cyprus	24 May 1989	25 May 1990
Greece	29 May 1989	1 February 1992
Uruguay	25 August 1989	1 July 1992
Kuwait	8 November 1989	1 March 1994
Spain	9 November 1989	1 August 1992
Norway	8 April 1991	4 December 1992
Israel	14 May 1991	14 September 1992
Australia	15 August 1991	10 May 1992

Country	Date of signature	Date of entry into force
China	29 May 1991	1 April 1993
Canada	3 October 1991	21 November 1993
Thailand	18 October 1991	18 October 1991
Morocco	12 December 1991	--
Turkey	14 January 1992	--
Portugal	28 February 1992	--
Indonesia	20 May 1992	12 September 1992
Poland	23 September 1992	--
Czech Republic	14 January 1993	--
Slovakia	15 January 1993	--
Argentina	5 February 1993	--
Malaysia	19 February 1993	--
Paraguay	11 August 1993	--
Romania	16 September 1993	--
Bulgaria	8 June 1994	--
Viet Nam	26 August 1994	--
Mongolia	13 September 1994	--
Ukraine	11 October 1994	--
Kazakhstan	7 December 1994	--
Iceland		
China	31 March 1994	--
India		
Germany	15 October 1964	15 October 1964
United Kingdom	14 March 1994	6 January 1995
Russian Federation	23 December 1994	--
Indonesia		
Denmark	30 January 1968	2 July 1968
Netherlands	7 July 1968	17 July 1971
Germany	8 November 1968	19 April 1971
Norway	24 November 1969	25 August 1970
Belgium	15 January 1970	17 June 1972
France	14 June 1973	29 April 1975
Switzerland	6 February 1974	9 April 1976
United Kingdom	27 April 1976	24 March 1977
Singapore	28 August 1990	28 August 1990
Republic of Korea	16 February 1991	10 March 1994
Italy	25 April 1991	--
Viet Nam	25 October 1991	3 December 1993
Norway	26 November 1991	--
Finland	7 February 1992	--
Tunisia	13 May 1992	12 September 1992
Hungary	20 May 1992	12 September 1992
Sweden	17 September 1992	18 February 1993
Poland	7 October 1992	1 July 1993
Australia	17 November 1992	29 July 1993
Egypt	19 January 1994	5 August 1994
Malaysia	22 January 1994	15 June 1994
Netherlands	6 April 1994	2 August 1994
Turkmenistan	2 June 1994	--
Slovakia	12 July 1994	20 September 1994

Country	Date of signature	Date of entry into force
Lao People's Democratic Republic	18 October 1994	--
China	18 November 1994	1 April 1995
Iran, Islamic Republic of		
Germany	11 November 1965	6 April 1968
Iraq		
Kuwait	25 October 1964	7 June 1966
Morocco	18 July 1990	--
Israel		
Germany	24 June 1976	Provisional application
France	9 June 1983	11 January 1985
Romania	2 September 1991	26 August 1992
Hungary	14 May 1991	14 September 1992
Poland	22 May 1991	1 January 1992
Bulgaria	6 December 1993	--
Latvia	27 February 1994	--
Estonia	14 March 1994	--
China	10 April 1995	--
Italy		
Guinea	20 February 1964	20 February 1964
Malta	28 July 1967	15 October 1973
Gabon	18 November 1968	--
Chad	11 June 1969	11 June 1969
Côte d'Ivoire	23 July 1969	--
China	28 January 1985	28 August 1987
Tunisia	17 October 1985	24 June 1989
Hungary	17 February 1987	23 February 1990
Sri Lanka	25 March 1987	20 March 1990
Kuwait	17 December 1987	21 May 1990
Malaysia	4 January 1988	25 October 1990
Philippines	17 June 1988	4 November 1993
Bulgaria	5 December 1988	27 December 1990
Republic of Korea	10 January 1989	26 June 1992
Egypt	2 March 1989	--
Poland	10 May 1989	9 January 1992
Soviet Union	30 November 1989	8 July 1991
Czechoslovakia	1 August 1990	--
Uruguay	21 February 1990	--
Bangladesh	20 March 1990	--
Bolivia	30 April 1990	22 February 1992
Viet Nam	18 May 1990	--
Argentina	22 May 1990	14 October 1993
Venezuela	4 June 1990	--
Morocco	18 July 1990	--
Romania	6 December 1990	14 October 1993
Indonesia	25 April 1991	--
Algeria	18 May 1991	--
Albania	12 September 1991	--

Country	Date of signature	Date of entry into force
Mongolia	15 January 1993	--
Chile	8 March 1993	--
Cuba	7 May 1993	--
Oman	23 June 1993	--
Jamaica	29 September 1993	--
Congo	17 March 1994	--
Peru	5 May 1994	--
Kazakhstan	22 September 1994	--
Ethiopia	23 December 1994	--
Turkey	23 March 1995	--
Jamaica		
United Kingdom	20 January 1987	14 May 1987
Switzerland	11 December 1990	21 November 1991
Netherlands	18 April 1991	1 August 1992
Germany	24 September 1992	--
France	25 January 1993	15 September 1994
Italy	29 September 1993	--
United States	4 February 1994	--
Argentina	8 February 1994	--
China	26 October 1994	--
Japan		
Egypt	28 January 1977	14 January 1978
Sri Lanka	1 March 1982	7 August 1982
China	27 August 1988	14 May 1989
Turkey	12 February 1992	12 March 1993
Jordan		
Germany	15 July 1974	10 October 1977
Switzerland	11 November 1976	2 March 1977
France	23 February 1978	18 October 1979
United Kingdom	10 October 1979	24 April 1980
Romania	2 July 1992	--
Turkey	2 August 1993	--
Kazakhstan [a]		
Turkey	1 May 1992	--
United States	19 May 1992	12 January 1994
China	10 August 1992	13 August 1994
Germany	22 September 1992	--
France	25 September 1992	--
Finland	29 September 1992	--
Egypt	24 December 1992	--
Spain	23 March 1994	--
Switzerland	12 May 1994	--
Poland	21 September 1994	--
Italy	22 September 1994	--
Mongolia	1 December 1994	--
Hungary	7 December 1994	--

Country	Date of signature	Date of entry into force
Kenya		
Netherlands	11 September 1970	11 June 1979
Korea, Republic of		
Germany	4 February 1964	15 January 1967
Switzerland	7 April 1971	7 April 1971
Netherlands	16 October 1974	1 June 1975
Belgium/Luxembourg	20 December 1974	3 September 1976
Tunisia	23 May 1975	28 November 1975
United Kingdom	4 March 1976	4 March 1976
France	28 December 1977	1 February 1979
Sri Lanka	28 March 1980	15 July 1980
Senegal	12 July 1984	2 September 1985
Bangladesh	18 June 1986	6 October 1988
Malaysia	11 April 1988	31 March 1989
Pakistan	24 May 1988	15 April 1990
Denmark	2 June 1988	2 June 1988
Hungary	28 December 1988	1 January 1989
Italy	10 January 1989	26 June 1992
Thailand	24 March 1989	29 September 1989
Poland	1 November 1989	2 February 1990
Zaire	19 July 1990	--
Romania	7 August 1990	30 December 1994
Soviet Union	14 December 1990	10 July 1991
Indonesia	16 February 1991	10 March 1994
Austria	14 March 1991	1 November 1991
Mongolia	28 March 1991	30 April 1991
Turkey	14 May 1991	4 June 1994
Czechoslovakia	27 April 1992	--
Uzbekistan	17 June 1992	20 November 1992
China	30 September 1992	4 December 1992
Paraguay	22 December 1992	6 August 1993
Viet Nam	13 May 1993	4 September 1993
Peru	3 June 1993	20 April 1994
Lithuania	24 September 1993	9 November 1993
Finland	21 October 1993	--
Spain	17 January 1994	19 July 1994
Philippines	7 April 1994	--
Argentina	17 May 1994	--
Portugal	3 May 1995	--
Kuwait		
Iraq	25 October 1964	7 June 1966
United Arab Emirates	12 February 1966	--
Egypt	2 May 1966	9 August 1966
Tunisia	14 September 1973	--
Morocco	3 April 1980	--
Pakistan	17 March 1983	--
China	23 November 1985	24 December 1986
Italy	17 December 1987	21 May 1990
Turkey	27 October 1988	25 April 1992
France	27 September 1989	16 May 1991
Hungary	8 November 1989	1 March 1994

Country	Date of signature	Date of entry into force
Poland	5 March 1990	18 December 1993
Romania	21 May 1991	26 July 1992
Republic of Moldova	4 February 1993	--
Germany	30 March 1994	--
Kyrgyzstan [a]		
Turkey	28 April 1992	--
China	14 May 1992	--
United States	19 January 1993	11 January 1994
France	2 June 1994	--
United Kingdom	8 December 1994	--
Lao People's Democratic Republic		
France	12 December 1989	8 March 1991
Thailand	22 August 1990	7 December 1990
China	31 January 1993	1 June 1993
Mongolia	3 March 1994	--
Australia	6 April 1994	--
Indonesia	18 October 1994	--
Latvia [a]		
Finland	5 March 1992	7 December 1992
Sweden	10 March 1992	6 November 1992
Denmark	30 March 1992	18 November 1994
France	15 May 1992	1 October 1994
Norway	16 June 1992	1 December 1992
Taiwan Province of China	17 September 1992	8 October 1993
Switzerland	22 December 1992	16 April 1993
Germany	20 April 1993	Provisional application
Poland	26 April 1993	19 July 1993
United Kingdom	24 January 1994	15 February 1995
Israel	27 February 1994	--
Netherlands	14 March 1994	1 April 1995
Austria	17 November 1994	--
Czech Republic	25 October 1994	--
United States	13 January 1995	--
Lesotho		
United Kingdom	18 February 1981	18 February 1981
Germany	11 November 1982	17 August 1985
Liberia		
Germany	12 December 1961	22 October 1967
Switzerland	23 July 1963	22 September 1964
France	23 March 1979	22 January 1982
Belgium/Luxembourg	5 June 1985	--
Libyan Arab Jamahiriya		
Malta	8 February 1973	19 December 1973

Country	Date of signature	Date of entry into force
Tunisia	6 June 1973	--
Morocco	25 January 1984	18 September 1993
Egypt	3 December 1990	4 July 1991
Lithuania [a]		
United States	28 October 1991	7 February 1992
Germany	28 February 1992	Provisional application
Sweden	17 March 1992	1 September 1992
Denmark	30 March 1992	9 December 1992
France	14 May 1992	17 February 1995
Finland	12 June 1992	8 January 1993
Norway	16 August 1992	19 December 1992
Poland	28 September 1992	6 August 1993
Switzerland	23 December 1992	13 May 1993
United Kingdom	17 May 1993	21 September 1993
Republic of Korea	24 September 1993	9 November 1993
Turkey	15 October 1993	--
China	8 November 1993	1 June 1994
Netherlands	26 January 1994	--
Spain	6 July 1994	--
Czech Republic	27 October 1994	--
Madagascar		
Germany	21 September 1962	21 March 1966
Switzerland	17 March 1964	31 March 1966
Denmark	10 December 1965	26 July 1967
Norway	13 May 1966	28 September 1967
Sweden	2 April 1966	23 June 1967
Malawi		
Denmark	1 August 1966	1 August 1966
Malaysia		
Germany	22 December 1960	6 July 1963
Netherlands	15 June 1971	13 September 1972
France	24 April 1975	1 September 1976
Switzerland	1 March 1978	9 June 1978
Sweden	3 March 1979	6 July 1979
Belgium/Luxembourg	22 November 1979	8 February 1982
United Kingdom	21 May 1981	21 October 1988
Norway	6 November 1984	7 January 1986
Austria	12 April 1985	1 January 1987
Finland	15 April 1985	3 January 1988
Italy	4 January 1988	25 October 1990
Republic of Korea	11 April 1988	31 March 1989
China	21 November 1988	31 March 1990
United Arab Emirates	11 October 1991	--
Denmark	6 January 1992	18 September 1992
Chile	11 November 1992	--
Hungary	19 February 1993	--
Poland	21 April 1993	23 March 1994

Country	Date of signature	Date of entry into force
Indonesia	22 January 1994	15 June 1994
Argentina	6 September 1994	--
Bangladesh	12 October 1994	--
Mali		
Germany	28 June 1977	16 May 1980
Switzerland	8 March 1978	8 December 1978
Tunisia	1 July 1986	--
Malta		
Switzerland	20 January 1965	23 February 1965
Italy	28 July 1967	15 October 1973
Libyan Arab Jamahiriya	8 February 1973	19 December 1973
Germany	17 September 1974	14 December 1975
France	11 August 1976	1 January 1978
Bulgaria	12 June 1984	4 December 1984
Netherlands	10 September 1984	1 July 1985
United Kingdom	4 October 1986	4 October 1986
Belgium/Luxembourg	5 March 1987	--
Mauritania		
Switzerland	9 September 1976	30 May 1978
Germany	8 December 1982	26 April 1986
Belgium/Luxembourg	23 November 1983	--
Tunisia	11 March 1986	--
Mauritius		
Germany	25 May 1971	27 August 1973
France	22 March 1973	1 April 1974
United Kingdom	20 May 1986	13 October 1986
Moldova, Republic of [a]		
Romania	14 August 1992	--
China	7 November 1992	1 March 1995
Kuwait	4 February 1993	--
United States	21 April 1993	25 November 1994
Turkey	14 February 1994	--
Germany	28 February 1994	Provisional application
Poland	16 November 1994	--
Mongolia		
Republic of Korea	28 March 1991	30 April 1991
Germany	26 June 1991	--
China	26 August 1991	1 November 1993
United Kingdom	4 October 1991	4 October 1991
France	8 November 1991	22 December 1993
Belgium/Luxembourg	3 March 1992	--
Ukraine	5 November 1992	5 November 1992
Italy	15 January 1993	--

Country	Date of signature	Date of entry into force
Lao People's Democratic Republic	3 March 1994	--
Hungary	13 September 1994	--
United States	6 October 1994	--
Kazakhstan	1 December 1994	--
Netherlands	9 March 1995	--
Denmark	13 March 1995	--
Morocco		
Germany	31 August 1961	21 January 1968
Belgium/Luxembourg	28 April 1965	18 October 1967
Netherlands	23 December 1971	27 July 1978
France	15 July 1975	13 December 1976
Egypt	3 June 1976	7 September 1978
Gabon	13 January 1979	7 November 1979
Kuwait	3 April 1980	--
United Arab Emirates	16 June 1982	--
Libyan Arab Jamahiriya	25 January 1984	18 September 1993
United States	22 July 1985	29 May 1991
Switzerland	17 December 1985	12 April 1991
Portugal	18 October 1988	13 February 1990
Spain	27 September 1989	15 January 1992
Iraq	18 July 1990	--
Italy	18 July 1990	--
Sweden	26 September 1990	Provisional application
United Kingdom	30 October 1990	Provisional application
Hungary	12 December 1991	--
Austria	2 November 1992	--
Romania	28 January 1994	--
Tunisia	28 January 1994	--
Greece	16 February 1994	--
Poland	24 October 1994	--
China	27 March 1995	--
Namibia		
Germany	21 January 1994	--
Switzerland	1 August 1994	--
Nepal		
France	2 May 1983	13 June 1985
Germany	20 October 1986	7 July 1988
United Kingdom	2 March 1993	2 March 1993
Netherlands [g]		
Tunisia	23 May 1963	19 December 1964
Côte d'Ivoire	26 April 1965	8 September 1966
Cameroon	6 July 1965	7 May 1966
Indonesia	7 July 1968	17 July 1971
United Republic of Tanzania	14 April 1970	28 July 1972
Uganda	24 April 1970	--

Country	Date of signature	Date of entry into force
Sudan	22 August 1970	27 March 1972
Kenya	11 September 1970	11 June 1979
Malaysia	15 June 1971	13 September 1972
Morocco	23 December 1971	27 July 1978
Singapore	16 May 1972	7 September 1973
Thailand	6 June 1972	3 March 1973
Republic of Korea	16 October 1974	1 June 1975
Yugoslavia	16 February 1976	1 April 1977
Egypt	30 October 1976	1 January 1978
Senegal	3 August 1979	5 May 1981
Sri Lanka	26 April 1984	1 May 1985
Malta	10 September 1984	1 July 1985
Philippines	27 February 1985	1 October 1987
Yemen	18 March 1985	1 September 1986
China	17 June 1985	1 February 1987
Turkey	27 March 1986	1 November 1989
Hungary	2 September 1987	1 June 1988
Oman	19 September 1987	1 February 1989
Bulgaria	8 March 1988	24 May 1990
Uruguay	22 September 1988	1 August 1991
Pakistan	4 October 1988	1 October 1989
Ghana	31 March 1989	1 July 1991
Soviet Union	5 October 1989	20 July 1991
Jamaica	18 April 1991	1 August 1992
Czechoslovakia	29 April 1991	1 October 1992
Venezuela	22 October 1991	1 November 1993
Cape Verde	11 November 1991	25 November 1992
Bolivia	10 March 1992	1 November 1994
Poland	7 September 1992	1 February 1994
Argentina	20 October 1992	1 October 1994
Estonia	27 October 1992	1 September 1993
Paraguay	29 October 1992	1 August 1994
Nigeria	2 November 1992	1 February 1994
Hong Kong	19 November 1992	1 September 1993
Lithuania	26 January 1994	--
Viet Nam	10 March 1994	1 February 1995
Latvia	14 March 1994	1 April 1995
Indonesia	6 April 1994	2 August 1994
Albania	15 April 1994	--
Ukraine	14 July 1994	--
Bangladesh	1 November 1994	--
Peru	27 December 1994	--
Romania	19 April 1994	--
Mongolia	9 March 1995	--
Belarus	11 April 1995	--
South Africa	9 May 1995	--
New Zealand		
China	22 November 1988	25 March 1989
Nicaragua		
Spain	16 March 1994	--
Denmark	13 March 1995	--

Country	Date of signature	Date of entry into force
Niger		
Switzerland	28 March 1962	17 November 1962
Germany	29 October 1964	10 January 1966
Tunisia	5 June 1992	--
Nigeria		
France	27 February 1990	19 August 1991
United Kingdom	11 December 1990	11 December 1990
Netherlands	2 November 1992	1 February 1994
Norway		
Madagascar	13 May 1966	28 September 1967
Indonesia	24 November 1969	25 August 1970
Malaysia	6 November 1984	7 January 1986
China	21 November 1984	10 July 1985
Sri Lanka	13 June 1985	13 June 1985
Poland	5 June 1990	24 October 1990
Hungary	8 April 1991	4 December 1992
Czechoslovakia	21 May 1991	6 August 1992
Romania	11 June 1991	23 March 1992
Indonesia	26 November 1991	--
Estonia	15 June 1992	15 June 1992
Latvia	16 June 1992	1 December 1992
Lithuania	16 August 1992	19 December 1992
Chile	1 June 1993	7 September 1994
Peru	10 March 1995	5 May 1995
Oman		
Germany	25 June 1979	4 February 1986
Egypt	28 April 1985	9 October 1985
Netherlands	19 September 1987	1 February 1989
Tunisia	19 October 1991	--
Italy	23 June 1993	--
France	17 October 1994	--
China	18 March 1995	--
Pakistan		
Germany	25 November 1959	28 April 1962
Romania	21 January 1978	26 June 1979
Sweden	12 March 1981	14 June 1981
Kuwait	17 March 1983	--
France	1 June 1983	14 December 1984
Netherlands	4 October 1988	1 October 1989
Republic of Korea	24 May 1988	15 April 1990
China	12 February 1989	30 September 1990
Tajikistan	31 March 1994	--
Spain	15 September 1994	--
Turkmenistan	26 October 1994	--
United Kingdom	30 November 1994	30 November 1994

Country	Date of signature	Date of entry into force
Singapore	8 March 1995	--
Turkey	16 March 1995	--
Panama		
United States	27 October 1982	30 May 1991
France	5 November 1982	9 October 1985
United Kingdom	7 October 1983	7 November 1983
Switzerland	19 October 1983	22 August 1985
Germany	2 November 1983	10 March 1989
China	26 March 1992	14 July 1992
Papua New Guinea		
Germany	12 November 1980	3 November 1983
United Kingdom	14 May 1981	22 December 1981
Australia	3 September 1990	20 October 1991
China	12 April 1991	12 February 1993
Paraguay		
France	30 November 1978	11 December 1980
United Kingdom	4 June 1981	23 April 1992
Switzerland	31 January 1992	28 September 1992
Taiwan Province of China	6 April 1992	--
Belgium/Luxembourg	6 October 1992	--
Netherlands	29 October 1992	1 August 1994
Republic of Korea	22 December 1992	25 July 1993
Denmark	22 April 1993	--
Hungary	11 August 1993	--
Germany	11 August 1993	--
Austria	13 August 1993	--
Spain	11 October 1993	--
Ecuador	28 January 1994	--
Peru	31 January 1994	--
Peru		
Switzerland	22 November 1991	23 November 1993
Thailand	15 November 1991	15 November 1991
Republic of Korea	3 June 1993	20 April 1994
Bolivia	30 July 1993	--
United Kingdom	4 October 1993	21 April 1994
France	6 October 1993	--
Paraguay	31 January 1994	--
Norway	10 March 1994	5 May 1995
Czech Republic	16 March 1994	--
Colombia	26 April 1994	--
Sweden	3 May 1994	1 August 1994
Italy	5 May 1994	--
Romania	16 May 1994	--
China	9 June 1994	1 February 1995
Argentina	10 November 1994	--
Spain	17 November 1994	--
Portugal	22 November 1994	--
Denmark	23 November 1994	--

Country	Date of signature	Date of entry into force
Netherlands	27 December 1994	--
Germany	30 January 1995	--
Philippines		
United Kingdom	3 December 1980	2 January 1981
Netherlands	27 February 1985	1 October 1987
Italy	17 June 1988	4 November 1993
China	20 July 1992	--
Poland	9 September 1992	--
Spain	19 October 1993	21 September 1994
Republic of Korea	7 April 1994	--
France	13 September 1994	--
Australia	25 January 1995	--
Poland		
Belgium/Luxembourg	19 April 1987	2 August 1991
United Kingdom	8 December 1987	14 April 1988
China	7 June 1988	8 January 1989
Austria	14 November 1988	1 November 1989
France	14 February 1989	10 February 1990
Italy	10 May 1989	9 January 1992
Sweden	13 October 1989	4 January 1990
Republic of Korea	1 November 1989	2 February 1990
Switzerland	8 November 1989	17 April 1990
Germany	10 November 1989	24 February 1991
Kuwait	5 March 1990	18 December 1993
Finland	5 April 1990	21 February 1991
Denmark	1 May 1990	13 October 1990
Norway	5 June 1990	24 October 1990
United States	21 March 1990	6 August 1994
Canada	6 April 1990	22 November 1990
Australia	7 May 1991	27 March 1992
Israel	22 May 1991	1 January 1992
Argentina	31 July 1991	1 September 1992
Uruguay	2 August 1991	--
Turkey	21 August 1991	19 August 1994
Belarus	24 April 1992	18 January 1993
Cyprus	4 June 1992	1 July 1993
Greece	14 October 1992	--
Spain	30 July 1992	1 May 1993
Netherlands	7 September 1992	1 February 1994
Philippines	9 September 1992	--
Hungary	23 September 1992	--
Lithuania	28 September 1992	6 August 1993
Russian Federation	2 October 1992	--
Indonesia	6 October 1992	1 July 1993
Thailand	18 December 1992	10 August 1993
Ukraine	12 January 1993	14 September 1993
United Arab Emirates	31 January 1993	9 April 1994
Albania	5 March 1993	9 August 1993
Portugal	11 March 1993	--
Tunisia	29 March 1993	22 September 1993
Malaysia	21 April 1993	23 March 1994
Latvia	26 April 1993	19 July 1993

Country	Date of signature	Date of entry into force
Estonia	6 May 1993	6 August 1993
Singapore	3 June 1993	29 December 1993
Czech Republic	16 July 1993	29 June 1994
Bulgaria	11 April 1994	9 March 1995
Slovenia	12 April 1994	--
Croatia	15 April 1994	--
Romania	23 June 1994	--
Slovakia	18 July 1994	--
Viet Nam	31 August 1994	--
Kazakhstan	21 September 1994	--
Morocco	24 October 1994	--
Republic of Moldova	16 November 1994	--
Uzbekistan	11 January 1995	--
Portugal		
Germany	16 September 1980	23 April 1982
Morocco	18 October 1988	13 February 1990
Cape Verde	26 October 1990	4 October 1991
Guinea Bissau	24 June 1991	--
China	3 February 1992	1 December 1992
Hungary	28 February 1992	--
Tunisia	11 May 1992	--
Poland	11 March 1993	--
Bulgaria	27 May 1993	--
Czech Republic	11 November 1993	--
Romania	17 November 1993	--
Brazil	9 February 1994	--
Zimbabwe	5 May 1994	--
Venezuela	17 June 1994	--
Argentina	6 October 1994	--
Peru	22 November 1994	--
Chile	28 April 1995	--
Republic of Korea	3 May 1995	--
Romania		
United Kingdom	19 March 1976	22 November 1976
Austria	30 September 1976	8 November 1977
France	16 December 1976	1 August 1978
Egypt	10 May 1976	22 January 1977
Pakistan	21 January 1978	26 June 1979
Belgium/Luxembourg	8 May 1978	1 May 1980
Sudan	8 December 1978	18 September 1982
Gabon	11 April 1979	5 December 1979
Germany	12 October 1979	10 January 1981
Senegal	19 June 1980	20 May 1984
Denmark	12 November 1980	9 April 1981
Cameroon	30 August 1980	16 December 1981
Sri Lanka	9 February 1981	3 June 1982
Morocco	11 September 1981	--
China	10 February 1983	12 January 1984
Bangladesh	13 March 1987	--
Tunisia	23 September 1987	--
Ghana	14 September 1989	--
Republic of Korea	7 August 1990	30 December 1994

Country	Date of signature	Date of entry into force
Uruguay	23 November 1990	--
Italy	6 December 1990	--
Turkey	24 January 1991	--
Kuwait	21 May 1991	26 July 1992
Norway	11 June 1991	23 March 1992
Cyprus	26 July 1991	10 July 1993
Israel	2 September 1991	26 August 1992
Greece	16 September 1991	21 October 1992
Finland	26 March 1992	6 January 1993
United States	28 May 1992	15 January 1994
Jordan	2 July 1992	--
Republic of Moldova	14 August 1992	--
Thailand	30 April 1993	--
Australia	21 June 1993	22 April 1994
Argentina	29 July 1993	--
Hungary	16 September 1993	--
Russian Federation	29 September 1993	--
Switzerland	25 October 1993	30 July 1994
Czech Republic	8 November 1993	28 July 1994
Portugal	17 November 1993	--
Morocco	28 January 1994	--
Netherlands	19 April 1994	--
Peru	16 May 1994	--
Bulgaria	1 June 1994	--
Denmark	14 June 1994	--
Poland	23 June 1994	--
China	12 July 1994	--

Russian Federation [a]

United States	17 June 1992	--
Poland	2 October 1992	--
Bulgaria	8 June 1993	--
Greece	30 June 1993	--
Cuba	7 July 1993	--
Romania	29 September 1993	--
Denmark	4 November 1993	--
Slovakia	30 November 1993	--
Czech Republic	5 April 1994	--
India	23 December 1994	--

Rwanda

Switzerland	15 October 1963	15 October 1963
Germany	18 May 1967	28 February 1969
Belgium/Luxembourg	2 November 1983	1 August 1985

Saint Lucia

United Kingdom	18 January 1983	18 January 1983
Germany	16 March 1985	22 July 1987

Saint Vincent and the Grenadines

Germany	25 March 1986	8 January 1989

Country	Date of signature	Date of entry into force
Saudi Arabia		
Germany	2 February 1979	15 March 1980
Egypt	13 March 1990	15 September 1992
Senegal		
Switzerland	16 August 1962	13 August 1964
Germany	24 January 1964	16 January 1966
Sweden	24 February 1967	23 February 1968
France	29 March 1974	--
Netherlands	3 August 1979	5 May 1981
United Kingdom	7 May 1980	9 February 1984
Romania	19 June 1980	20 May 1984
United States	6 December 1983	25 October 1990
Tunisia	17 May 1984	--
Republic of Korea	12 July 1984	2 September 1985
Argentina	6 April 1993	--
Sierra Leone		
Germany	8 April 1965	10 December 1966
United Kingdom	8 December 1981	--
Singapore		
Netherlands	16 May 1972	7 September 1973
Germany	3 October 1973	1 October 1975
United Kingdom	22 July 1975	22 July 1975
France	8 September 1975	18 October 1976
Switzerland	6 March 1978	3 May 1978
Belgium/Luxembourg	17 November 1978	27 November 1980
Sri Lanka	9 May 1980	30 September 1980
China	21 November 1985	7 February 1986
Indonesia	28 August 1990	28 August 1990
Viet Nam	29 October 1992	25 December 1992
Poland	3 June 1993	29 December 1993
Pakistan	8 March 1995	--
Slovakia [e]		
Czech Republic	23 November 1992	--
Hungary	15 January 1993	--
Russian Federation	30 November 1993	--
Indonesia	12 July 1994	20 September 1994
Poland	18 July 1994	--
Bulgaria	21 July 1994	9 March 1995
Slovenia		
Sweden	10 November 1978	21 November 1979
Germany	28 October 1993	--
Czech Republic	4 May 1993	21 May 1994
China	13 September 1993	1 January 1995
Poland	12 April 1994	--

Country	Date of signature	Date of entry into force
Somalia		
Germany	27 November 1981	15 February 1985
South Africa		
United Kingdom	20 September 1994	--
Netherlands	9 May 1995	--
Switzerland	27 June 1995	--
Soviet Union [a]		
Finland	8 February 1989	15 August 1991
Belgium/Luxembourg	9 February 1989	13 October 1991
United Kingdom	6 April 1989	3 July 1991
Germany	13 June 1989	5 August 1991
France	4 July 1989	18 July 1991
Netherlands	5 October 1989	20 July 1991
Canada	20 November 1989	27 June 1991
Italy	30 November 1989	8 July 1991
Austria	8 February 1990	1 September 1991
Denmark	1 May 1990	--
China	21 July 1990	--
Spain	26 October 1990	28 November 1991
Switzerland	1 December 1990	26 August 1991
Republic of Korea	14 December 1990	10 July 1991
Turkey	14 December 1990	--
Spain		
Morocco	27 September 1989	15 January 1992
Hungary	9 November 1989	1 August 1992
Bolivia	24 April 1990	12 May 1992
Soviet Union	26 October 1990	28 November 1991
Czechoslovakia	12 December 1990	28 November 1991
Argentina	3 October 1991	28 September 1992
Chile	2 October 1991	28 March 1994
China	6 February 1992	1 May 1994
Uruguay	7 April 1992	6 May 1994
Tunisia	28 May 1991	20 June 1994
Poland	30 July 1992	1 May 1993
Egypt	3 November 1992	26 April 1994
Paraguay	11 October 1993	--
Philippines	19 October 1993	21 September 1994
Republic of Korea	17 January 1994	19 July 1994
Nicaragua	16 March 1994	--
Honduras	18 March 1994	--
Kazakhstan	23 March 1994	--
Cuba	27 May 1994	--
Lithuania	6 July 1994	--
Pakistan	15 September 1994	--
Peru	17 November 1994	--
El Salvador	14 February 1995	--
Turkey	15 February 1995	--

Country	Date of signature	Date of entry into force
Sri Lanka		
Germany	8 November 1963	7 December 1966
United Kingdom	13 February 1980	18 December 1980
Republic of Korea	28 March 1980	15 July 1980
France	10 April 1980	19 April 1982
Singapore	9 May 1980	30 September 1980
Romania	9 February 1981	3 June 1982
Switzerland	23 September 1981	12 February 1982
Japan	1 March 1982	7 August 1982
Belgium/Luxembourg	5 April 1982	26 April 1984
Sweden	30 April 1982	30 April 1982
Netherlands	26 April 1984	1 May 1985
Finland	27 April 1985	25 October 1987
Denmark	4 June 1985	4 June 1985
Norway	13 June 1985	13 June 1985
China	13 March 1986	25 March 1987
Turkey	27 March 1986	--
Italy	25 March 1987	20 March 1990
United States	20 September 1991	1 May 1993
Sudan		
Germany	7 February 1963	24 November 1967
Netherlands	22 August 1970	27 March 1972
Switzerland	17 February 1974	14 December 1974
Egypt	28 May 1977	14 March 1978
France	31 July 1978	5 July 1980
Romania	8 December 1978	5 December 1979
Swaziland		
Germany	5 April 1990	--
Sweden g		
Côte d'Ivoire	27 August 1965	3 November 1966
Madagascar	2 April 1966	23 June 1967
Senegal	24 February 1967	23 February 1968
Egypt	15 July 1978	29 January 1979
Yugoslavia	10 November 1978	21 November 1979
Slovenia	10 November 1978	21 November 1979
Malaysia	3 March 1979	6 July 1979
Pakistan	12 March 1981	14 June 1981
China	29 March 1982	29 March 1982
Sri Lanka	30 April 1982	30 April 1982
Yemen	29 October 1983	23 February 1984
Tunisia	15 September 1984	13 May 1985
Hungary	21 April 1987	21 April 1987
Poland	13 October 1989	4 January 1990
Bolivia	20 September 1990	3 July 1992
Morocco	26 September 1990	Provisional application
Czechoslovakia	13 November 1990	23 September 1991
Argentina	22 November 1991	28 September 1992
Latvia	10 March 1992	6 November 1992
Lithuania	17 March 1992	1 September 1992

Country	Date of signature	Date of entry into force
Estonia	31 March 1992	20 May 1992
Indonesia	17 September 1992	18 February 1993
Chile	24 May 1993	--
Viet Nam	8 September 1993	2 August 1994
Bulgaria	19 April 1994	1 April 1995
Hong Kong	27 May 1994	26 June 1994
Peru	3 May 1994	1 August 1994
Belarus	20 December 1994	--
Switzerland [h]		
Tunisia	2 December 1961	19 January 1964
Niger*	28 March 1962	17 November 1962
Guinea*	26 April 1962	29 July 1963
Côte d'Ivoire*	26 June 1962	18 November 1962
Senegal*	16 August 1962	13 August 1964
Congo*	18 October 1962	11 July 1964
Cameroon*	28 January 1963	6 April 1964
Liberia*	23 July 1963	22 September 1964
Rwanda*	15 October 1963	15 October 1963
Togo*	17 January 1964	9 August 1966
Madagascar*	17 March 1964	31 March 1966
Malta*	20 January 1965	23 February 1965
United Republic of Tanzania	3 May 1965	16 September 1965
Costa Rica	1 September 1965	18 August 1966
Benin*	20 April 1966	6 October 1973
Chad*	21 February 1967	31 October 1967
Ecuador	2 May 1968	11 September 1969
Burkina Faso*	6 May 1969	15 September 1969
Republic of Korea	7 April 1971	7 April 1971
Uganda	23 August 1971	8 May 1972
Gabon*	28 January 1972	18 October 1972
Zaire	10 March 1972	10 May 1973
Central African Republic*	28 February 1973	4 July 1973
Egypt	25 July 1973	4 June 1974
Indonesia	6 February 1974	9 April 1976
Sudan	17 February 1974	14 December 1974
Mauritania*	9 September 1976	30 May 1978
Jordan	11 November 1976	2 March 1977
Syria	22 June 1977	10 August 1978
Malaysia	1 March 1978	9 June 1978
Singapore	6 March 1978	3 May 1978
Mali	8 March 1978	8 December 1978
Sri Lanka	23 September 1981	12 February 1982
Panama	19 October 1983	22 August 1985
Morocco	17 December 1985	12 April 1991
China	12 November 1986	18 March 1987
Bolivia	6 November 1987	13 May 1991
Turkey	3 March 1988	21 February 1990
Hungary	5 October 1988	16 May 1989
Uruguay	7 October 1988	22 April 1989
Poland	8 November 1989	17 April 1990
Czechoslovakia	5 October 1990	7 August 1991
Soviet Union	1 December 1990	26 August 1991

Country	Date of signature	Date of entry into force
Jamaica	11 December 1990	21 November 1991
Argentina	12 April 1991	6 November 1992
Ghana	8 October 1991	16 June 1993
Bulgaria	28 October 1991	26 October 1993
Cape Verde	28 October 1991	6 May 1992
Chile	11 November 1991	--
Peru	22 November 1991	23 November 1993
Paraguay	31 January 1992	28 September 1992
Viet Nam	3 July 1992	3 December 1992
Albania	22 September 1992	30 April 1993
Estonia	21 December 1992	18 August 1993
Latvia	22 December 1992	16 April 1993
Lithuania	23 December 1992	13 May 1993
Uzbekistan	16 April 1993	5 November 1993
Belarus	28 May 1993	13 July 1994
Honduras	14 October 1993	--
Romania	25 October 1993	30 July 1994
Venezuela	18 November 1993	30 November 1994
Gambia	22 November 1993	--
Kazakhstan	12 May 1994	--
Namibia	1 August 1994	--
Zambia	3 August 1994	--
Hong Kong	22 September 1994	22 October 1994
Brazil	11 November 1994	--
El Salvador	8 December 1994	--

Syrian Arab Republic

Switzerland	22 June 1977	10 August 1978
Germany	2 August 1977	20 April 1980
France	28 November 1977	1 March 1979

Tajikistan [a]

Czech Republic	11 February 1994	--
Pakistan	31 March 1994	--
China	9 March 1993	20 January 1994

Taiwan Province of China

Paraguay	6 April 1992	--
Latvia	17 September 1992	8 October 1993

Tanzania, United Republic of

Germany	30 January 1965	12 July 1968
Switzerland	3 May 1965	16 September 1965
Netherlands	14 April 1970	28 July 1972
United Kingdom	7 January 1994	--

Thailand

Germany	13 December 1961	10 April 1965

Country	Date of signature	Date of entry into force
Netherlands	6 June 1972	3 March 1973
United Kingdom	28 November 1978	11 August 1979
China	12 March 1985	13 December 1985
Belgium/Luxembourg	19 March 1986	--
Bangladesh	13 March 1988	--
Republic of Korea	24 March 1989	29 September 1989
Lao People's Democratic Republic	22 August 1990	7 December 1990
Czechoslovakia	16 October 1991	--
Hungary	18 October 1991	18 October 1991
Viet Nam	30 October 1991	7 February 1992
Peru	15 November 1991	15 November 1991
Poland	18 December 1992	10 August 1993
Romania	30 April 1993	--
Czech Republic	12 February 1994	--
Finland	18 March 1994	--
Togo		
Germany	16 May 1961	21 December 1964
Switzerland	17 January 1964	9 August 1966
Tunisia	13 September 1987	--
Trinidad and Tobago		
United Kingdom	23 July 1993	8 October 1993
France	28 October 1993	--
United States	26 September 1994	--
Tunisia		
Switzerland	2 December 1961	19 January 1964
Netherlands	23 May 1963	19 December 1964
Germany	20 December 1963	6 February 1966
Belgium/Luxembourg	15 July 1964	9 March 1966
France	30 June 1972	30 June 1972
Libyan Arab Jamahiriya	6 June 1973	--
Kuwait	14 September 1973	--
Republic of Korea	23 May 1975	28 November 1975
Senegal	17 May 1984	--
Sweden	15 September 1984	13 May 1985
Italy	17 October 1985	24 June 1989
Mauritania	11 March 1986	--
Mali	1 July 1986	--
Togo	13 September 1987	--
Romania	23 September 1987	--
United Kingdom	14 March 1989	4 January 1990
Egypt	8 December 1989	2 January 1991
United States	15 May 1990	7 February 1993
Guinea	18 November 1990	--
Spain	28 May 1991	20 June 1994
Turkey	29 May 1991	7 February 1993
Oman	19 October 1991	--
Portugal	11 May 1992	--
Indonesia	13 May 1992	12 September 1992

Country	Date of signature	Date of entry into force
Niger	5 June 1992	--
Argentina	17 June 1992	--
Greece	31 October 1992	--
Burkina Faso	7 January 1993	--
Poland	29 March 1993	22 September 1993
Albania	30 October 1993	--
Morocco	28 January 1994	--
Turkey		
Germany	20 June 1962	16 December 1965
United States	3 December 1985	18 May 1990
Netherlands	27 March 1986	1 November 1989
Sri Lanka	27 March 1986	--
Belgium/Luxembourg	27 August 1986	4 May 1990
Bangladesh	12 November 1987	21 June 1990
Austria	16 September 1988	1 January 1992
Switzerland	3 March 1988	21 February 1990
Kuwait	27 October 1988	25 April 1992
Denmark	7 February 1990	1 August 1992
China	13 November 1990	19 August 1994
Soviet Union	14 December 1990	--
Romania	24 January 1991	--
United Kingdom	15 March 1991	--
Republic of Korea	14 May 1991	4 June 1994
Tunisia	29 May 1991	7 February 1993
Poland	21 August 1991	19 August 1994
Hungary	14 January 1992	--
Japan	12 February 1992	12 March 1993
Kyrgyzstan	28 April 1992	--
Uzbekistan	28 April 1992	--
Czechoslovakia	30 April 1992	--
Kazakhstan	1 May 1992	--
Turkmenistan	2 May 1992	--
Argentina	8 May 1992	--
Albania	1 June 1992	--
Georgia	31 July 1992	--
Finland	13 May 1993	--
Jordan	2 August 1993	--
Lithuania	15 October 1993	--
Azerbaijan	9 February 1994	--
Republic of Moldova	14 February 1994	--
Bulgaria	6 July 1994	--
Spain	15 February 1995	--
Pakistan	16 March 1995	--
Italy	22 March 1995	--
Turkmenistan [a]		
Turkey	2 May 1992	--
China	21 November 1992	6 June 1995
France	28 April 1994	--
Indonesia	2 June 1994	--
Pakistan	26 October 1994	--
United Kingdom	9 February 1995	9 February 1995

Country	Date of signature	Date of entry into force
Uganda		
Germany	29 November 1966	19 August 1968
Netherlands	24 April 1970	--
Switzerland	23 August 1971	8 May 1972
Ukraine [a]		
Finland	14 May 1992	30 January 1993
Denmark	23 October 1992	29 April 1994
China	31 October 1992	29 May 1993
Mongolia	5 November 1992	5 November 1992
Egypt	21 December 1992	10 October 1993
Poland	12 January 1993	14 September 1993
United Kingdom	10 February 1993	10 February 1993
Germany	15 February 1993	Provisional application
Bulgaria	1 January 1994	--
United States	4 March 1994	--
Czech Republic	17 March 1994	--
France	3 May 1994	--
Netherlands	14 July 1994	--
Hungary	11 October 1994	--
Canada	24 October 1994	--
Switzerland	20 April 1995	--
United Arab Emirates		
Kuwait	12 February 1966	--
Morocco	16 June 1982	--
Egypt	19 June 1988	--
France	9 September 1991	18 December 1992
Malaysia	11 October 1991	--
United Kingdom	8 December 1992	13 December 1993
Poland	31 January 1993	9 April 1994
China	1 July 1993	--
Czech Republic	23 November 1994	--
United Kingdom		
Egypt	11 June 1975	24 February 1976
Singapore	22 July 1975	22 July 1975
Republic of Korea	4 March 1976	4 March 1976
Romania	19 March 1976	22 November 1976
Indonesia	27 April 1976	24 March 1977
Thailand	28 November 1978	11 August 1979
Jordan	10 October 1979	24 April 1980
Sri Lanka	13 February 1980	18 December 1980
Senegal	7 May 1980	9 February 1984
Bangladesh	19 June 1980	19 June 1980
Philippines	3 December 1980	2 January 1981
Lesotho	18 February 1981	18 February 1981
Papua New Guinea	14 May 1981	22 December 1981
Malaysia	21 May 1981	21 October 1988
Paraguay	4 June 1981	23 April 1992
Sierra Leone	8 December 1981	--
Yemen	25 February 1982	11 November 1983

Country	Date of signature	Date of entry into force
Belize	30 April 1982	30 April 1982
Cameroon	4 June 1982	7 June 1985
Costa Rica	7 September 1982	--
Saint Lucia	18 January 1983	18 January 1983
Panama	7 October 1983	7 November 1983
Haiti	18 March 1985	--
China	15 May 1986	15 May 1986
Mauritius	20 May 1986	13 October 1986
Malta	4 October 1986	4 October 1986
Jamaica	20 January 1987	14 May 1987
Dominica	23 January 1987	23 January 1987
Hungary	9 March 1987	28 August 1987
Antigua and Barbuda	12 June 1987	12 June 1987
Benin	27 November 1987	27 November 1987
Poland	8 December 1987	14 April 1988
Grenada	25 February 1988	25 February 1988
Bolivia	24 May 1988	16 February 1990
Tunisia	14 March 1989	4 January 1990
Ghana	22 March 1989	25 October 1991
Soviet Union	6 April 1989	3 July 1991
Congo	25 May 1989	9 November 1990
Guyana	27 October 1989	11 April 1990
Czechoslovakia	10 July 1990	26 October 1992
Burundi	13 September 1990	13 September 1990
Morocco	30 October 1990	Provisionally in force
Argentina	11 December 1990	19 February 1993
Nigeria	11 December 1990	11 December 1990
Turkey	15 March 1991	--
Mongolia	4 October 1991	4 October 1991
Uruguay	21 October 1991	--
Bahrain	30 October 1991	30 October 1991
United Arab Emirates	8 December 1992	13 December 1993
Ukraine	10 February 1993	10 February 1993
Nepal	2 March 1993	2 March 1993
Barbados	7 April 1993	7 April 1993
Lithuania	17 May 1993	21 September 1993
Armenia	22 May 1993	--
Trinidad and Tobago	23 July 1993	8 October 1993
Peru	4 October 1993	21 April 1994
Uzbekistan	24 November 1993	24 November 1993
Honduras	7 December 1993	--
United Republic of Tanzania	7 January 1994	--
Latvia	24 January 1994	15 February 1995
Belarus	1 March 1994	28 December 1994
Colombia	9 March 1994	
India	14 March 1994	6 January 1995
Albania	30 March 1994	--
Ecuador	10 May 1994	--
Estonia	12 May 1994	--
Brazil	19 July 1994	--
South Africa	20 September 1994	--
Pakistan	30 November 1994	30 November 1994
Kyrgyzstan	8 December 1994	--
Cuba	30 January 1995	--
Turkmenistan	9 February 1995	9 February 1995

Country	Date of signature	Date of entry into force
Georgia	15 February 1995	15 February 1995
United States		
Panama	27 October 1982 [i]	30 May 1991
Senegal	6 December 1983	25 October 1990
Haiti	13 December 1983	--
Zaire	3 August 1984	28 July 1989
Morocco	22 July 1985	29 May 1991
Turkey	3 December 1985	18 May 1990
Cameroon	26 February 1986	6 April 1989
Egypt	11 March 1986	27 June 1992
Bangladesh	12 March 1986	25 July 1989
Grenada	2 May 1986	3 March 1989
Congo	12 February 1990	13 August 1994
Poland	21 March 1990	6 August 1994
Tunisia	15 May 1990	7 February 1993
Sri Lanka	20 September 1991	1 May 1993
Czechoslovakia	22 October 1991	19 December 1992
Lithuania	28 October 1991	7 February 1992
Argentina	14 November 1991	20 October 1994
Kazakhstan	19 May 1992	12 January 1994
Romania	28 May 1992	15 January 1994
Russian Federation	17 June 1992	--
Armenia	23 September 1992	--
Bulgaria	23 September 1992	2 June 1994
Kyrgyzstan	19 January 1993	12 January 1994
Republic of Moldova	21 April 1993	25 November 1994
Ecuador	27 August 1993	--
Belarus	15 January 1994	--
Jamaica	4 February 1994	--
Ukraine	4 March 1994	--
Georgia	7 March 1994	--
Estonia	19 April 1994	--
Trinidad and Tobago	26 September 1994	--
Mongolia	6 October 1994	--
Uzbekistan	16 December 1994	--
Albania	10 January 1995	--
Latvia	13 January 1995	--
Uruguay		
Germany	4 May 1987	29 June 1990
Netherlands	22 September 1988	1 August 1991
Switzerland	7 October 1988	22 April 1991
Hungary	25 August 1989	1 July 1992
Italy	21 February 1990	--
Romania	23 November 1990	--
Canada	16 May 1991	--
Poland	2 August 1991	--
United Kingdom	21 October 1991	--
Belgium/Luxembourg	4 November 1991	--
Spain	7 April 1992	6 May 1994
France	14 October 1993	--
China	2 December 1993	--

Country	Date of signature	Date of entry into force
Uzbekistan [a]		
China	13 March 1992	--
Turkey	28 April 1992	--
Republic of Korea	17 June 1992	20 November 1992
Finland	1 October 1992	22 October 1993
Egypt	16 December 1992	
Switzerland	16 April 1993	5 November 1993
Germany	28 April 1993	Provisional application
Denmark	23 September 1993	--
France	27 October 1993	--
United Kingdom	24 November 1993	24 November 1993
United States	16 December 1994	--
Poland	11 January 1995	--
Venezuela		
Italy	4 June 1990	--
Netherlands	22 October 1991	1 November 1993
Chile	2 April 1993	11 January 1994
Argentina	16 November 1993	--
Ecuador	18 November 1993	1 February 1995
Switzerland	18 November 1993	30 November 1994
Portugal	17 June 1994	--
Barbados	15 July 1994	--
Denmark	28 November 1994	--
Viet Nam		
Italy	18 May 1990	--
Belgium/Luxembourg	24 January 1991	--
Australia	5 March 1991	11 September 1991
Indonesia	25 October 1991	3 December 1993
Thailand	30 October 1991	7 February 1991
France	26 May 1992	10 August 1994
Switzerland	3 July 1992	3 December 1992
Singapore	29 October 1992	25 December 1992
China	2 December 1992	1 September 1993
Republic of Korea	13 May 1993	4 September 1993
Germany	3 April 1993	Provisional application
Denmark	23 July 1993	7 August 1994
Sweden	8 September 1993	2 August 1994
Finland	13 September 1993	--
Netherlands	10 March 1994	1 February 1995
Hungary	26 August 1994	--
Poland	31 August 1994	--
Yemen		
Germany	21 June 1974	19 December 1978
United Kingdom	25 February 1982	11 November 1983
Sweden	29 October 1983	23 February 1984
France	27 April 1984	1 October 1991
Netherlands	18 March 1985	1 September 1986
Egypt	19 October 1988	3 March 1990

Country	Date of signature	Date of entry into force
Yugoslavia		
France	28 March 1974	3 March 1975
Netherlands	16 February 1976	1 April 1977
Egypt	3 June 1977	--
Sweden	10 November 1978	21 November 1979
Germany	10 July 1989	26 October 1990
Austria	25 October 1989	1 June 1991
Zaire		
Germany	18 March 1969	22 July 1971
Switzerland	10 March 1972	10 May 1973
France	5 October 1972	1 March 1975
Belgium/Luxembourg	28 March 1976	1 January 1977
United States	3 August 1984	28 July 1989
Republic of Korea	19 July 1990	--
Zambia		
Germany	10 December 1966	25 August 1972
Switzerland	3 August 1994	--
Zimbabwe		
Portugal	5 May 1994	--

a   In accordance with the Alma Ata Declaration, all international obligations from treaties concluded up until 25 December 1991, concluded by the former Sovient Union, have been assumed by the successor States.

b   Signed by Belgium only.

c   Signed by Belgium and Luxembourg, but not as an Economic Union.

d   Canada has also signed 33 bilateral investment guarantee agreements.

e   Obligations from treaties concluded by Czechoslovakia have been assumed as of 1 January 1993 by both the Czech Republic and Slovakia.

f   Includes commercial agreements.

g   Includes economic cooperation agreements.

h   Includes agreements on commerce, investment protection and technical cooperation. These are marked with an asterix.

i   See 1986 consolidated text (Senate Treaty Doc. 99-24) established following signature of the supplementary protocol.

ANNEX C
Non-governmental Instruments

Draft Statutes of the Arbitral Tribunal for Foreign Investment and of the Foreign Investments Court*

> The Draft Statutes of the Arbitral Tribunal for Foreign Investment were drafted by the International Law Association and published in 1948. Also reproduced in this volume are the Draft Statutes of the Foreign Investments Court. The Introductory Comments on the Draft Statutes of the Arbitral Tribunal for Foreign Investment and the Draft Statutes of the Foreign Investment Court have not been reproduced in this volume.

Article 1

The present Convention aims to provide machinery for the settling:

(a)   of any dispute arising out of any unreasonable or discriminatory impairment within the territory of any Contracting Party of the property of nationals of the other Parties;

(b)   of any dispute concerning the observance or interpretation of any undertaking which a Party may have given in relation to investments made by nationals of any other Party.

Article 2

(1)   The Parties agree that any such dispute may, with the consent of the interested Parties, be submitted to an Arbitral Tribunal set up in accordance with the provisions set out below. Such consent may take the form of specific agreements or of unilateral declarations. In the absence of such consent or of agreement for settlement by other specific means, the dispute may be submitted by either Party to the International Court of Justice.

(2)   The Parties may at any time declare that they recognize as compulsory *ipso facto* and without special agreement in relation to any other State accepting the same obligation the jurisdiction of the Tribunal in all disputes mentioned in Article 1.

Article 3

(1)   A national of one of the Parties claiming that between him and a Party there exists a dispute within the meaning of Art. 1 may institute proceedings against this Party before the Arbitral Tribunal provided that the Party against which the claim is made had declared that it accepts the jurisdiction of the said Arbitral Tribunal in respect of claims by nationals of one or more Parties, including the Party concerned.

---

*Source: International Law Association, "Draft Statutes of the Arbitral Tribunal for Foreign Investment and the Foreign Investments Court," mimeo. [Note added by the editor].

(2)   Article 2 (2) shall apply *mutatis mutandis*.

Article 4

The Arbitral Tribunal shall consist of three persons appointed as follows: one arbitrator shall be appointed by each of the Parties to the arbitration proceedings and a third arbitrator (hereinafter sometimes called "the Umpire") shall be appointed by agreement of the Parties or, if they shall not agree, by the President of the International Court of Justice or, failing appointment by him, by the Secretary-General of the United Nations. If either of the Parties shall fail to appoint an arbitrator, such arbitrator shall be appointed by the Umpire.

Article 4a

The arbitrator and the Umpire may only be selected from the panel of arbitrators to be established within a month after the coming into force of the present treaty. For this purpose each Party nominates three persons having a recognized competence in international law or international economic life. Only one of these persons may be a national of the party concerned.

Article 4b

Access to the tribunal presupposes the exhaustion of local remedies except where other rules of international law or an agreement between the Parties provides otherwise.

Article 5

(1)   Arbitration proceedings may be instituted upon notice by the Party instituting such proceedings (whether a Party to the Convention or a national of a Party to the Convention, as the case may be) to the other Party. Such notice shall contain a statement setting forth the nature of the relief sought and the name of the arbitrator appointed by the Party instituting such proceedings. Within 30 days after the giving of such notice, the adverse Party shall notify the Party instituting proceedings the name of the arbitrator appointed by such adverse Party.

(2)   If, within 60 days after the giving of such notice instituting the arbitration proceedings, the Parties shall not have agreed upon an Umpire, either Party may request the appointment of an Umpire as provided in Article 4.

(3)   The Arbitral Tribunal shall convene at such time and place as shall be fixed by the Umpire. Thereafter, the Arbitral Tribunal shall determine where and when it shall sit.

Article 6

In case any arbitrator appointed in accordance with Article 4 to 5 shall resign, die or become unable to act, a successor arbitrator shall be appointed in the same manner as herein prescribed for the appointment of the original arbitrator and such successor shall have all the powers and duties of such original arbitrator.

Article 7

(1)   A Party may propose the disqualification of one of the arbitrators on account of a fact arising subsequently to the constitution of the tribunal. It may only propose the disqualification of one of the arbitrators on account of a fact arising prior to the constitution of the tribunal if it can show that the appointment was made without knowledge of that fact or as a result of fraud. In either case, the decision shall be taken by the other members of the tribunal.

(2)   In the case of the Umpire the question of disqualification shall, in the absence of agreement between the Parties, be decided by the President of the International Court of Justice or -- if the Umpire was appointed by the Secretary-General of the United Nations -- by the latter.

(3)   Any resulting vacancy shall be filled in accordance with the procedure prescribed for the original appointments.

Article 8

When a vacancy has been filled after the proceedings have begun, the proceedings shall continue from the point they had reached at the time the vacancy occurred. The newly appointed arbitrator may, however, require that the oral proceedings shall be recommenced from the beginning, if these have already been started.

Article 9

It shall be sufficient to establish the Tribunal under the conditions set out in Articles 2 to 8 if a Party or national of a Party, as the case may be, alleges that there exists a dispute within the meaning of Art. 1.

Article 10

The Arbitral Tribunal is the judge of its own competence.

Article 11

(1)   The Arbitral Tribunal shall apply to the dispute any law or rules which were declared applicable to the subject-matter of the dispute concerned in any treaty or agreement concluded between the Parties to the dispute provided that such treaty or agreement was not in violation of international law.

(2)   In the absence of or to supplement such rules the tribunal shall apply:

   (*a*)   International conventions, whether general or particular, establishing rules expressly recognised by the contesting States;

(*b*)   International custom, as evidence of a general practice accepted as law;

(*c*)   The general principles of law recognized by civilized nations;

(*d*)   Judicial decisions and the teachings of the most highly qualified publicists of the various nations, as subsidiary means for the determination of rules of law.

(3)   If, however, subsequently to the coming into force of the treaty or agreement referred to in para. 1 any rule contained therein had been modified or abrogated by any rule originating from a source of law mentioned in para. 2 lit. a).......c) above, the latter shall be applied by the tribunal.

(4)   By agreement of the Parties the tribunal may also decide *ex aequo et bono*.

Article 12

The tribunal may not bring in a finding of *non liquet* on the ground of the silence or obscurity of the law to be applied.

Article 13

All decisions shall be taken by a majority vote of the members of the tribunal.

Article 14

(1)   The tribunal shall be competent to formulate or complete the rules of procedure.

(2)   The tribunal may fix reasonable time limits for the various acts to be performed by the Parties in the course of the proceedings. At the expiration of any such time-limit it may either apply the rule on default or grant an extension of the time limit concerned.

Article 15

The tribunal shall decide which language shall be employed before it.

Article 16

(1)   The Parties shall appoint agents before the tribunal to act as intermediaries between them and the tribunal.

(2)   They may retain counsel and advocates for the prosecution of their rights and interests before the tribunal.

(3)   The Parties shall be entitled through their agents, counsel or advocates to submit

in writing and orally to the tribunal any arguments they may deem expedient for the prosecution of their case. They shall have the right to raise objections and incidental points. The decisions of the tribunal on such matters shall be final.

(4)   The members of the tribunal shall have the right to put questions to agents, counsel or advocates and to ask them for explanations. Neither the questions put nor the remarks made during the hearing are to be regarded as an expression of opinion by the tribunal or by its members.

Article 17

(1)   The arbitral procedure shall in general comprise two distinct phases; pleading and hearing.

(2)   The pleadings shall consist in the communication by the respective agents to the members of the tribunal and to the opposite Party of memorials, counter-memorials and, if necessary, of replies and rejoinders. Each Party must attach all papers and documents cited by it in the case.

(3)   The hearing shall consist in the oral development of the Parties' arguments before the tribunal.

(4)   A certified true copy of every document produced by either Party shall be communicated to the other Party.

Article 18

(1)   The hearing shall be conducted by the Umpire. It shall be public only if the tribunal so decides with the consent of the Parties.

(2)   Records of the hearing shall be kept and signed by the Umpire; only those so signed shall be authentic.

Article 19

(1)   After the tribunal has closed the written pleadings, it shall have the right to reject any papers and documents not yet produced which either Party may wish to submit to it without the consent of the other Party. The tribunal shall, however, remain free to take into consideration any such Papers and documents which the agents, advocates or counsel of one or other of the Parties may bring to its notice, provided that they have been made known to the other Party. The latter shall have the right to require a further extension of the written pleadings so as to be able to give a reply in writing.

(2)   The tribunal may also require the Parties to produce all necessary documents and to provide all necessary explanations. It shall take note of any refusal to do so.

Article 20

(1)   The tribunal shall decide as to the admissibility of the evidence that may be adduced and shall be the judge of its probative value. It shall have the power, at any stage of the proceedings, to call upon experts and to require the appearance of witnesses. It may also, if necessary, decide to visit the scene connected with the case before it.

(2)   The Parties shall co-operate with the tribunal in dealing with the evidence and in the other measures contemplated by para. 1. The tribunal shall take note of the failure of any Party to comply with the obligations of this paragraph.

Article 21

The tribunal shall decide on any ancillary claims which it considers to be inseparable from the subject-matter of the dispute and necessary for its final settlement.

Article 22

(1)   When, subject to the control of the tribunal, the agents, advocates and counsel have completed their presentation of the case, the proceedings shall be formally declared closed.

(2)   The tribunal shall, however, have the power, so long as the award has not been rendered, to re-open the proceedings after their closure, on the ground that new evidence is forthcoming of such a nature as to constitute a decisive factor, or if it considers, after careful consideration, that there is a need for clarification on certain points.

Article 23

(1)   Except where the claimant admits the soundness of the defendant's case, discontinuance of the proceedings by the claimant Party shall not be accepted by the tribunal without the consent of the defendant.

(2)   If the case is discontinued by agreement between the Parties, the tribunal shall take note of the fact.

Article 24

If the Parties reach a settlement, it shall be taken note of by the tribunal. At the request of either Party, the tribunal may, if it thinks fit, embody the settlement in an award.

Article 25

(1)   Whenever one of the Parties has not appeared before the tribunal or has failed to present its case, the other Party may call upon the tribunal to decide in favour of its case.

(2)   The arbitral tribunal may grant the defaulting Party a period of grace before rendering the award.

(3)   On the expiry of this period of grace, the tribunal shall render an award after it has satisfied itself that it has jurisdiction. It may only decide in favour of the submissions of the Party appearing, if satisfied that they are well founded in fact and in law.

Article 26

The deliberations of the tribunal shall remain secret.

Article 27

(1)   The award shall be rendered by a majority vote of the members of the tribunal. It shall be drawn up in writing and shall bear the date on which it was rendered. It shall contain the names of the arbitrators and shall be signed by the Umpire and by the members of the tribunal who have voted for it.

(2)   Any member of the tribunal may attach his separate or dissenting opinion to the award.

(3)   The award shall be deemed to have been rendered when it has been read in open court, the agents of the Parties being present or having been duly summoned to appear.

(4)   The award shall immediately be communicated to the Parties.

Article 28

The award shall, in respect of every point on which it rules, state the reasons on which it is based.

Article 29

Once rendered, the award shall be binding upon the Parties. It shall be carried out in good faith immediately, unless the tribunal has allowed a time limit for the carrying out of the award or of any part of it.

Article 30

During a period of one month after the award has been rendered and communicated to the Parties, the tribunal may, either of its own accord or at the request of either Party, rectify any clerical, typographical or arithmetical error in the award, or any obvious error of a similar nature.

Article 31

The arbitral award shall constitute a definitive settlement of the dispute.

Article 32

(1)   Any dispute between the Parties as to the meaning and scope of the award shall, at the request of either Party and within three months of the rendering of the award, be referred to the tribunal which rendered the award.

(2)   In the event of a request for interpretation, it shall be for the tribunal to decide whether and to what extent execution of the award shall be stayed pending a decision on the request.

Article 33

Failing a request for interpretation, or after a decision on such a request has been made, all pleadings and documents in the case shall be deposited by the Umpire with the International Bureau of the Permanent Court of Arbitration.

Article 34

(1)   An application for the revision of the award may be made by either Party on the ground of the discovery of some fact of such a nature as to constitute a decisive factor, provided that, when the award was rendered, that fact was unknown to the tribunal and to the Party requesting revision, and that such ignorance was not due to the negligence of the Party requesting revision.

(2)   The application for revision must be made within six months of the discovery of the new fact and, in any case, within ten years of the rendering of the award.

(3)   In the proceedings for revision, the tribunal shall, in the first instance, make a finding as to the existence of the alleged new fact and rule on the admissibility of the application.

(4)   If the tribunal finds the application admissible, it shall then decide on the merits of the dispute.

(5)   The tribunal or the Court may, at the request of the interested Party and if circumstances so require, grant a stay of execution pending the final decision on the application for revision.

Article 35

(1)   The application for revision shall, whenever possible, be made to the tribunal

which rendered the award.

(2)   If, for any reason, it is not possible to make the application to the tribunal which rendered the award, a new tribunal shall be appointed according to the procedure provided in Art. 4.

Article 36

The tribunal shall determine the manner in which the costs and disbursements shall be apportioned.

Article 37

For the purposes of the Convention:

(*a*)   "Nationals" in relation to a Party includes (i) companies which, under the municipal law of that Party, are considered national companies of that Party and (ii) companies in which nationals of that Party have directly or indirectly a controlling interest. "Companies" includes both juridical persons recognized as such by the law of a Party and associations even if they do not possess legal personality.

(*b*)   "Property" includes all property, rights and interests, whether held directly or indirectly. A member of a company shall be deemed to have an interest in the property of the company.

FOREIGN INVESTMENTS COURT

Article I

The Parties agree to establish by the present Convention the Foreign Investments Court in order to provide machinery for the settling (*a*) of any dispute arising out of any unreasonable or discriminatory impairment within the territory of any Contracting Party of the property of nationals of the other Parties; (*b*) of any dispute concerning the observance or interpretation of any undertaking which a Party may have given in relation to investments made by nationals of any other Party.

Article II

(1)   The Parties agree that any such dispute may, with the consent of the interested Parties, be submitted to this Court. Such consent may take the form of specific agreements or of unilateral declarations. In the absence of such consent or of agreement for settlement by other specific means, the dispute may be submitted by either Party to the International Court of Justice.

(2)   The Parties may at any time declare that they recognize as compulsory *ipso facto*

and without special agreement in relation to any other State accepting the same obligation the jurisdiction of the Court in all disputes mentioned in Article I.

Article III

(1)   A national of one of the Parties claiming that between him and a Party there exists a dispute within the meaning of Art. 1 may institute proceedings against this Party before the Court, provided that the Party against which the claim is made has declared that it accepts the jurisdiction of the Court in respect of claims by nationals of one or more Parties, including the Party concerned.

(2)   Article II (2) shall apply *mutatis mutandis.*

Article IV

The Court shall be composed of a body of independent judges, elected regardless of their nationality from among persons of high moral character, who possess the qualifications required in their respective countries for appointment to the highest judicial offices or are jurisconsults of recognized competence in international law or are persons of recognized competence in international economic life.

Article V

(1)   The Court shall consist of fifteen members, no two of whom may be nationals of the same State.

(2)   A person who, for the purposes of membership in the Court, could be regarded as a national of more than one State, shall be deemed to be a national of the one in which he ordinarily exercises civil and political rights.

Article VI

Each Party to the Convention has the right to present three candidates. Only one of these candidates may be a national of the Party concerned.

Article VII

From amongst these candidates the members of the Court shall be elected by those Parties who have accepted the compulsory jurisdiction of the Court in accordance with Art. II (2) and Art. III (2).

Article VIII

(1)   A vote shall be passed on each candidate. A candidate having obtained more than 3/4 of the votes cast shall be considered as elected provided there is a vacancy to be filled.

(2)   If more candidates obtain such a majority than there are vacancies to be filled, the candidate having obtained the largest number of votes shall fill the first vacancy, and so on.

(3)   If two candidates are nationals of the same State and if both fulfil the conditions under para. 1 above, only the candidate having obtained the larger number of votes shall be elected. In case of a tie the decision shall be by lot.

(4)   The decision shall also be by lot if there are more candidates all having obtained the same number of votes than there are vacancies remaining to be filled.

Article IX

If after this procedure there remain vacancies to be filled, a record of the vote shall be transmitted to the President of the International Court of Justice. He shall fill the remaining vacancies from among the candidates. In doing so, he shall not only take into account the number of votes each of these candidates has obtained in the presentation and voting procedure but also the necessity to ensure that, if possible, all legal systems to which the several Parties to the Convention adhere and their several forms of civilisation are fairly represented on the Court.

Article X

(1)   The members of the Court shall be elected for nine years and may be re-elected, provided, however, that, of the judges elected at the first election, the terms of five judges shall expire at the end of three years and the terms of five more judges shall expire at the end of six years.

(2)   The judges whose terms are to expire at the end of the above-mentioned initial periods of three and six years shall be chosen by lot.

(3)   The members of the Court shall continue to discharge their duties until their places have been filled. Though replaced, they shall finish any cases which they may have begun.

(4)   In the case of the resignation of a member of the Court, the resignation shall be addressed to the President of the Court.

Article XI

The provisions of Art. VIII and IX shall apply if a member of the Court shall resign, die or become unable to act.

Article XII

A member of the Court elected to replace a member whose term of office has not expired shall hold office for the remainder of his predecessor's term.

Article XIII

(1)   No member of the Court may exercise any political or administrative function or engage in any other occupation of a professional nature.

(2)   Any doubt on this point shall be settled by the decision of the Court.

Article XIV

(1)   No member of the Court may act as agent, counsel or advocate in any case.

(2)   No member may participate in the decision of any case in which he has previously taken part as agent, counsel or advocate for one of the Parties or as a member of a national or international court or of a commission of enquiry or in any other capacity.

(3)   Any doubt on this point shall be settled by the decision of the Court.

Article XV

No member of the Court can be dismissed unless, in the unanimous opinion of the other members, he has ceased to fulfil the required conditions.

Article XVI

The Court shall elect its President and Vice-President for a period of three years; they may be re-elected.

Article XVII

(1)   If, for some special reason, a member of the Court considers that he should not take part in the decision of a particular case, he shall so inform the President.

(2)   If the President considers that for some special reason one of the members of the Court should not sit in a particular case, he shall give him notice accordingly.

(3)   If in any such case the member of the Court and the President disagree, the matter shall be settled by the decision of the Court.

Article XVIII

(1)   The full Court shall sit except when it is expressly provided otherwise in the present Statute.

(2)   Subject to the condition that the number of judges available to constitute the Court is not thereby reduced below eleven, the Rules of the Court may provide for allowing one or

more judges, according to circumstances and in rotation, to be dispensed from sitting.

(3)   A quorum of nine judges shall suffice to constitute the Court.

Article XIX

(1)   The Court may from time to time form one or more Chambers, composed of three or more judges as the Court may determine, for dealing with particular categories of cases.

(2)   Cases shall be heard and determined by the Chambers provided for in this Article if the Parties so request.

Article XX

A judgment given by any of the Chambers provided for in Article XIX shall be considered as rendered by the Court.

Article XXI

The Chambers provided for in Article XIX may, with the consent of the Parties, sit and exercise their functions elsewhere than at [The Hague].

Article XXII

The Court shall frame rules for carrying out its functions. In particular, it shall lay down rules of procedure.

Article XXIII

(1)   Judges of the nationality of each of the Parties shall retain their right to sit in the case before the Court.

(2)   If the Court includes upon the Bench a judge of the nationality of one of the Parties, the other Party may choose a person to sit as judge. Such person shall be chosen preferably from among those persons who have been nominated as candidates as provided in Article VI.

(3)   If the Court includes upon the Bench no judge of the nationality of the Parties, each of these Parties may proceed to choose a judge, as provided in paragraph 2 of this Article.

(4)   The provisions of this Article shall apply to the case of Article XIX. In such cases, the President shall request one or, if necessary, two of the members of the Court forming the Chamber to give place to the members of the Court of the nationality of the Parties concerned and failing such, or if they are unable to be present, to the judges specially chosen by the Parties.

(5)   Judges chosen as laid down in paragraphs 2, 3 and 4 of this Article shall fulfil the conditions required by Articles IV, XIV and XVII of the present Statute. They shall take part in the decision on terms of complete equality with their colleagues.

Article XXIV

Each member of the Court shall receive an annual salary.

Article XXV

(1)   The costs of the Court shall be borne by the Parties so as to correspond proportionally to the respective percentages of their contribution to the costs of the United Nations.

(2)   The Parties will establish by majority vote a schedule of fees and costs to be borne by the litigants. This schedule shall not discriminate between private Parties and States. On the strength of this schedule the Court shall determine the costs to be borne by each litigant in each particular case.

Article XXVI

Cases are brought before the Court, as the case may be, either by the notification of the special agreement of the Parties to submit the dispute to the jurisdiction of the Court or by a written application addressed to the President. In either case the subject of the dispute and the Parties shall be indicated.

Note

Art. 4b, 10-34 and 37 of the Draft on the Arbitral Tribunal shall apply *mutatis mutandis*: instead of "(Arbitral) Tribunal" read "Court"; instead of "Umpire" read "President"; instead of "award" read "sentence". The second sentence of Article 24 shall be deleted. In Art. 32 (1) the words "which rendered the award" shall be deleted.

*   *   *

INTERNATIONAL CODE OF FAIR TREATMENT FOR FOREIGN INVESTMENTS[*]

> The International Code on Fair Treatment for Foreign Investments was prepared jointly by the International Chamber of Commerce's Committee on Foreign Investments and its Committee on Foreign Establishments. The Code was published in 1949. The Code was endorsed by a resolution adopted by the International Chamber of Commerce's Quebec Congress. The resolution and the Introductory Report of the International Chamber of Commerce's Committee on Foreign Investments have not been reproduced in this volume.

International Code of Fair Treatment
for Foreign Investments

**drawn up by the I.C.C.'s Committees
on Foreign Investments and Foreign Establishments
and approved by the I.C.C.'s Quebec Congress
(June 1949)**

PREAMBLE

The High Contracting Parties, desirous of promoting an expanding world economy and convinced that an ample flow of private investments is essential to the economic and industrial growth of their countries and to the welfare of their peoples, decide to establish, by the provision of civil, legal and fiscal safeguards, conditions of fair and non-discriminatory treatment for investments made in their territories by the nationals (physical or legal persons) of the other High Contracting Parties.

Article 1

The High Contracting Parties undertake to give effect to the provisions set out hereafter within their metropolitan and overseas territories as well as within those territories where, either by treaty or by virtue of powers conferred upon them by an international authority acting within the limits of its competence, they are entitled so to do.

Article 2

By the terms of this Treaty the High Contracting Parties agree to apply fair treatment, as

---

[*]Source: International Chamber of Commerce (1949). *Fair Treatment for Foreign Investment. International Code*, Brochure 129 (Paris: Lecraw Press) [Note added by the editor].

hereinafter defined, to investments of any kind made in their territories by the nationals of the other High Contracting Parties, including *inter alia* the following types:

-- direct investments in real property, natural resources, commercial, financial, agricultural, industrial or transport enterprises, as well as in public utilities or enterprises connected therewith;

-- equity investments in company shares and similar holdings;

-- credits and advances to private and public borrowers and fixed-interest investments in private and public loans.

Article 3

The High Contracting Parties shall take no discriminatory political, legal or administrative measures designed to hamper investments in their territories by the nationals of the other High Contracting Parties. They shall give to investments originating with the other High Contracting Parties treatment no less favourable than to investments made by their own nationals. In the case, however, of investments immediately concerned with national defence, special conditions may, if necessary, be imposed.

Article 4[1]

No High Contracting Party shall discriminate on grounds of nationality in its legislative or administrative treatment of investments, between the investments made by the nationals of one of the High Contracting Parties and the investments made by the nationals of any other of the High Contracting Parties.

Article 5

In the territories of each of the High Contracting Parties, the treatment extended to the nationals of the other High Contracting Parties shall be not less favourable than that applied to their own nationals, in respect of the legal and judicial protection of their person, property, rights and interests, and in respect of the acquisition, purchase, sale and assignment of moveable and immoveable property of any kind.

They shall have access to the domestic courts as plaintiff or defendant under the same conditions as nationals and be entitled to appear before the competent administrative authorities for the purpose of safeguarding their rights and interests in accordance with the laws in force on the said territories, such laws being applied without any distinction to their own nationals and

---

[1] This Article is concerned exclusively with legislative or administrative action by governments and is in no way intended to interfere with the negotiation of special terms between investor and investee for any specific investment.

those of the other High Contracting Parties.

In all cases they shall have the right to receive reasonable prior notice of any proceedings before such domestic courts or competent administrative authorities.

Should the nationals of one of the High Contracting Parties not enjoy the full benefit of the civil rights generally recognized by the other High Contracting Parties or by international law, the nationals of the other High Contracting Parties shall be entitled to such rights and this protection shall not be denied to them on the ground that a preferential system would thus be established in their favour.

Article 6[2]

The High Contracting Parties shall not introduce any legislative or administrative provisions of a discriminatory character placing restrictions on:

-- the nationality of the shareholders;
-- the composition of the board of Directors and the choice of the Directors;
-- the selection or introduction into their territories of such administrative, executive and technical officers and staff, not nationals of those territories, as shall be deemed by the enterprises concerned to be requisite for their efficient operation.

In the case, however, of enterprises directly concerned with national defence, special conditions may, if necessary, be imposed.

Article 7

The High Contracting Parties shall not give less favourable treatment in respect of taxation to the nationals of the other High Contracting Parties than to their own nationals.

Article 8

In order to eliminate the serious deterrents to the development of foreign investments resulting from double taxation, the High Contracting Parties shall seek to conclude bilateral agreements for the prevention of the double taxation of income, and of capital, estates and successions on the basis of the two Model Bilateral Conventions of London drawn up for that purpose by the League of Nations.

---

[2] This Article is necessary and important, because before investors are willing to transfer capital to another country for the purpose of establishing and developing an enterprise, they desire to know that the administrative, financial and technical management will be under the direction of those whom they consider to be most suitably qualified without regard to nationality. In addition to the obligation on the High Contracting Parties not to introduce new discriminatory legislation, it is also necessary that the High Contracting Parties endeavour as soon as practicable to withdraw or modify any existing legislative or administrative restrictions of the kind referred to in the Article, which deter the investment of foreign capital.

Article 9

Subject to such restrictions and exceptions as may be authorized under the Agreement of the International Monetary Fund, the High Contracting Parties in whose territories sums have been invested by nationals of the other High Contracting Parties shall allow to such nationals freedom of transfer:

a) of current payments arising out of their investments including *inter-alia* interest, dividends, profits, royalties (derived from enterprises in the case of direct investment);

b) of payments of principal, payments in respect of redeemable shares, loan certificates and like securities, as well as payments in respect of amortization of loans and, in the case of direct investments, depreciation;

c) of all payments necessary for the upkeep and renewal of assets maintained in such territories.

A national of one of the High Contracting Parties owning shares or having interests in the territory of another High Contracting Party shall, in the event of his surrendering for a consideration the rights vested by him in such shares or interests, or in the event of liquidation or reduction of capital, be entitled to transfer, within a reasonable period, the proceeds of such surrender, liquidation or reduction.

All such transfers shall be authorized either in the currency of the creditor or in some other currency agreed upon by the creditor and debtor.

Article 10

The conditions of transfer defined in Article 9 shall also apply to investments in any public loan or loan guaranteed by a public authority, which shall have been issued in the territory of one of the High Contracting Parties:

a) by another High Contracting Party;

b) by a public body situated in the territory of another High Contracting Party;

c) by any other person or body, with the guarantee of another High Contracting Party or of one of its agencies or of the International Bank for Reconstruction and Development.

In the case of such international loans, bondholders of creditor High Contracting Parties shall have the right to appoint representatives in the territories of the debtor High Contracting Parties to defend their interests and endeavour to reach settlement of difficulties that may arise through default of payment or measures of alleged discrimination by private or public bodies.

These representatives shall likewise have the right to apply to the competent courts in the event of disputes and, if the courts fail to act within a reasonable period or in the case of unfair treatment not amenable to the jurisdiction of a court, to carry the matter before the International Court of Arbitration for which provision is made in Article 13 and 14 below.

Article 11

High Contracting Parties who may decide to take measures for the expropriation or dispossession of private property, involving the transfer of the ownership or management of property belonging in whole or in part to nationals of the other High Contracting Parties either to governmental authorities or to their own nationals, shall apply the following principles:

a) the property of investors who are nationals of the other High Contracting Parties shall in no circumstances be liable to measures of expropriation or dispossession except in accordance with the appropriate legal procedure and with fair compensation according to international law;

b) any national law enacting expropriation or dispossession of the property of the nationals of another High Contracting Party shall state explicitly the purpose and conditions of such expropriation or dispossession;

c) the introduction in the territory of one of the High Contracting Parties of a system of exchange control shall not exempt the said High Contracting Party from its obligation to carry out the transfer of the compensation due for expropriation or dispossession;

d) the basis of the compensation shall be determined before expropriation or dispossession takes place. The compensation shall be payable in cash or in readily marketable securities of an equivalent value. The cash or the proceeds of the sale of the securities shall be freely transferable forthwith at the rates of exchange prevailing at the time of expropriation or dispossession. The transfer shall be in the currency of the foreign creditor, unless otherwise agreed.

Article 12

The High Contracting Parties shall afford all reasonable facilities to the investors of the other High Contracting Parties to obtain the information required for a correct estimate of economic conditions within their territories as well as information concerning their law and their legal, political and administrative systems.

Article 13

The High Contracting Parties agree that any differences that may arise between them respecting the interpretation or application of this Convention shall, unless settled within a short and reasonable period by direct negotiation or by any other form of conciliation, be submitted for decision to the International Court of Arbitration in accordance with the procedure laid down in Article 14.

Article 14

(This Article should contain detailed provisions for the composition and working of the International Court of Arbitration to which all disputes and differences are to be referred under Article 13. The details are, however, left to be worked out by the negotiating governments).

Article 15

(This Article should contain detailed provisions governing the interpretation of the word "nationals" so as to ensure that that expression shall include not only physical persons but also incorporated or unincorporated associations).

Article 16

(This Article would contain the customary provisions for entry into force and ratification, the details of which are left to the negotiating governments).

* * *

Guidelines for International Investment*

The Guidelines for International Investment were adopted unanimously by the Council of the International Chamber of Commerce at its 120th Session on 29 November 1972.

INTRODUCTION

Private international investment is an increasingly important factor in the world economy. It contributes to a more effective allocation of resources and integration of markets in both industrialized and developing countries. Moreover, for a number of developing countries it is already the major external source of capital and technology and may well become increasingly important generally, in view of the relatively slow growth of official assistance.

While the benefits of international investment are generally recognized, there exists none the less concern that the international economic interdependence which it involves may conflict with aspirations for national economic independence. On the one hand, the independent management of domestic economic affairs is desired; on the other, it is recognized that a large measure of participation in the international economy serves the general welfare. This dilemma lies at the heart of the tensions which sometimes arise between international investors and the governments of both host countries and investor countries.

It is generally agreed that, in an increasingly interdependent world, all resources -- public and private, domestic and international -- capable of making a contribution to economic and social welfare must be effectively marshalled. There are however genuine differences of view among governments regarding the forms and amounts of private international investment required and the terms and priorities which should be accorded to it in various sectors of the economy. International investors also have differing policies and priorities which they must review from time to time in the light of changing requirements and attitudes.

The ICC believes that, if international investment is to make its optimum contribution to economic and social progress alongside a strong and efficient domestic private sector, it is essential that mutual understanding between private international investors and governments on basic issues affecting their relationship be promoted. Accordingly, it has drawn up the recommendations in the Guidelines which follow.

Practical Recommendations

It must be strongly emphasized that these Guidelines should not be regarded as a rigid

---

*Source: International Chamber of Commerce (1972). *Guidelines for International Investment* No. 272 (Paris: Lecraw-Servant) [Note added by the editor].

code of conduct. They are, rather, a set of practical recommendations based upon experience, designed to facilitate consultation between investors and governments and to promote a better understanding of each other's needs and objectives. Furthermore, because they are all interrelated, specific recommendations must not be considered in isolation from others, nor should they be understood in isolation from their object which is to promote a climate of mutual confidence.

While some of the recommendations contained herein may be particularly relevant to an investment in a developing country, the Guidelines generally apply to all private international direct investments whether they originate in or are destined for developed or developing countries. In fact, the largest flows of international direct investment are at present among the developed market economies and these, therefore, provide the largest field of application for the recommendations; these countries are thus host countries as well as capital exporting countries. As developing countries progressively become capital exporters, they will find themselves increasingly in the same situation.

UN Development Decade

In so far as they do apply to relations between less developed countries and international investors, the Guidelines reflect strongly the basic principles set out in the Action Programme of the United Nations Development Decade II:

"Developing countries will adopt appropriate measures for inviting, stimulating and making effective use of foreign private capital, taking into account the areas in which such capital should be sought and bearing in mind the importance for its attraction of conditions conducive to sustained investment. Developed countries, on their part, will consider adopting further measures to encourage the flow of private capital to developing countries. Foreign private investment in developing countries should be undertaken in a manner consistent with the development objectives and priorities established in their national plans. Foreign private investors in developing countries should endeavour to provide for an increase in the local share in management and administration, employment and training of local labour including personnel at the managerial and technical levels, participation of local capital and reinvestment of profits. Efforts will be made to foster better understanding of the rights and obligations of both host and capital-exporting countries, as well as of individual investors."

The ICC is of the opinion that the general acceptance of the recommendations contained in the Guidelines would tend to create a climate of mutual confidence conducive to an increased, and mutually satisfactory, flow of international investment. It is hoped also that these Guidelines will be helpful to the United Nations and other intergovernmental organizations in their efforts to promote constructive discussions on the relationships between international investors, the governments of host countries and the investors' governments.

I. INVESTMENT POLICIES

1. The Investor[*]

a) Should ensure in consultation with the competent authorities that the investment fits satisfactorily into the economic and social development plans and priorities of the host country.

b) Should be prepared in any negotiations with the government of the host country to make known his expectations concerning the expansion of the enterprise, employment and marketing prospects and the financing of its operations.

c) Should in appropriate cases, where the government of the host country so wishes, be prepared to enter into contractual arrangements with that government.

d) Should, in response to the interest shown by the public of the host country in his activities, take steps to provide relevant information about the operations of the enterprise, subject to any exclusions necessary for competitive reasons.

2. The Investor's Country's Government

a) Should, in the formulation or modification of policies that affect foreign investments by its nationals, take the fullest possible account of the need of investors for stability, continuity and growth in their operations as well as of the general interests of the host country.

b) Should seek to enter into binding obligations under international law with other governments either on a bilateral or multilateral basis, in respect of the reciprocal treatment to be accorded to the property, rights, and interests of its nationals.

c) Should offer, either nationally or through participation in an international investment insurance agency, guarantee facilities against non-commercial risks encountered by the investor.

d) Should examine the possibility of providing special aid for relevant economic and social infrastructure projects in developing countries which

---

[*]Wherever the circumstances are such that a recommendation addressed to "the Investor" falls for implementation to the enterprise operating in the host country, it should be regarded as addressed to that enterprise.

will facilitate private investment of significance to the economic development of the host country.

3. The Host Country's Government

a) Should, in the formulation or modification of policies that affect foreign investments, take the fullest possible account of the need of investors for stability, continuity and growth in their operations.

b) Should, with regard to sectors not reserved to domestic ownership, make known to prospective investors its economic priorities and the general conditions that it wishes to apply to incoming direct private investment, and should provide an opportunity for consultation with the private sector during the development of national plans.

c) Should make known the treatment that it will accord to the proposed investment and any limitations or financial charges that it will impose.

d) Should not discriminate on the grounds of its foreign ownership in the treatment accorded to the enterprise, it being understood that the government has a right to accord special treatment to any enterprise or enterprises, whether domestic or foreign owned, in the interest of the economy.

e) Should, in appropriate cases and where the foreign investor so wishes, be prepared to enter into contractual arrangements with the investor concerned.

f) Should be prepared to enter into binding obligations under international law with other governments either on a bilateral or multilateral basis, in respect of the reciprocal treatment to be accorded to the property, rights, and interests of nationals of the other state or states.

II. OWNERSHIP AND MANAGEMENT

1. The Investor

a) Should, in presenting his investment proposals to the authorities of the host country, examine favourably suitable proposals concerning forms of association with local interests, public or private.

b) Should, in developing countries where the necessary institutional facilities exist, offer part of the equity of the subsidiary for purchase or subscription by local investors, wherever this is compatible with the long-term economic interest of the enterprise.

c) Should encourage local participation in the management of the enterprise, promoting nationals to posts of increasing responsibility and providing the training and experience that are a prerequisite for such promotion.

d) Should, if he finds himself in a dominant market position, refrain from abuse of that position by actions that are to the detriment of the economy of the host country.

2. The Investor's Country's Government

Should, in the framework of foreign aid, support financial, educational and other institutions, including those providing managerial training, thus preparing the ground for more local private participation in the financing and management of enterprises established in developing countries.

3. The Host Country's Government

a) Should, once the details of the implementation of an investment project have been accepted and the ownership and management structure of the enterprise has been established, refrain subsequently from modifying such arrangements otherwise than through negotiation and agreement.

b) Should recognise that joint ventures are much more likely to be successful if they are entered into voluntarily and if the terms of the contracts are left to the free negotiation of the parties, and that there may be cases where investments which deserve high priority are only feasible on the basis of total foreign ownership.

c) Should take appropriate measures, principally by encouraging the creation or development of an effective capital market, to facilitate the purchase of equity in domestic and foreign-owned enterprises by local interests.

d) In so far as laws or regulations requiring local participation are judged to be necessary, should frame these laws in such a way that the rights of existing enterprises are respected, new investment is not discouraged and flexible application is possible.

e) Should rely on economic, fiscal and commercial policy measures applying to all business operations, national and foreign, for the exercise of controls in the public interest rather than seek to do this through compulsory governmental participation in the equity or management of enterprises.

f) If there is abuse of a dominant market position, should, in preference to the immediate application of restrictive regulations, seek to remedy the situation either by stimulating competition, especially through the encouragement of new investment and the lowering of import tariffs, or by recommending a change in the investor's practices.

III. FINANCE

1. The Investor

a) Should, without prejudice to the freedom of transfer of financial resources, where there is government concern about the balance of payments of the host country, take this situation into account in shaping his commercial and other policies.

b) Should assist the enterprise to comply with the requirements for disclosure of profits and other financial information imposed generally on companies by the host country.

c) Should, when having substantial recourse to local sources of capital, take into account the impact which his requirements may have on the availability of funds to local enterprise.

d) Should consider favourably the reinvestment of part of his profits, whether in the enterprise or in other economic activities in the host country which he considers suitable.

2. The Investor's Country's Government

a) Should not interfere in the financial management of the enterprise by, for example, insisting upon a given level of remittances in any period unless an adverse balance of payments situation forces it to do so.

b) Should remove as speedily as possible any existing restrictions on the outflow of capital in the form of direct investment by companies, and should refrain from introducing new restrictions except where exceptional circumstances make short term regulation necessary.

3. The Host Country's Government

a) Should place no restrictions on the remittance of loan interest, redemption payments, service and advisory fees, license fees, royalties and similar payments except in circumstances where the laws of the country require prior approval of the underlying agreement between payor and payee and such approval has not been obtained.

b) Should allow the investor liberty to remit his profit, in particular avoiding the imposition of restrictions not notified at the time of the investment, and should respect any engagements entered into with the investor. Similar conditions should apply to the repatriation of capital, although it is recognised that developing countries may find it necessary to require that remittances be spread over a reasonable period of time.

c)   Should, if faced with balance of payments difficulties which justify the temporary imposition of restrictions, follow the principles of the International Monetary Fund and the General Agreement on Tariffs and Trade.

d)   Should, in devising any special exemptions or incentives aimed at attracting foreign investment or encouraging new investment in general, have regard to the need to avoid undue distortion of competition between enterprises operating within its territory, whether domestic or foreign.

e)   Should allow the unrestricted transfer of the personal savings of the investor's expatriate personnel and the funds necessary to meet pension and family commitments.

f)   Should, where restrictions on local borrowing are necessary, make them equally applicable to all enterprises without any discrimination as between foreigners and nationals, except that developing countries may in special circumstances be justified in restricting long and medium term borrowing by foreign-owned enterprises.

IV. FISCAL POLICIES

1.   The Investor

a)   Should observe the laws and regulations of the host country in relation to the submission of returns, and provision of information in connection with the assessment and collection of taxes.

b)   Should, to the extent that such information is not available to the enterprise that is under the tax jurisdiction of the host country, be prepared to assist that enterprise to provide justification for its export and import prices.

2.   The Investor's Country's Government

a)   Should seek to enter into effective arrangements for avoidance of double taxation with capital importing countries.

b)   Should ensure that when, in double taxation arrangements, the host country retains a primary right to tax dividends, interest, royalties, etc., such tax is fully relieved by tax credit or reimbursement according to the legal status or personal circumstances of the beneficiary deriving the income directly or through an intermediate company.

c) Should ensure that, even in the absence of double taxation arrangements, the aggregate of foreign and domestic tax imposed on income from foreign sources (including, in the case of a dividend from direct investment, the foreign tax on profits underlying the dividends) does not exceed the greater of the foreign tax or the tax imposed on similar income from domestic sources.

d) Should introduce arrangements, unilaterally if necessary, to avoid any double taxation on the salaries and other incomes of expatriate employees.

e) Should refrain from frustrating the effects of development reliefs granted by host countries in respect of new investment by affording appropriate matching reliefs.

3. **The Host Country's Government**

a) Should seek to enter into effective arrangements for avoidance of double taxation with capital-exporting countries.

b) Should ensure that taxes on income are imposed on no more than the net income arising in the host country after deducting all expenses properly attributable thereto incurred within or outside the country, whether such expenses are payable to associated or non-associated enterprises.

c) Should not impose on enterprises wholly or partially foreign-owned, taxes which are higher or more burdensome than those to which purely domestic enterprises are subject.

d) Should provide a stable tax system with profits and other income being taxed at rates which do not discourage private investment and enterprise.

V. LEGAL FRAMEWORK

1. The Investor

a) Should respect the national laws, policies and economic and social objectives of the host country in the same way as would a good citizen of that country, and abide by undertakings given to the government of the host country in connection with the investment.

b) Should be willing to enter into arrangements for the settlement by international conciliation or arbitration of disputes with the government of the host country.

2. The Investor's Country's Government

Should not seek to interfere with the legal order of the host country by extending the application of its national laws, directives and regulations to the investor's operations in the host country.

3. The Host Country's Government

a) Should respect the recognised principles of international law, reflected in many international treaties regarding the treatment of foreign property, concerning in particular:

    i.   Fair and equitable treatment for such property;

    ii.   The avoidance of unreasonable and discriminatory measures;

    iii.   The observance of contractual and other undertakings given to the investor;

    iv.   In the event of expropriation or nationalisation the effective payment, without undue delay, of just compensation.

b) Should in suitable circumstances enter into arrangements for the settlement by international conciliation or arbitration of disputes with the investor.

c) Should provide in its national laws for suitable protection for minority share-holdings in those cases where appropriate provisions do not as yet exist.

VI. LABOUR POLICIES

1. The Investor

a) Should make the maximum practicable use of qualified local personnel.

b) Should co-operate with the host government, labour unions and local educational and vocational training institutions in programmes for the upgrading and training of local labour.

c) Should, to the extent consistent with the efficient operation of the enterprise, take into account the host government's efforts to create employment opportunities in the localities where they are most needed.

d) Should, in all matters directly affecting the interests of labour, to the extent appropriate to local circumstances, consult and co-operate with organizations representing its employees.

e) When the necessity for the closure of factories or the laying off of redundant employees becomes apparent, should give adequate advance information, and in consultation with the employees, arrange the timing and conditions of such action in a way that will cause the minimum social damage.

f) Should, in fixing wage and salary levels, act as a good employer, participating constructively as a member of national employers associations where these exist, and providing, according to local circumstances, the best possible wages, social benefits, retirement provisions and working conditions within the framework of the government's policies.

2. The Investor's Country's Government

a) Should, in formulating policies aimed at securing full employment, rely on stimulating domestic demand through appropriate economic and social policies, rather than on restrictions on the outflow of direct investment.

b) Should consider making available aid for educational and vocational training of local personnel in the skills needed by the enterprise and elsewhere in the economy of the host country, especially if it is a developing country.

3. The Host Country's Government

a) Should seek, in co-operation with investors and with appropriate national and foreign organisations, to assess future needs for skilled employees and to develop adequate programs for technical and managerial training.

b) Should permit the employment of qualified foreign personnel where this is needed for the efficient operation of the enterprise or for training purposes.

VII. TECHNOLOGY
(Including inventions, know-how and skills)

1. The Investor

a) Should, whenever practicable, promote the development of the technological capacity of the host country, particularly if it is a developing country, for example by the training of local staff, assistance to educational institutions, and provided that conditions for efficient research so allow, by establishment in the host country of suitable research activities.

b) Should, when granting licenses for the use of industrial property rights or when otherwise transferring technology, do so on reasonable terms and conditions and with an adequate market area.

c) Should make the latest suitable technology available in return for appropriate payments, and keep it up to date in accordance with the circumstances of the host country.

d) Should not, without prejudice to existing contracts, require payment for the use of industrial property rights or technology of no real value to the enterprise.

e) Should support its investment with appropriate services and advice to ensure the full contribution of the investment to the development of the economy of the host country.

f) Should co-operate with the government of the host country in examining the impact of his operations on the environment and take steps to minimize damage so far as is economically and technically practical in the local situation.

2. The Investor's Country's Government

a) Should, in so far as it has not already done so, accede to relevant international treaties relating to Industrial Property and seek to conclude bilateral agreements that will facilitate the transfer of technology by private enterprises in return for appropriate remuneration.

b) Should, where applicable, provide assistance to the host country, especially if it is a developing country, with a view to promoting the scientific and educational infrastructure necessary to facilitate the transfer and development of technology.

3. The Host Country's Government

a) Should, in the formulation of its policies, take into account the fact that technology is mainly developed by private enterprises in the principal industrial and scientific centres of the world, and that its successful international transfer by such enterprises depends not only upon appropriate compensation being provided but also upon suitable conditions in the receiving country.

b) Should facilitate the continuing acquisition on appropriate terms of the additional know-how necessary to sustain competitive efficiency.

c) Should, if it wishes to encourage the investor to establish research facilities in its territory, take account of the need for an adequate scientific and educational infrastructure, and of the practical limits to dispersing research activities.

d)   Should ensure effective legal protection for industrial property rights and encourage freedom of contract for licensing, subject to legislation for preventing abuses of industrial property rights such as failure to put them to use.

e)   Should, in so far as it has not already done so, accede to relevant international treaties relating to Industrial Property and seek to conclude bilateral agreements that will facilitate the transfer of technology by private enterprises in return for appropriate remuneration.

f)   Should not impose witholding taxes on licence fees, royalties and payments for services and advice at such a level that they materially increase the cost of the technology, make its transfer difficult, or even prevent it altogether.

VIII.   COMMERCIAL POLICIES

1.   The Investor

a)   Should not seek undue protection from competition from imports nor require unjustified guarantees against competition from new manufacturers in the same market.

b)   Should assist the enterprise in its efforts to develop its export business and should not place any obstacle to such exports unless he is prevented by existing obligations to third parties or by sound economic reasons which he should be prepared to disclose to the government of the host country.

c)   Should practice fair pricing policies for goods and services in dealings with associated companies which take into consideration the tax, customs and competition regulations of the countries involved.

d)   If prices and quality are competitive, should give preference to local sources of supply for components and raw materials, particularly where the host country is a developing country.

2.   The Investor's Country's Government

a)   Should open its frontiers as fully as possible to foreign imports and in particular improve access to its markets for the industrial and agricultural products of developing countries.

b)   Should not seek to extend the application of its national laws, directives and regulations to restrict the exports of the enterprise from the host country to any third market.

3.   **The Host Country's Government**

a)   Should co-operate in worldwide and regional initiatives towards liberalization of international trade to the fullest extent that its level of economic development permits and in this connection avoid cost raising policies inconsistent with sound development.

b)   Should not impose export obligations on the enterprise beyond those contractually entered into.

c)   Should permit the enterprise to import the equipment, spare parts, components and materials which it requires for efficient production without undue formalities and without excessive Customs and other duties.

*   *   *

CHARTER OF TRADE UNION DEMANDS FOR THE LEGISLATIVE CONTROL OF MULTINATIONAL COMPANIES*

> The Charter of Trade Union Demands for the Legislative Control of Multinational Companies was adopted by the Eleventh International Confederation of Free Trade Unions World Congress, held in Mexico between 17-25 October 1975.

CONTENTS

Preamble

Trade union objectives

Trade union proposals for action

---

*Source: International Confederation of Free Trade Unions (1975). "Charter of Trade Union Demands for the Legislative Control of Multinational Companies adopted by the Eleventh World Congress", *Multinational Charter* (Brussels: International Confederation of Free Trade Unions), pp. 17-67. The sample table on page 57 in the original source has not been reproduced in this volume [Note added by the editor].

Appendix IX: ICFTU and ICFTU-ARO on operations of multinationals
Appendix X: ORIT policy on multinational companies

PREAMBLE

1.   From an early stage in its history, the labour movement has been acutely aware of the dangers which the international operations of capital could beget for the exercise of trade union rights, as well as for the earnings and job security of the workers. It is now more than 100 years since international solidarity was first proclaimed as a weapon, not only for the achievement of social justice, but also -- more immediately and concretely -- for the defeat of employers' attempts to break strikes by transferring production abroad. International labour solidarity was the motive force behind the formation of the first international labour groupings in the third quarter of the nineteenth century. And today international labour solidarity is being given ever more concrete shape in the new forms of organization which our movement is seeking to evolve for meeting the even greater challenge posed by the activities of multinational companies.

2.   What is a multinational company? For trade union purposes, the simplest definition is one which carries on activities other than marketing its own products in more than one country. Companies doing that have, of course, existed for a long time. What is new is the rapid growth in their number and size, the varied fields into which they have moved, the use made by some of them of modern technology and communications in order to set up integrated production facilities sited in various countries and, above all, the economic, social and political problems they pose, not only to the trade unions but to many national governments too. These problems do not arise exclusively from any misdeeds of the companies (such as those mentioned in the following two paragraphs). They can be a consequence of their "normal" industrial, financial and commercial activities and of the private planning in their own interest which they are often able to impose to the detriment of public planning in the interest of the community as a whole. They collect financial resources from all over the world and invest them where and how it is most profitable to themselves: in so doing they may in many cases virtually decide whether a country is to expand its production and employment or, alternatively, to stagnate. Or again, with their built-in tendency to boost cash flow and their easy access to international capital markets, they may have an inherent inflationary effect, quite apart from any price-hiking possibilities arising from their position of market domination. From the global viewpoint, they are also very largely responsible for perpetuating the world's economic imbalance and further widening the gap between rich and poor nations: two thirds of international investment still goes to the older industrial countries, despite all the brave talk about the multinationals' role in promoting economic growth in the Third World.

3.   These companies owe no allegiance to any nation-state. They mostly seek to escape any form of democratic control or social responsibility: they are guided primarily by motives of expansion and profit-maximization. Conceiving company policies on a world-wide basis, and with production and assembly facilities in many different countries, they can juggle exports and imports by fixing artificial prices for transfers between the parent firm and/or its foreign

subsidiaries. They can also manipulate dividends, tax payments and capital movements in ways which often escape the control of national authorities. There is no doubt that some of the financial and trading practices of these companies have had serious repercussions on the implementation of the policies of many governments in respect of the balance of payments, domestic industrial development, inflation and national economic planning in general. Some of these companies, moreover, have used their enormous resources to interfere in the internal political affairs of countries in which they have established subsidiaries: the methods used have ranged from the large-scale bribery of politicians to the active promotion of subversive movements aiming at the overthrow of democratically elected governments.

4.   The activities of the multinationals in certain developing countries have given rise to especially sharp criticism from the trade union movement. Profiting from the urgent need of these countries for industrial investment -- and, in a predominantly capitalist world economy, there is no visible alternative for the supply of the necessary capital and know-how -- the companies have extracted far-reaching concessions which such countries can ill afford to make: tax holidays for up to ten years, exemption from import duties, even the provision of ready-built factories and -- most despicable of all from the labour viewpoint -guarantees against trade union "interference" in the shape of restrictive legislation for ensuring the trouble-free exploitation of vast pools of cheap labour. Add to those incentives the attraction of freedom from the increasingly stringent antipollution and health-protection measures being adopted in the older industrialized countries, and the motives of the companies for investing in some parts of the Third World become clearer. In return the developing countries, it is true, receive some badly needed industrial investment -- but not necessarily that best suited to their real development needs -- some access to scarce foreign currency from increased exports -- after deduction, of course, of profits whose repatriation they have had to guarantee to the companies. And, in the final analysis, there is no certainty that the companies will stay once their tax holiday has expired, or increasing trade union pressure -despite all the restrictions -- has begun to eat into their super profits. A side effect of the superprofit-making activities of the multinationals in the Third World is the stimulus they give to protectionist feelings and the jeopardizing of support for development aid policies among workers in industries affected by unfair competition in the older industrial countries. Another prediliction of some multinational companies is for investments in countries with dictatorial regimes, where elementary human and labour rights are systematically flouted.

5.   In the absence of coordinated international trade union action, it is obvious that the growth and concentration of international capital must tip the balance of bargaining power in favour of management and against labour. Strikes can be broken by the transfer of production to other factories of the same company; the introduction of industrial democracy can be rendered null and void, if the board of directors on which the workers are granted representation is not autonomous but subject to control from a parent body in another country. Hence the efforts of the international trade secretariats to build up a countervailing power to that of the companies, in particular through the creation of world councils representing the workers in the various concerns. The ICFTU recognises the primordial role of the international trade secretariats in strengthening union bargaining capacity vis-à-vis the companies and in seeking to evolve new

forms of organisation based on international workers' solidarity in order to meet the multinational challenge.

6.　　There is general recognition throughout the international labour movement, however, that collective bargaining procedures are not in themselves sufficient for dealing with all the various problems raised by the activities of multinational companies. As in the case of certain other trade union objectives, political action for securing appropriate legislation is also required. The immediate aim of this action is to protect the general interests of the workers and the peoples by imposing social controls on the activities of the companies. Its long-term aim is to substitute for the international division of labour which the multinationals have imposed on the world a more just and humane system of international cooperation under democratic control. We wish to put an end to the frantic competition between nations to secure investment and jobs from the multinationals. Only when industrial production is geared to satisfying the basic needs of the masses, not the private profit of a few, will it be possible to give really effective aid to the industrial development of the Third World countries. Such development would thus complement that of the industrially advanced countries; it would not have the effect, which much multinational investment has at present, of simply transferring jobs from the industrial to developing countries, with consequently higher unemployment in the former. An essential element in the kind of democratic control mentioned above will be the introduction or extension of systems of industrial democracy giving the workers a greater say in economic decision-making at all levels. As for the mechanics of transferring capital and technical know-how to the countries which need them most through channels other than the multinationals, there are vast untapped possibilities in cooperation between countries with a well-developed public sector, as well as in international investment by the cooperative movement with its basic philosophy of production for use rather than profit.

Trade union objectives

7.　　Recognising the need for a common trade union strategy towards the multinationals, particularly for the attainment of our political objectives, the 10th ICFTU World Congress in July 1972 called for the creation of a joint working party together with the international trade secretariats. Set up in February 1973, the ICFTU/ITS Working Party on Multinational Companies has concentrated its main endeavours on the promotion of legislation, national and international, for controlling the activities of these companies. Our studies of the problems involved have confirmed our belief that national legislation in many cases needs to be complemented -- and sometimes even preceded -- by international agreements with machinery for supervision and enforcement. This is true where the nature of the practices calling for control is intimately connected with the international character of the multinationals. It is also true in respect of almost any control measures to be applied by small countries whose total budget may be less than one tenth of the annual turnover of some of the huge concerns they have to deal with. Such countries obviously need the moral, material and institutional support of the international community.

8.　　Ideally, we would have wished to see a general multilateral treaty under United Nations auspices, with a new fully-fledged UN agency for supervising its application. It would be the task of this agency to elaborate the international agreements of a social, economic, commercial, technological, fiscal and financial nature required to co-ordinate, complement and reinforce national legislation in the matter. It would do so in close cooperation with other United Nations specialized agencies and regional bodies concerned with particular aspects of the problem. In addition, the agency would provide technical assistance to governments of developing countries to help them in dealing with the companies. Without such an agency, concerned exclusively with multinational company problems and having the power to promote socially useful solutions, the companies will continue to hold their present license to blackmail the developing countries, to disrupt the economies of the industrial countries, to export pollution and in general to act without regard for trade union rights, the health and job security of the workers, or for the national sovereignty and economic independence of whole peoples. Such an agency would need, moreover, to be based on tripartite representation of governments, workers and employers, as is the ILO, and equipped with a similar complaints procedure.

9.   As a possible first step in that direction, the trade unions welcomed the decision of the UN Economic and Social Council to set up a Commission on Transnational Corporations, to be backed up with an Information and Research Centre. Obviously, however, that Commission will never be in a position to elaborate and apply effective social controls on the multinationals unless it finds ways and means of realistically associating the trade union movement with its work.

10.   Certain United Nations specialised agencies have for some time been studying various particular aspects of the problem: the ILO (social aspects), UNCTAD (transfer of technology and unfair business practices in developing countries). So, too, have some intergovernmental regional groupings: the six Andean Pact countries of South America have evolved a common policy regarding foreign investment; the European Economic Community has a rather timid project for a very rudimentary code of conduct which has been awaiting the approval of its Council of Ministers for about two years; while the Organisation for Economic Cooperation and Development has been studying the problem in a number of expert committees for some three years without evolving any definite proposals.

11.   In all these intergovernmental bodies, as well as in the United Nations, the ICFTU -- in cooperation with the international trade secretariats and in support of their action at the level of the various companies -- will continue to urge the early adoption of policies which can really control multinational company activities. Pending the creation of an effective international agency with trade union participation for the control of the multinationals, we believe that they should follow four lines of action: firstly to establish guidelines and machinery for effective cooperation between governments in their relations with multinational enterprises; secondly, to promote co-ordinated national legislation in the various fields where government control is needed; thirdly, to adopt international conventions imposing enforceable standards and rules on the companies; and, finally, to keep under constant review the impact of the multinationals on industrial structures and social and economic development in all countries, as well as on international trade and the international monetary system.

12.   We believe that the approach generally adopted by intergovernmental bodies -- that is towards a voluntary "code of conduct" -- is too timid and inadequate in face of the challenge posed by the activities of multinational companies. We could accept such a code only as a first step towards binding regulations set out in international conventions to which the governments can give legal force by embodying them in national legislation.

13.   An essential element of these conventions would be the establishment of tripartite committees with equal representation of governments, trade unions and employers' organizations. Infringements of the conventions, especially in regard to social standards, would be reported to these committees whose hearings would be public.

14.   The conventions would become binding upon ratification by a specified number of states. By the same conventions, the governments would be obliged to adopt common measures in such fields as employment and social policy capital movements, investment incentives, control of mergers, safeguarding of competition and taxation.

15.   Responsibility for the overall promotion and co-ordination of such international agreements would obviously be the task of the United Nations and its Economic and Social Council under which a Commission on Transnational Corporations together with an Information and Research Centre has been set up. We have welcomed the establishment of this Commission, but only as a step in the direction of an international agency with executive powers and with effective trade union participation. Progress towards the conclusion of a global international convention covering all aspects of the problems raised by the activities of multinational companies should not, however, preclude the promotion of regulations covering certain aspects of those problems by UN specialised agencies, or by regional bodies such as the OECD, the European Community or the Andean Pact. The ILO, in particular, has had the question of the social impact of multinational companies on its agenda since 1968 and the trade union movement is now awaiting some concrete proposals from that quarter.

16.   In the advance towards the international control of the activities of multinational companies, we believe a very important role could be played by the UN Information and Research Centre when it becomes operative. Its major priority task will obviously be the elaboration of a global multilateral agreement defining the areas in which binding regulations should be applied. In order to facilitate intergovernmental co-operation, another priority task for the Centre would be a close examination of different industrial sectors in order to assess the degree and pattern of domination by the multinationals; "ad hoc" working groups could be set up for particular industries. In general, the Centre's studies of the impact of multinationals should be undertaken with the effective tripartite cooperation of governments, trade unions and employers and in close liaison with the appropriate UN specialised agencies: those, for example, concerning the impact on employment and other social problems could obviously not be effectively pursued without the collaboration of the ILO.

17.   Another very important and continuing task for the Centre would be the organizing of technical assistance projects for developing countries in order to equip their governments better for dealing with the companies.

Trade union proposals for action

18.   The ICFTU and the international trade secretariats associated with it propose that the appropriate intergovernmental organizations take steps for the adoption of international conventions concerning multinational companies on the subjects listed below. The legal form and scope of such agreements are clearly matters for the agencies concerned. As for the content, in the light of trade union experience in dealing with these companies, we believe that our proposals represent the minimum of regulations required. We are ready and willing to discuss them with any intergovernmental agency which is ready to come to grips with the problem of elaborating realistic international social controls on the activities of the multinational companies.

(i) Public accountability

19.   Not only are the trade unions often hindered in their collective bargaining activities by the lack of basic financial information on the operations of the multinationals; the governments of many countries, too, need much more ample and specific data on these operations for purposes of national economic and social planning, as well as for cooperating in the international control of the companies.

20.   What is needed is legislation obliging multinational concerns to provide detailed financial accounts and other data not only for the branch in any particular country but also for the parent company. This information should accurately reflect all aspects of production development, including the worldwide breakdown of production operations, profits, cash flow, investment expenditure and projects, capital borrowing, participations, taxes, employment, wages, corporate ownership, etc.

21.   Our proposals for the substance of the legislation required in order to enforce public accountability are contained in Appendix I, to which are attached three further sub-appendices outlining a suggested model form of financial reporting to be required from the companies.

22.   In signing an international convention on legislative measures for enforcing public accountability, it is understood that the signatory states would thereby also agree to make the resultant information available to the United Nations and/or appropriate specialized agencies or intergovernmental regional organisations.

23.   It is furthermore strongly recommended that, with a view to facilitating the enforcement of those regulations, in order to ensure that the trade unions concerned have the essential information and in the general public interest, governments should appoint special auditors for checking the information supplied by the companies.

(ii) Social obligations of the companies

24.   It is clear that multinational companies are expected to comply with the social legislation of every country in which they operate. Any derogations granted by way of investment incentives are obviously socially and economically undesirable and should be expressly forbidden in the international conventions adopted in this field. Furthermore, such companies should be subject to certain additional social obligations not applicable to exclusively domestic concerns. This is not a question of discriminating against the multinationals, but rather of redressing to some extent the balance of power of the companies with their vast international ramifications, on the one hand and, on the other hand, their workers who are limited within a national context, just as indeed are the governments. This is particularly true of the developing countries, where trade unions are generally weak, while many of the governments concerned may have national budgets as little as one tenth the size of the annual turnover of some of the companies with which they have to deal.

25.   Our proposals for the content of a series of conventions laying down the social obligations incumbent upon the companies are contained in Appendix II.

(iii) Control of international direct investment and takeovers

26.   The period since the end of the second world war has been characterised so far as the international movement of capital is concerned, by an increasingly liberal "laissez-faire" attitude on the part of most governments. In the OECD area this found expression in a Code of Liberalisation of Capital Movements. In recent years this tendency has also been discernible even in the countries of centrally planned economies. Very few governments, on the other hand, took any steps to safeguard the interests of the labour force which were often jeopardised by the lack of minimum social and labour standards in many of the countries to which investments were freely flowing. This policy of liberalising capital movements provided the essential condition for the mushrooming growth of multinational companies, which undoubtedly contributed a good deal to economic development in many countries. This progress was achieved, however at the cost of a tremendous concentration of economic power in the hands of a relatively small group of industrial and financial interests, with all the obvious social and political dangers inherent in such a violent upheaval in the balance of social forces.

27.   The trade union movement believes that the time has come to call a halt to the unbridled freedom of international investment and to insist that stricter control be imposed with a view to safeguarding the economic independence and national sovereignty of all nations, as well as to ensuring that certain social obligations are attached to such operations. Controls are even more necessary when the international investment involves the takeover of an existing concern. Apart from the social considerations involved, the job security and trade union rights of the workers, for example, such operations may conflict with national economic, industrial and science policies (research workers are usually among the first victims of the rationalisation measures which frequently accompany an international takeover). The trade unions of the OECD countries have already made concrete proposals for the amendment of the OECD Code of Liberalisation in the

sense outlined above. Non-OECD countries, however, are certainly at least as much in need of protection from the effects of uncontrolled foreign economic penetration. This, in fact, is eminently a case for concerted international action:one unfortunate result of isolated national attempts to deal with the situation will be to divert multinational investment to the countries with the least controls.

28. The ICFTU and the international trade secretariats associated with it consequently submit the following elements which they believe should enter into an international convention on the control of foreign direct investment and takeovers.

(a) Prior authorisation by the competent national authorities shall be required for all inward foreign direct investment or acquisition of existing undertakings, such authorization only being granted when it is deemed to be in the national interest, after consultation with the trade union movement.

(b) As a condition for the establishment or acquisition of an undertaking the competent authorities may impose limitations in time or other conditions, reserving for example the right for public participation, with or without the further right to subsequent partial or total ownership.

(c) Authorization shall be granted only on condition that the investor agrees to comply fully with the terms of the conventions on social obligations outlined in (ii) above.

(d) In the case of acquisition of an existing undertaking, the views of the workers concerned shall be an essential factor to be taken into consideration by the competent authorities in deciding if the operation is in the national interest.

(e) As a guarantee for the fulfillment of the foregoing conditions the investor shall be required to deposit a certain sum (the amount being mutually agreed with the competent authorities in accordance with criteria to be established by international agreement), which may, in particular, be used for the compensation of the workers in the event of subsequent retrenchment or close-down.

(f) In respect of outward investment, authorization will, as in the case of inward investment, only be granted on condition the investor complies fully with the terms of the conventions or social obligations outlined in (ii) and such compliance shall furthermore be a condition for benefiting from any outward investment guarantee scheme.

(iv) Restrictive business practices and oligopolistic pricing

29. The use of economic power to dominate the market and restrict competition --in the matter not only of prices, but also of conditions for the sale or purchase of goods and services, access to patents and licenses, the physical removal of competitors either through mergers or the acquisition of control over rival enterprises and similar cartel practices -- was certainly not an invention of the multinational companies. They have been able to use such practices to vastly greater effect, however, thanks to their world-wide ramifications and thus to set up international cartels for the boosting of profits and the building of economic empires.

30.   These practices are not only socially and politically undesirable, but also economically disastrous in their long-term effects. There is no doubt that the near-monopoly control of prices administrated by many multinationals has been a major factor in the violent upsurge of inflation which by the mid '70's was rocking the world economy to its very foundations.

31.   What is also clear is that purely national legislation has in many respects proved ineffective for controlling the restrictive business practices of the big multinationals. An international convention for the suppression of these practices is urgently required. That convention would also provide the basis for the closer collaboration between the taxation and customs authorities -- at regional and world levels -- which would certainly be needed to translate the good intentions of such a convention into reality.

32.   Our proposals for the main elements of a convention on restrictive business practices and oligopolistic pricing are contained in Appendix III.

(v) Taxation of the multinationals

33.   It is common knowledge, although not always easy to prove in any particular case, that existing tax law and regulations in most countries fail to keep a grip on the slippery --if not strictly illegal -- financial practices of some multinational companies. This inadequacy is due to a number of resources and subterfuges which, by the very nature of their structure, are available only to multinational companies in their dealings with national tax authorities. These include:the ability to withhold or give insufficient information on their operations outside the national territory; the use of fictitious transfer prices, royalties, debt repayments and the division of overhead expenses between the parent company and/or its branches in various countries; the switching, thanks to the foregoing devices, of the lion's share of total profits to low-tax or tax-haven countries; and, finally, the perfectly legal, but morally indefensible, tax advantages granted as incentives to invest, particularly in developing countries.

34.   What may well be necessary in taxing multinational companies would be to take as the basis, not apparent gross profits, but the size of the investment, expenses and the turnover as criteria for arriving at a realistic estimation.

35.   We therefore propose that regional and international conventions on the principles and rules for the taxation of multinational companies be elaborated to include the elements set out in Appendix IV.

(vi) Transfer of technology and the role of multinationals in development

36.   Apologists for the multinational companies are wont to harp on the benefits by way of industrialisation they have brought, especially to the developing countries, thanks to the spread of modern technology of which they have a virtual monopoly. What is not usually mentioned is the tremendous cost this has involved, especially to developing countries which can ill afford to pay the exorbitant sums demanded as royalties and patent rights.

37.   The instrument whereby patent holders in the rich countries have established their right to exact their pound of flesh from the poor countries is the Paris Convention for the Protection of Industrial Property of 1883. This lays down the principle of temporary monopoly of production and sale to the license owner or patentee of an industrial process. Most developing countries have refused to sign this convention, but are nevertheless obliged to comply with it, faced as they are with the enormous power of the multinational license holders. They rightly regard it as an instrument of exploitation whereby they are expected to strengthen the position of foreign firms on their own territories through the payment or royalties unilaterally fixed by the companies themselves.

38.   There is no doubt that the Paris Convention, with its sanctification of technological monopoly, has been instrumental in promoting a tremendous concentration of economic power in the hands of a few powerful companies. The international trade union movement has consequently called for the drastic revision of the Paris Convention and its replacement by a system of fees to be fixed by negotiation or arbitration.

39.   Even where the transfer of technology takes place within the company itself and involves no direct charge on a developing country, this is not necessarily an unmixed blessing. It usually means that an industrial process has been foisted willy-nilly on that country without regard to its real development needs or its national planning objectives. Furthermore, it generally does little to raise the level of technological knowledge in the country, but on the contrary reinforces its economic and technological dependence on monopoly capital.

40.   We consequently recommend to the attention of the United Nations and intergovernmental regional bodies the conclusions of the Group of Twenty regarding technology in their report "The Impact of Multinational Corporations on Development and International Relations". (See Appendix V).

41.   We also recommend the common regulations evolved by the Andean Group of countries, which seek to render null and void contracts containing clauses which permit the supplier to interfere directly or indirectly in the management of the purchasing company, establish the obligation to transfer to the supplier improvements developed by the purchasing company, establish the obligation to purchase from certain suppliers only, or limit the volume of production. (See Appendix VI).

42.   We furthermore recommend, as one possible and obviously socially useful alternative to the transfer of technology by multinationals, the studies which the International Cooperative Alliance is pursuing on the possibility of joint cooperative productive investment in developing countries for the benefit of the workers and peoples concerned.

(vii) Short-term capital movements

43.   The breakdown in the early 1970's of the international monetary system set up by the Bretton Woods agreement for the stabilisation of exchange rates is one of the main factors

behind the present world economic crisis. And there is no doubt that the financial operations of multinational companies have played a big part in the collapse of that system. They were able to do this because of the huge cash flow which they controlled: by the end of 1971 multinational companies and international banks held more than twice the liquid assets of all the world's central banks and financial institutions put together. Their ability to move these vast sums round the world, switching millions at the lift of a telephone from one currency into another, was used not only for normal commercial transactions but also for purely speculative purposes directed against the principal reserve currencies -- the US dollar and the pound sterling. The successive devaluations of these currencies affected not only the two countries directly concerned, but also and perhaps even more acutely a good many developing countries which had a great part of their monetary reserves in those currencies and whose economies were ill-equipped to stand such speculative buffeting.

44.   The ICFTU believes that international agreement is essential on a new, stable monetary system and on the co-ordinated control of international capital markets in order to prevent governments losing control of their countries' economies through the actions of speculators, including multinational companies. A fuller analysis of the whole problem of the international monetary system, together with ICFTU proposals for its reform, will be found in the Congress document "Economic security and social justice:ICFTU policies 1975-78". Here we are concerned only with the special controls needed to prevent multinational companies abusing their financial power to indulge in currency speculations. Such control, would have to be applied also to other firms with international financial ramifications such as insurance companies, building societies and international banks.

45.   The ICFTU believes that the International Monetary Fund should take the initiative in preparing guide-lines to assist governments in setting up adequate reporting systems in order to identify financial transactions made by multinational enterprises. In most countries the information is already available on a daily basis through the reporting system of the banks to the national exchange authorities. Some countries, however, have no appropriate reporting systems:even those with such highly developed economies and financial structures as Canada, Germany and the USA, while in Switzerland special legislation would be needed to authorise it.

46.   In order to reinforce national reporting systems in this matter international cooperation between the appropriate national authorities would be necessary, just as we have proposed in the matter of taxation controls. Such cooperation should be more immediately feasible on a regional basis, especially where a fully structured intergovernmental regional organisation already exists. In the OECD, for example, the Trade Union Advisory Committee has submitted a proposal in this connection to the Organisation, together with a project of a questionnaire for gathering the required information (see Appendix VII).

Appendix I
MAIN DATA REQUIRED ON MULTINATIONALS

There should be ample, detailed and precise public accountability of multinationals on consolidated and subsidiary level. In addition, further information should be available to the workers and their representatives (see below, sub-headings "Information on the Future" and "Annual Social Report").

The scope of the public accountability in the form of the annual company report should be as follows:

-- The composition of principal shareholders is to be shown together with all the ramifications of the whole group, including minority participations and other financial, marketing or technical links with other companies.

-- Public reporting must cover the geographical location of all plants in the entire group with indications of the types of production, including subcontracting, in each of them and a breakdown of employment figures for individual companies and establishments.

-- The economic and financial information given should provide, at the various levels of operations and overall, the necessary elements for a clear judgement on capital structure, profitability, and ability to pay, as well as indications of capital movements within the group.

-- A clear picture is to be given of the balance sheet and the profit and loss account, both in the consolidated report and in reports for each individual company within the group.

-- The necessary data and explanations should be given to reveal clearly the company's solvency and liquidity.

-- There should be exact indications on the financial state of affairs and on all items reflecting the profit situation. The gross operating profit with its breakdown, net cash flow (depreciation, provisions and ploughed back profits), dividends, interest payments and taxes, is to be stated for the entire group and the individual subsidiaries. The consequences of these financial results for individual operating units contributing to the various financial outcomes are to be described.

-- Concrete information is to be given on the planning of future projects, overall and in various locations, with indications on short and long-term investment policies.

-- There must be a list of fundamental items which allow an appropriate comparative view covering all the various companies that make up the group structure. This list comprises:

-- Sales income (with and without turnover tax)

--   Number of units produced and share (value and/or units) of national markets and worldwide
--   Export figures
--   Rate of capacity utilization
--   Number of employees (total manual / non-manual)
--   Total wage costs
--   Raw material costs, services and general expenses
--   Value added, including income and corporation tax
--   Gross operating profit (net cash flow, interest payments, dividends and taxes)
--   Capital expenditure for plant and machinery (investment amount for fixed assets).

--   Social data and indicators must be an integral part of the public accountability of multinationals: concise information should be given on employment and wages, indicating the various component costs and actual benefits reaching the workers.
This should comprise specific data on wages and salaries by categories, statutory social contributions and contractual and other social charges with separate indications for the main social services such as pension schemes, sickness insurance, income security funds, educational training costs, etc.
Information on employment should cover total employment, worldwide, by subsidiary companies and by individual plant units. It should be further broken down into manual and non-manual workers; men and women; skilled, semi-skilled and unskilled; indigenous workers, nationals from the parent company and other foreign workers.

--   Information on employment and other relevant social data is to be given by main product groups belonging to particular industries. This industrial or major product data should include a profit and loss account, employment figures with their breakdown into categories, wage costs, production figures, in value and if possible in units, and indications of investment projects. The elements necessary to permit an assessment of productivity should be given, in particular, hours worked and the number or value of units produced.

--   Financial disclosure must embrace fundamental data that throw light upon the security of employment, both short and long-term, by indications with regard to capital expenditure for plant and machinery, net cash flow (both already mentioned as fundamental data on the company structure), long-term debts, including loans from the parent company, evolution of reserve capital and the whole net worth and, as an item of particular importance, research and development costs.

--   Financial reports should reveal any financial incentives, reimbursements, subsidies and grants from governments by information on government loans, tax rebates and fiscal exemptions as well as all other advantages which might be provided in the form of export bonuses, transport subsidies, etc.

-- All the above mentioned data should be contained in the yearly report of the multinational company as figures with explanations. There is to be full and distinct accountability of both the parent company itself and the whole consolidated group, with separate statements of the financial and economic facts. Individual reports must be produced on the subsidiary companies wherever they operate and be made internationally available.

-- The yearly reports must be issued as rapidly as possible, with a time limit on their publication of up to a maximum of three months after the end of the financial year.

-- There should be condensed half-yearly or quarterly interim statements revealing the basic facts of the employment and profit situation and indicating special features which arise in the operations of the multinationals, having some immediate bearing on employment and income security or on national economic and social policy.

-- The annual reports must be certified by a registered accountant.

Special obligations with regard to the issuing of data by multinational companies

The balance sheet

The balance sheet is to be drawn up in accordance with the following overall standards:

There is to be a distinction made between different kinds of credit and debit. Particular attention should be paid to the following points:

-- A uniform evaluation system is needed for greater clarity and ease of comparison.
-- Hidden or secret reserves are not allowed.
-- The present value of assets must be declared.
-- A distinction must be made between provision and reserves.
-- There must be accurate and up-to-date evaluation of assets and stocks.
-- A distinction must be made between the determination and the allocation of profits.

Solvency and liquidity

The balance sheet gives, together with explanations, the extent and composition of the assets at a given moment. The liquidity and solvency position can be more easily understood if the figures are set out vertically and the items arranged in order of liquidity. (See Sub-Appendix 1 - page 42)**.

_____

** Page numbers referred to in the text correspond to the relevant pagination in the original source document [Note added by the editor].

Liabilities must be shown as fully as possible in the balance sheet, otherwise the picture is incomplete.

For the same reason there is need for a statement of the origin and destination of resources from the recent past, as well as a similar budgetary statement.

In the budgetary statement will be included all investment plans, even if they have not yet reached the stage where the firm has undertaken definite liabilities. (See Sub-Appendix 2 - page 43)**.

It is also desirable that the balance sheet mentions some ratios with an explanation of their use, as for example:

--   short-term liquidity $\dfrac{\text{floating assets}}{\text{floating liabilities}}$
(current ratio):

--   solvency (debt ratio): $\dfrac{\text{external financing}}{\text{total financing}}$

Profit and loss statement

A distinction has to be made between different sorts of assets and liabilities in order to get a good idea of gross operating profit (trading results). Particular attention has to be paid to the following points:

--   Figures about profits and losses must be reported by industrial sector and by geographical establishment.

--   Sales income should be shown according to the industrial branch and capacity of the firm, while changes in sales income should be broken down by quantity and by prices. They should range over several years so as to allow comparisons. These requirements hold for the subsidiaries too.

--   Exceptional financial results and other windfalls should be distinguished from the normal gross operating profit of the firm.

--   Income and expenditure in respect of interest should be shown separately, as well as interest relating to resources outside of normal trading activities.

--   Allocations granted by public authorities, whatever their form, should be shown separately: subsidies, establishment grants, export subsidies, etc.,; grants in respect of temporary short-time working; orders placed by public authorities with a view to maintaining the level of employment.

-- Company tax should bear a normal relation to profits declared. The relation between profits and those declared for tax purposes should be explained. There is to be complete publication of the company tax paid by all the national subsidiaries of the multinational group and of the parent company itself. This is to reveal the final results obtained by every subsidiary and in this field the inter-relations among different subsidiaries and between them and the parent company.

-- There is to be a clear distinction between taxes on financial results, taxes on capital and other taxes.

-- Changes in profits or losses between the current and previous years should receive detailed comment and, in this respect, care should be taken to distinguish as far as possible between changes due to variations in volume and those due to price fluctuations.

-- All profits and losses, including extraordinary profits and losses, should figure in the statement. Direct incorporation of certain profits into the net worth should be forbidden.

-- Regarding the distribution of profits clear statements should be made with the figures necessary for comparison with preceding periods.

-- The vertical setting out of profit and loss accounts and the use of uniform terminology can facilitate the understanding of accounts and their comparison over several years. (An example is given in Sub-Appendix 3 - page 10).

-- With the help of ratios a clearer picture can be given of profitability, of levels of activity and of the reciprocal relations between the two, for example, in respect of:

   -- the rate of sales income,
   -- average periods of credit,
   -- output per labour unit (indication of value),
   -- development of labour productivity (indication of quantity),
   -- value added per employee,
   -- value added compared with wages,
   -- rate of return on investment capital,
   -- rate of return on self-financing,
   -- gross profit margins (gross profit as percentage of sales income),
   -- rate of return on certain investments,
   -- labour costs as percentage of sales income.

Information on the employment situation

Information is required on employment both on the present situation and on long and short-term plans with particular reference to: quantity (breakdown for each establishment); quality (training, age, sex, structure, etc.); regional development; development by industrial branch.

The management of the company should provide information on the effects on the employment situation of all measures planned for the immediate future.

In this connection particular attention should be paid to investment decisions, since these are taken for long periods and are difficult or impossible to influence at a later stage.

Various kinds of investment may be distinguished according to their effect on the employment situation: replacement investment; technological investment; expansion investment; diversification investment; other investment in the form of participation in other firms (e.g. portfolio investment); and disinvestment.

Indicators of the process of capital generation and capital movements

On the basis of accurate information on all data required for public accountability some indicators can be established showing the visible capital generating process at various levels of the multinational concern and capital movements within the group.

This can be dome by compiling from the parent and all its subsidiary companies the following ratios and specific financial information:

-- Net cash flow as a percentage of sales	
-- Net cash flow as a percentage of value added	Indicators of the financial returns declared by the company at various levels
-- Net profit before tax as a percentage of net worth	
-- Taxation as a percentage of net profit before tax	Indicator for management motivation to channel cash flow
-- Dividends as a percentage of gross cash flow	Indicator of the shareholders' portion of the company's income
-- Income from outside investments and other payments as a percentage of net profits before tax	Indicator of the holding function of the company or subsidiaries
-- Evolution -- total volume and index -- of net worth, i.e., shareholders' equity (share capital plus legal capital and special reserve funds)	Indicator of the capital equity growth

-- Ratio share capital: reserves	Indicator of self-earned capital accumulating or excessive movement of reserves at various levels within the group
-- Evolution -- total volume and index -- of capital employed (total fixed assets and current assets minus current liabilities)	Indicator of growth
-- Capital employed per worker	Indicator of the total long-term capital input
-- Ratio sales: capital employed	Indicator of the yearly turnover rate of the long-term capital
-- Long-term debts as a percentage of capital employed	Indicator of the structure of long-term capital at the disposal of the company
-- Loans from the parent company with indications of the rate of interest to be payed -- Loans from the parent company in relation to the dividends paid during the last 10 years	Indications of the degree of domination by the parent company
-- Payments for royalties, patents and specialised services from parent company	Indicator of some capital flow

Information on the future

The annual report contains information on the recent past. For the workers, and also for shareholders and creditors, information about the future is very important. That is why the workers or their representatives must in all cases receive the following information:

-- The directors' report must have a section dealing with the future. This should provide forecasts in increases or decreases in production, product development and market penetration.

-- Long-term reports are to be provided about the effects of existing and projected investments on profitability and production, by industrial sector and by establishment. The effects on past and future employment should be quantified.

-- Budgets should be presented for the coming year with the same break-down as for the annual report so as to allow comparison. The effects of projected output and price changes should be given separately. The difference between past and projected achievements should be analysed. The basis of calculation of the budget should also be indicated.

Annual social report

A social report at least once a year should be submitted to the workers with regard to each company and its establishments. It should comprise:

-- The company's annual profit and loss account, as published in pursuance of the above system, with specific explanations.
-- Information on economic and social trends.
-- Information on the development of the employment situation, especially with regard to the state of the order book, on main types of products, reorganisation and investment plans.
-- Information on working conditions.

Generally information must be available at the level of each company within the multinational group on:

-- Labour-management relations with special regard to trade union recognition.
-- Remuneration systems.
-- Working conditions, including:
    -- work organisation, working hours, overtime work;
    -- safety and health standards (accident rates, sickness rates, noise, pollution, the use of dangerous materials).
-- Labour policy concerning hiring, selection, evaluation, training, retraining, promotion and dismissal and especially with regard to special categories of workers.
-- Social conditions: legal, contractual and unilateral.

Balance sheet as at ....

(with comparable figures of previous balance sheet)

	Comparable figures
CURRENT ASSETS	
Cash	000
Accounts receivable (debts)	000
	+ 000
CURRENT LIABILITIES	000
(short-term debts at less than one year, except bank credit)	./.
	000
Net current assets	000
FIXED ASSETS	+ 000
	000
PROVISIONS	./. 000
	000

Financed with:		
At short-term: bank credit		000
At long-term:		
EXTERNAL CAPITAL		000
OWN CAPITAL: capital	000	
reserves	+ 000	
		000
		000

Statement of source of revenue and disbursements
during the year ....

Source of revenue

Net profit	000	
Costs which are not an outlay of funds		
-- Depreciation	000	
-- Additions to provisions	000	
Sales of fixed assets	000	
Released from inventories and accounts receivable	000	
		000
Shares issued	000	
Long-term external capital taken up	000	
Short-term external capital taken up	000	
		000
		000

A. Result in movement of funds

EMPLOYMENT OF FUNDS

Investments in fixed means of production	000	
Increase of inventories and accounts receivable	000	
Utilization of provisions	000	
Investments	000	
		000
Redemption of long-term external capital	000	
Redemption of short-term external capital	000	
		000
Distribution of profit		000

B. Total disbursements — 000

Increase/decrease current assets (A - B) — 000

Profit and loss account

	Previous period	Present period
Output		000
Cost price of output		000
Gross profit		000
Staff expenditure		000
Other working costs		000
Depreciation fixed assets		000
Additions to provisions		000
Charges on interest		000
		000
Revenue from interest		000
		000
Trading result (or gross operating profits)		000
Special income		000
Special costs		000
Taxable result		000
Taxes		000
		000

SOCIAL OBLIGATIONS OF MULTINATIONAL COMPANIES

Regarding employment and industrial relations the following obligations should be imposed on the multinational companies:

(a)   multinational companies shall follow the laws, the rules and the practices of the host country regarding the labour market **only** if these are not inferior to the standards of the International Labour Organisation in which case those of the ILO shall be followed;

(b)   multinational companies shall not offer working conditions inferior to those provided for in the United Nations Charter of Human Rights and ILO Conventions;

(c)   multinational companies shall acknowledge the genuine trade unions of the host country as well as the right of negotiation of the employees, and shall endeavour to regulate the working conditions of the employees through collective agreements. Further the multinational companies shall not hinder, but facilitate, trade union work at the local as well as international level;

(d)   multinational companies shall continuously inform the authorities and the trade unions of the home and host country regarding ongoing or planned activities for the purpose of adjusting these to the economic and social planning of both countries;

(e)   multinational companies shall in their activities use such production methods and forms of cooperation as are in harmony with the economic and social conditions of the host country, and in a longer perspective contribute to a development consistent with the host country's interests. The criteria of such production methods shall be fixed by governmental authorities having regard for the worker's aspirations.

(f)   in cooperation with the trade unions, multinational companies shall provide the necessary facilities for the promotion of the principles of industrial democracy, both at the local, as well as headquarter level;

(g)   provision shall be made for the employees' representatives of the multinational to meet at least three times a year for consultation and exchanges of views;

(h)   the operating expenses of the employees' representatives shall be met by the management of the relevant subsidiary of the multinational;

(i)   no lay-off may be carried out by a multinational (in case of "rationalisation", transfer of production, etc.), without prior arrangement of a job, equivalent in income and skill, for the employee.

(j)   multinational companies shall in cooperation with the authorities and trade unions in the host country provide ample opportunities for the employees to further their education;

(k)   multinational companies, through active manpower planning, shall provide stable employment for their employees and accept negotiated obligations for job and social security;

(l)   multinational companies shall not exercise any discrimination on racial, political or religious grounds regarding, for example, employment, wages, housing, etc.;

(m)   multinational companies operating in a developing country shall make contributions to a fund for the development of that country's social infrastructure, the amount being fixed as a percentage (to be determined by the government in consultation with the company and the trade unions concerned) of the profits made by the company in that country. The fund shall be administered by a tripartite committee representing the government, trade unions and the company.

(n)   multinational companies operating in a developing country shall pay wages and fringe benefits which give their employees a fair share of the fruits of the higher productivity resulting from their superior technology and managerial skills.

In addition the ICFTU suggests modifications to national legislation regulating the right to strike and to take industrial action when existing laws create obstacles to solidarity action by trade unions across national borders, e.g. on issues such as trade union rights, transfer of production, etc.

The ICFTU holds that the right to undertake international sympathy trade union action should be clearly and unequivocally defined by legislation. Specifically the ICFTU proposes:

(a)   that trade unions which have not the right to take sympathy measures in favour of workers in a subsidiary of a multinational company should be given such a right;

(b)   that the question of the legality of the foreign conflict shall be judged on the basis of the law of the country where the sympathy measures are taken;

(c)   even if a primary conflict is not undertaken abroad but would be legal according to the law of the country in question, it should be possible to undertake sympathy measures in any country in favour of employees abroad in case of infringement of trade union or human rights.

(d)   in countries where boycotting is not authorised, the legislation should be changed and provision made to legalise it.

Appendix III
RESTRICTIVE BUSINESS PRACTICES AND OLIGOPOLISTIC PRICING

The ICFTU will support proposals aimed at making existing instruments work effectively or improving them so as to develop inter-governmental cooperation with a view to countering the harmful effects which acquisitions, mergers and absorptions might have on competition. The United Nations' Information and Research Centre on Transnational Corporations should explore the possibilities of starting vigorous anticartel actions by reviewing the situation in various sectors where cartels or dangers of cartellisation exist and drawing up recommendations for governments.

The ICFTU proposes that legislation on restrictive business practices should be revised and reinforced in coordinated form with the aim of permitting an effective defence of the interests of employees and consumers in the continuing process of concentration of the economies; in particular the following rules should be introduced in national legislation on restrictive business practices:

(a)   Official supervision and registration shall be obligatory for all enterprises with a predominant market position resulting from a company's share of the total production in the country in question, as well as the share of total turn-over of an importing enterprise in the market concerned.

(b)   There shall be obligatory declaration and public advance examination of projected mergers and take-overs of enterprises, as well as cooperation agreements with similar effect, with a view to prohibiting them as a general rule. Mergers and take-overs shall be subject to the agreement of employees in the firms concerned. The opinion of employees shall be part of the evaluation when the examination is made by the authorities. The terms of mergers and take-overs must serve the interests of the employees, the consumers and the community as a whole.

(c)   Provision shall be made for prohibiting

    (i)   cartels and cartel agreements
    (ii)   selective sales and delivery refusal as instruments of price maintenance
    (iii)   excessive selling prices or other abusive business conditions
    (iv)   the application of different conditions to commodities of the same value, as discriminatory pricing with regard to different customers.

(d)   Effective supervision of price policies shall be instituted, especially for firms with a dominant market position.

(e)   Provision shall be made for the fixing of legal maximum prices.

(f)   Provision shall be made for inflicting penalties on firms which, with the intention of obtaining excessive advantage, deliberately limit production, sales or technical development to the prejudice of the employees and/or consumers.

Appendix IV
TAXATION OF MULTINATIONAL COMPANIES

To come to grips with problems related to the taxation of the multinational companies, the ICFTU proposes that the existing tax laws and legislative regulations of business practices be reformed and in particular:

(i)   multinational companies which deal with a tax-haven based company must prove that their transactions are genuine and are within "normal" limits;

(ii)   the practice of multinational companies deferring liability for taxes to the parent tax authorities shall be abolished;

(iii)   "tax deduction" shall replace the existing "tax credit" practices;

(iv)   effective cooperation shall be established between the tax authorities of member States, via an exchange of information that could facilitate the combating of tax evasion and abuse of double taxation conventions; transfer pricing practices, the fixing of royalties, regulations regarding the allocation of over-heads between the parent company and the subsidiaries shall especially be the subject of extended cooperation between the tax authorities in order to harmonize their approach;

(v)   the evaluation of the profit of each distinct unit of an international company shall be based on the consolidated profit of the group: taxation can then be based on each subsidiaries share of the international company's total labour force and capital;

(vi)   homogeneous and strengthened provisions shall be introduced concerning taxation on assets and capital gains with a view to preventing non-taxed funds (e.g. stocks, reserves) from proceeding to other countries in connection with a take-over or a merger between enterprises in different countries;

(vii)   taxation shall be introduced on all dividends paid by holding companies beyond national frontiers;

(viii) taxation shall be established for all payments beyond national frontiers for royalties and payments of interest on bonds issued by holding companies in tax-havens;

(ix) the recognition of remittances in respect of royalties shall be on the condition that the enterprise paying the royalties proves that there exists an objective reason for the payment consistent with commercial usage;

(x) in case of litigation between a company and the tax authority, the onus of proof shall lie with the enterprise.

Appendix V
RECOMMENDATIONS OF THE UNITED NATIONS' GROUP OF TWENTY REGARDING TECHNOLOGY[1]

(1) **The Group recommends** that before a multinational corporation is permitted to introduce a particular product into the domestic market, the host Government should carefully evaluate its suitability for meeting local needs.

(2) **The Group recommends** that the machinery for screening and handling investment proposals by multinational corporations, recommended earlier, should also be responsible for evaluating the appropriateness of the technology, and that its capacity to do so should, where advisable, be strengthened by the provision of information and advisory services by international institutions.

(3) **The Group recommends** that host countries should require multinational corporations to make a reasonable contribution towards product and process innovation, of the kind most suited to national or regional needs, and should further encourage them to undertake such research through their affiliates. These affiliates should also be permitted to export their technology to other parts of the organisation at appropriate prices.

(4) **The Group draws attention** to the work of the Economic and Social Council and UNCTAD on technology (including decision 104 [XIII] of the Trade and Development Board on exploring the possibility of establishing a code of conduct for the transfer of technology) **and recommends** that international organisations should engage in an effort to revise the patent system and to evolve an over-all regime under which the cost of technology provided by multinational corporations to developing countries could be reduced.

(5) **The Group supports** the establishment of a world patents (technology) bank to which any public institution may donate for use in developing countries patents which it owns or purchases for this purpose.

---

[1]"The Impact of Multinational Corporations on Development and International Relations", United Nations, New York (1974). [In the original text, this note appears as an asterisk]

---

(6)   **The Group recommends** that host countries should explore alternative ways of importing technology other than by foreign direct investment, and should acquire the capacity to determine which technology would best suit their needs. **It also recommends** that international agencies should help them in this task.

Appendix VI
COMMON REGULATIONS OF THE ANDEAN GROUP OF COUNTRIES GOVERNING THE IMPORTATION OF TECHNOLOGY.

The following common regulations governing the importation of technology were contained in the Cartagena Treaty adopted in 1968 by Bolivia, Chile, Colombia, Ecuador and Peru and later adhered to by Venezuela. They could well serve as guidelines for other developing countries, although further study by the United Nations Information and Research Centre might eventually add to them.

(i)   Any contract regarding the importation of technology or the use of patents and trademarks shall be reviewed and submitted to the approval of the appropriate agency of the respective member country, which shall evaluate the effective contribution of the imported technology by means of an appraisal of its possible profit generation, the price of the goods embodying technology or other specific means of measuring the effect of the imported technology.

(ii)   Contracts for importing technology shall at least contain some clauses regarding the following:

    (a)   Identification of the manner in which the technology to be imported shall be transferred;

    (b)   Contractual value for each of the elements involved in the transfer of technology expressed in a similar way as that used in the registration of foreign direct investment; and

    (c)   Determination of the time period during which the contract shall be in force.

(iii)   The member countries shall not authorise contracts for the transfer of foreign technology or use of parents containing:

    (a)   Clauses stipulating that the provision of technology carries with it an obligation on the part of the receiving country or enterprise to purchase capital goods, intermediate products, raw materials or other technologies from some given sources or to make permanent use of staff appointed by the firm supplying the technology. In exceptional cases, the receiving country may accept clauses of this nature for the purchase of capital goods, intermediate products or raw materials provided that their price falls within the levels prevailing in the international market;

(b)   Clauses stipulating that the technology-supplying firm reserves the right of establishing the sale or resale prices of the products manufactured on the basis of the respective technology;

(c)   Clauses stipulating restrictions as to the volume and structure of production;

(d)   Clauses prohibiting the use of competitive technologies;

(e)   Clauses stipulating a total or partial purchase option in favour of the supplier of technology;

(f)   Clauses committing the buyer of technology to transfer to the supplier those inventions or improvements obtained through the use of the said technology;

(g)   Clauses stipulating payment of royalties for unused patents to the holders of said patents; and

(h)   Other clauses having equivalent effects.

With the exception of special cases, duly verified by the appropriate agency of the receiving country, clauses prohibiting or in any way limiting the export of the products manufactured on the basis of the respective technology will not be accepted.

(iv)   Intangible technological contributions will have a right to payment of royalties, with the prior authorisation of the appropriate national agency, but may not be registered as capital contributions.

When these contributions are made to a foreign enterprise by its parent company or some other affiliate of the same enterprise, payment of royalties shall not be authorised nor will any deduction be accepted for this reason for tax purposes.

(v)   National authorities shall undertake a continuous and systematic identification of the technologies available in the world market for the different industrial fields, for the purpose of having at their disposal the most favourable and convenient alternative solutions for their economic conditions.

(vi)   The technology receiving country should be able to levy taxes on those products using foreign trademarks which involve payment of royalties when easily available or known technology is used in their manufacture.

(vii)   Licensing agreements for the exploitation of foreign trademarks in the technology receiving country may not contain restrictive clauses such as:

(a)   Prohibition or limitations to export or sell products manufactured under the respective trademarks or similar products in certain countries;

(b)   Obligation to use raw materials, intermediate goods or equipment supplied by the trademark holder or its affiliates. In exceptional cases, the receiving countries may accept clauses of this type provided their price is within the levels currently prevailing in the international market;

(c)   Establishment of sale or resale prices of the products manufactured under the trademark;

(d)   Obligation to pay the trademark holder royalties for unused trademarks;

(e)   Obligation to provide permanent employment to personnel provided or appointed by the trademark holder, and

(f)   Other clauses having equivalent effect.

Appendix VII
TUAC PROPOSAL FOR THE INTRODUCTION OF A REPORTING SYSTEM ON SHORT-TERM CAPITAL MOVEMENTS BY MULTINATIONAL COMPANIES.

1. Data availability

In most countries, the information exists and is generally available on a daily basis through the reporting system of the banks (and firms) to the national exchange control authorities:

(i)   Hence, the proposed reporting system at the OECD level would not directly concern the firms or add an extra reporting burden on them;

(ii)   Some countries, however, have no appropriate reporting system: especially Canada, USA and Germany on purely financial movements. A big gap is Switzerland, but its role could be crosschecked through information originating from other national authorities;

(iii)   The only condition put on the feasibility of an OECD reporting system is that it would have to protect the confidentiality of the data (bank secrecy)[*];

(iv)   The main new feature in setting up such a system is not that it would collect new information, but that it would channel it and analyse it regularly at the OECD level.

---

[*]**Bank secrecy**: The problem No 1 is the willingness of the responsible authorities to forward information to such an institution as the OECD. This information in the respective countries is protected by law and tradition on bank secrecy. Indeed, the information is with the banks collectively. Banks are obliged to communicate information to the national exchange control authorities which are fully aware of its confidential character. Therefore, the reporting system to the OECD should respect this principle; otherwise even OECD will not have the cooperation of national authorities.

2.   The reporting system should have the following characteristics:

(i)   It should be a regular and coordinated system, on a continuing basis (the other possible approach of analysing what had happened during selected past periods of heavy movements is of limited interest, except historical);

(ii)   The system should cover a rather limited number of firms (50 to 200), selected on the basis of minimum volume of turnover (and not size of capital), and operating in industry, trade and banking.

(**Note**: We reject the wider solution of monitoring all "international" firms, because three quarters of the flows originate in a limited number of firms (50 to 200) which take the most conscious and organised decisions in this matter).

(iii)   It should cover cross-border flows, i.e. the creation or destruction of assets, and liabilities between parent companies and subsidiaries or branches, subsidiaries among themselves (intra-group transactions) and movements between companies and the foreign banking system. It should include commercial transactions.

(**Note**: It would not be feasible to cover transactions outside the group, since a corporation may have thousands of foreign clients and suppliers. It is necessary to include commercial as well as financial operations because of the importance of leads and lags. Furthermore, the comprehensive approach should also cover transactions concerning long-term assets and liabilities because of their potentially volatile behaviour through prepayments).

(iv)   Only spot transactions should be recorded. There is a real information problem about the evolution of credit lines (except in Belgium and may be other countries) and forward transactions which are often done and undone in another country than the one concerned;

(v)   Only flows are to be covered and not outstanding stocks of assets and liabilities (which have no real interest for the purpose).

3. Periodicity

The information should be recorded on a continuing basis, i.e. daily, reported monthly to the OECD and analysed on a monthly or quarterly basis.

4. Conclusion

TUAC is of the opinion that it is appropriate and possible to set-up a reporting system at the OECD level. There would be no additional burden put on the firms. There would not be any need for new legal authority to gather such information (except in Switzerland). The cost would not be heavy for national exchange authorities to sort out existing information in a way useful for the purpose. In summary, it would not consist in setting up a new system, but in channelling and analysing already existing information.

Furthermore, the imbalance produced by short-term capital movements constitutes a real problem for national authorities, which endangers national economic and social objectives and policies: multinational enterprises have in this respect their own behaviour distinct from other national corporations (or corporations with only limited international connections):it stems from their very nature, i.e.:

(i)   the number of money markets to which they have direct access;
(ii)   and the number' and different types of transactions they can operate intra-group, which multiply their possibilities (multiplechoice strategies).

*
* *

Finally, for the above reasons, TUAC has submitted a questionnaire to be used in the reporting system, which it believes can be usefully considered as a basis to start the system. To make such a decision, starting the system, it is not considered by TUAC to be appropriate to convene another ad hoc working party composed of experts. What is needed is the political will on the part of the monetary authorities of the respective countries.

Project for a questionnaire to be used by national exchange control authorities and answers returned to OECD reporting system

Principles

(a)   Information on transactions to be supplied in the currency dealt with (and not in equivalent of national currency, or $, or SDR)

(b)   Transactions to be ranked in **2 categories**:

| **Inflows**   and   **Outflows** |

and such **sub categories** as
  -- export receipts
  -- borrowing abroad
  -- receipts of dividends
  -- etc.
  -- import payments
  -- payments of licences/royalties
  -- etc.

(c)   Additional information concerning the time span of certain transactions (borrowing and lending abroad, ...)

(d)   Indication of

     (i)   the foreign country;

     (ii)   the type of institution with which the transaction is concluded (two types only:intra-group foreign economic unit or foreign banking institution); and

     (iii)   the domicile of the foreign banking institution with which a foreign affiliate is banking for the particular transaction.

Appendix VIII
WORKERS' RIGHT OF PARTICIPATION IN MULTINATIONAL COMPANIES

Resolution adopted by the Executive Committee of the European Trade Union Confederation

(Brussels, 6 February 1975)

Recognising that

--all multinational companies are increasingly expanding their worldwide activities,

--important decisions in multinational companies are made centrally,

--in almost every case the decisions taken centrally in multinational companies involve the interests of the employees in the dependent companies and establishments of these concerns, which are spread over several countries,

--the employees' rights of information, which are still limited to national frontiers, are being increasingly restricted by the decision-taking procedure of multinational companies,

--in the various countries the elected employees' representatives in the enterprises and establishments of multinational companies have no duly established rights to communicate amongst themselves,

--that in only a limited number of countries company law comprises special provisions governing the relations between dominant and dependent enterprises, the Executive Committee of the European Trade Union Confederation considers it absolutely essential to create international rights of representation for employees promoting, in particular, the information and consultation of employees in multinational companies.

Since one cannot expect to find an immediate world-wide solution to this problem, the Executive Committee of the European Trade Union Confederation appeals to both the institutions of the European Community of the Nine and those of EFTA, and to the Governments of all the Member States of the European Community and of EFTA to cooperate in this question, which is of importance not only for employees, but also for the States themselves.

The ETUC makes the following demands:

I.   The legislative should ensure that, at the request of the trade unions in the enterprises of a concern and of their international organisation, an institution or body for the information and consultation of employees is created. The relevant rights of the employees shall cover, both geographically and in subject matter, the field of competence of the managements of the respective concerns.

Provision should be made for the creation of a body for the information and consultation of employees

--at head office of every multinational company located in a Member State of the European Community or EFTA,

--at the registered office of every subsidiary concern of a multinational company located in one of these States, irrespective of whether the head office of the multinational company is located in one of these States or outside Europe,

--at the head office of every concern located in one of the Member States of the European Community or EFTA if enterprises or establishments located in more than one of these States belong to the concern as dependent enterprises.

II.   The legislative should further make the following provisions:

1.   Where company law does not provide for the representation of employees at concern level, the composition of the employees' representative body referred to under I shall be stipulated in an agreement to be concluded between the management of the concern in question and the trade unions represented in the various enterprises of the concern together with their international organisations. It must be ensured that the conclusion of an agreement of this nature cannot be willfully delayed by the management of the concern in question. It must also be guaranteed that every enterprise in the concern and its important establishments are represented on the employees' representative body.

327

2.   The members of the employees' representative body shall perform their duties during working hours and enjoy at least the same rights of protection as are in force in the companies by which they have been delegated.

3.   The operating expenses of the employees' representative body shall be met by the management of the relevant concern. The members of the body must be given the opportunity of expressing themselves in their mother tongue at meetings or talks.

4.   The employees' representative body to be created must be convened at least three times a year by an elected chairman. Further meetings are to be held wherever necessary. The body can also be convened at the request of the management of the concern.

5.   The rights of the employees' representative body shall cover the regular supply of oral and written information and regular consultation on the following questions:

--past and predictable production and market development in the various fields of activity, classified by branch of production and by country, and expressed in quantitative and monetary units,

--development of production costs and productivity in the individual branches of production and countries,

-- market developments and order books,

--financial situation of subcontracting firms; cooperation with subcontracting firms,

--investments which have been effected and those planned, classified by country; rationalisation plans classified by country,

--economic and financial situation;financial structure,

--production and working methods and the introduction of new production and working methods,

--development of research projects and their cost, utilisation of patents and licences,

--employment developments and predictable employment development classified by branch of production and by country,

--working conditions and payment, classified by country,

--other proceedings involving the interests of employees or which could affect employment.

The employee's representative body must be consulted prior to decisions on the part of the management of the concern on the following questions:

--changes in the organisation of the enterprise or in the purpose of the enterprise,

--reduction or expansion of the activities of the enterprise,

--closure, limitation, or takeover of the enterprise or parts of the enterprise,

--commencement and termination of cooperation with other enterprises (amalgamations) and their predictable effects on employment and the social situation of employees,

--introduction or abolition of social institutions for all employees of the concern.

6. The management of the concern shall be legally bound to submit and elucidate the consolidated annual statement of accounts to the members of the employees' representative body.

7. The employees' representative body can decide that representatives from the trade unions represented in the enterprises of the concern and from their international organisations will participate at its meetings.

The greater the economic power of the multinational companies and international concerns becomes, the more urgent is the need for the employees of these enterprises to protect their interests irrespective of frontiers. The rights of control necessary for this purpose can only be created if an internationally composed body of employees' representatives is set up at the head office of the concern and is vested with rights of information and consultation.

The European Trade Union Confederation stresses that it considers that these employees' rights must be guaranteed by legal regulations. Since the scope of these rights is supranational, it is essential that the regulations to be created be uniform. We thus call upon the institutions of the European Community and EFTA and the Governments of all the Member States to establish as soon as possible and in responsible cooperation a common legal basis for the realisation of the above demands.

Appendix IX
ICFTU AND ICFTU-ARO ON OPERATIONS OF MULTINATIONAL COMPANIES

Declaration adopted by the Tenth ICFTU Asian Regional Conference
Kuala Lumpur, 3-6 February 1973

The operations of multinational companies where these are conducted without any national or international control and supervision insofar as they affect socio-economic policies, are a source of increasing concern. Very often the operational and other decisions of the multinational companies are not taken in the host country itself, but emanate from centres outside local jurisdiction. The Asian Regional Organisation of the ICFTU and its affiliates will give their support to any initiative taken by the ICFTU, in collaboration with the ITS to study the operations of multinational companies in some depth, with a view to the formulation of an international labour strategy to meet the challenges posed to the interests of labour by the proliferation of these giant companies, which appear to be subordinate to no national or international modes of supervision or codes of socio-economic conduct.

In the formulation of such an international labour strategy, it is crucial to ensure that the legitimate interests of Asian labour are given due consideration and are incorporated as an integral part of any such international approach.

Emphatic attention must be drawn to the fact that the criticism of the activities of multinational companies, and the serious general concern generated by their freedom from national or international restraints are also being exploited, for their own purposes, by powerful protectionist groups in some of the highly developed industrial countries of the West and in Japan. A trenchant reminder is necessary that the growth of such protectionist sentiment in the developed countries will prove seriously detrimental to the real interests of developing countries.

The international free trade union movement has always committed itself to halt and to reverse the widening development gap between the developed and developing sectors of the international community. There is the widening income gap, generated by the ever-widening technological gap, and compounded by unfair, unequal, and unjust terms of trade between the developed and developing economies. The commitment of international free labour to the imperatives of economic and social development in the Third World imposes a corresponding obligation to fight the growth of protectionist sentiments and tendencies in the advanced industrial societies of the West. This means that the strategy to be developed by international free labour, in dealing with multinational companies should not in any way inhibit the still sluggish flow of investments of industrial capital to the Third World and the concomitant spread and diffusion of technological know-how.

A survey of the recent spurt in the economies of developing countries like Indonesia, Malaysia, Singapore, Taiwan, Hongkong and South Korea, will reveal the significant role played in this regard by movements of industrial capital and technological expertise from North America, Western Europe and Japan. Any discouragement or inhibition of this flow of industrial investment capital can only serve to damage and to detract from the fundamental commitment of international free labour to narrow the development gap between the developed and developing worlds.

In the circumstances, it is vital to ensure that the international free labour movement does not allow any distortion of its perspectives in relation to the operations of multinational companies by protectionist tendencies in the developed countries. Having emphasised this, an objective study of the activities of multinational companies, not only insofar as they adversely affect the rights and interests of labour in the developing countries, but also in all other relevant aspects, is nonetheless urgent and vital.

An obvious danger posed by multinational companies to developing societies is the political risk which ensues if a single multinational company and its auxiliaries, are allowed to secure an overwhelming domination and stranglehold over the economic life of any developing country. The governments of developing countries will, therefore, be well advised to diversify, as a matter of principle and as much as possible, multinational investments in their own countries. The proverbial wisdom of not keeping all one's eggs in one basket should serve to guide the approach of governments to all foreign investments.

Trade unions in developing countries are more immediately concerned with the failure, under one pretext or another, of several multinational companies to respect basic ILO standards and conventions, and in particular the right of their employees to organised representation through bona fide trade unions. Organised labour in the developing world deserves and expects that the full strength of international public opinion in general, and of international free labour in particular, is brought to bear in order to ensure that ILO standards and conventions are strictly observed by all foreign investors in the developing countries.

Another serious complaint against multinational companies is the exploitation of cheap labour in developing countries at sweated rates of remuneration, taking advantage, as they do, of the lack of any adequate social infrastructure. Equally reprehensible, however, is the fact that the governments of developing countries themselves, in the competition between them to attract foreign investments to their own countries, aggravate such exploitation by offering the lowest possible wage costs. It is incumbent on multinational companies operating in developing countries, to make significant contributions to the progressive development of the socio-economic infrastructure.

It is recognised that it would be neither feasible nor desirable to claim that employees of multinational companies in developing countries should enjoy the higher rates of pay and standards of living prevalent in the developed industrial societies of the West. The only result of such an unrealistic approach would be to upset local wage relativities in the developing countries and to distort their economies. However, a strong case can and should be made out of the laying down of appropriate standards of remuneration and conditions of employment for employees of multinational companies in the developing countries by an international institution like the ILO. This would protect the workers against exploitation and help to eliminate the present unhealthy competition between the governments of developing countries to attract foreign capital investments.

Appendix X
ORIT POLICY ON MULTINATIONAL COMPANIES

The following conclusions and recommendations of an ICFTU/ORIT Seminar on Multinational Companies were adopted by the 8th ORIT Congress (Mexico, January 1974):

1. The Seminar ratifies and adopts on its own account the decisions taken by the ICFTU Executive Board at its meeting from 8 to 10 December 1974, those taken at the World Economic Conference held in Geneva from 24 to 26 June 1971 and those at the 10th ICFTU World Congress, held in July 1972, together with the resolutions of the ICFTU/ITS Working Party, and supports the demands put forward at the United Nations for a multilateral agreement on multinational companies with trade union participation.

2. It recommends to the ORIT Congress the setting up within the ORIT secretariat of a Committee to examine the various aspects of the adverse effects of the activities of multinational companies in our continent.

Each affiliated national trade union centre is to appoint one of its members to supply information on a continuous basis to the ORIT Committee, and is to publicise material which expresses the point of view of the labour movement in the continent on these problems.

3. The Seminar reaffirms its stoutest opposition to the economic systems in the various countries being adversely affected by the investments being made in the said countries by multinational companies, and denounces violations of freedom of association to the ILO. It calls for the setting up at the ILO of a tripartite committee to examine the pernicious effects exercised by multinationals on the national economies, on the standard of living of the working class and on working conditions. It further calls for the control of new production techniques, to ensure that they are not detrimental to the moral and physical well being of the workers, do not result in the restriction of trade unions rights, do not adversely affect conditions of employment, and comply with legislation in each country.

4. The Seminar brings to the notice of the International Labour Organisation the disagreement of the labour movement in the continent over the fact that representatives of the international free trade union movement have not been included among the members of the group of "eminent persons" which is studying the problem of multinational corporations, and it supports the attitude of the ICFTU, which has declined to state its point of view to the said group.

5. The Seminar calls upon the UN and the Organisation of American States to set up a working party to consider ways and means of keeping a check on the activities of multinational corporations, as a means of helping to secure respect for the sovereignty and integrity of the countries in the region, and to ensure that the multinationals strictly abide by the ILO Conventions in their industrial relations, and that they pay their workers a decent wage.

6. It calls upon the governments to adopt legislation governing foreign investments made by multinational corporations, so designed as to prevent the sovereignty of the Latin American States being flouted, the impoverishment of their peoples and the blocking of the road towards development. The governments must set clear-cut standards guaranteeing adequate wages and that part of the funds of multinationals are used for social welfare projects on behalf of the community, and making it compulsory for them to make reinvestments which favour development planning.

7. The Seminar denounces before public opinion in the continent the unbridled concentration of multinational capital, which is done without the governments in the various countries

exercising any effective tax legislation. This state of affairs represents a danger, when it comes to surmounting the economic backwardness afflicting our countries.

8. The Seminar calls for the mounting of a continent-wide publicity drive to denounce the negative aspects of multinationals and to exhort all the affiliated national centres to train their members in the study of these problems, and urges the ORIT and the ICFTU to conduct seminars and conferences on the challenge of multinational corporations.

9. It alerts the governments, trade unions and people of the continent to the monopolising effect of the mass media which, in the hands of these corporations, deny freedom of expression and give out tendentious information to the millions of inhabitants in our nations, thereby misrepresenting the ideology and activities of the free trade union movement and its fight for social justice, freedom and democracy.

10. The Seminar calls for co-ordinated action at the very earliest opportunity between the ICFTU and the ITS to denounce the practices of multinational corporations and to study possibilities of instituting international trade union means of bringing pressure to bear on multinationals and to reinforce the unity, ideology and action of the world labour movement.

11. It calls for ways and means of arriving at a regional agreement between our trade union organisations, progressive parties and democratic governments, with a view to initiating co-ordinated action against this type of international monopolistic practices, stemming from the concentration of capital in these economic power groups which have jeopardised the future of our peoples and the economic integration of Latin America.

12. The Seminar recommends the 8th Congress to arrange for the coordination of a large-scale campaign by ORIT-ICFTU-ITS, to call upon the International Labour Conference to adopt measures to secure adequate control of pernicious practices of this sort which distort international trade, the production of the countries, and the standards of living, education, housing and health of the workers.

13. It calls for the attainment of the maximum solidarity between the workers of Latin America and others throughout the world, as a means of fostering the aforesaid ideals. For this purpose there should be ORIT representation on the ICFTU/ITS Working Party.

14. The Seminar draws attention to the major contribution made by the ICFTU in the study of these problems and in sponsoring the Seminar Conference on Multinational Companies and in its attitude towards the trade unions in Latin America and recommends ORIT to continue with studies of this sort.

*   *   *

INTERNATIONAL CHAMBER OF COMMERCE RULES OF CONCILIATION AND ARBITRATION[*]

> The International Chamber of Commerce Rules of Conciliation and Arbitration were adopted in 1975. The New Conciliation Rules and amended Arbitration Rules reproduced in this volume have been in operation since 1 January 1988. The amended Rules of Arbitration have three appendices: Appendix I - Statutes of the Court; Appendix II - Internal Rules of the Court of Arbitration; and Appendix III - Schedule of Conciliation and Arbitration costs. The Appendices have not been reproduced in this volume.

Rules of Optional Conciliation

PREAMBLE

Settlement is a desirable solution for business disputes of an international character.

The International Chamber of Commerce therefore sets out these Rules of Optional Conciliation in order to facilitate the amicable settlement of such disputes.

Article 1

All business disputes of an international character may be submitted to conciliation by a sole conciliator appointed by the International Chamber of Commerce.

Article 2

The party requesting conciliation shall apply to the Secretariat of the International Court of Arbitration of the International Chamber of Commerce setting out succinctly the purpose of the request and accompanying it with the fee required to open the file, as set out in Appendix III hereto.

Article 3

The Secretariat of the International Court of Arbitration shall, as soon as possible, inform the other party of the request for conciliation. That party will be given a period of 15 days to inform the Secretariat whether it agrees or declines to participate in the attempt to conciliate.

---

[*]Source: International Chamber of Commerce (1993). *ICC Rules of Conciliation and Arbitration* (Paris: International Chamber of Commerce) Publication ICC No. 447-3 [Note added by the editor].

If the other party agrees to participate in the attempt to conciliate it shall so inform the Secretariat within such period.

In the absence of any reply within such period or in the case of a negative reply the request for conciliation shall be deemed to have been declined. The Secretariat shall, as soon as possible, so inform the party which had requested conciliation.

Article 4

Upon receipt of an agreement to attempt conciliation, the Secretary General of the International Court of Arbitration shall appoint a conciliator as soon as possible. The conciliator shall inform the parties of his appointment and set a time-limit for the parties to present their respective arguments to him.

Article 5

The conciliator shall conduct the conciliation process as he thinks fit, guided by the principles of impartiality, equity and justice.

With the agreement of the parties, the conciliator shall fix the place for conciliation.

The conciliator may at any time during the conciliation process request a party to submit to him such additional information as he deems necessary.

The parties may, if they so wish, be assisted by counsel of their choice.

Article 6

The confidential nature of the conciliation process shall be respected by every person who is involved in it in whatever capacity.

Article 7

The conciliation process shall come to an end:

(a)   Upon the parties signing an agreement. The parties shall be bound by such agreement. The agreement shall remain confidential unless and to the extent that its execution or application require disclosure.

(b)   Upon the production by the conciliator of a report recording that the attempt to conciliate has not been successful. Such report shall not contain reasons.

(c)   Upon notification to the conciliator by one or more parties at any time during the conciliation process of an intention no longer to pursue the conciliation process.

Article 8

Upon termination of the conciliation, the conciliator shall provide the Secretariat of the International Court of Arbitration with the settlement agreement signed by the parties or with his report of lack of success or with a notice from one or more parties of the intention no longer to pursue the conciliation process.

Article 9

Upon the file being opened, the Secretariat of the International Court of Arbitration shall fix the sum required to permit the process to proceed, taking into consideration the nature and importance of the dispute. Such sum shall be paid in equal shares by the parties.

This sum shall cover the estimated fees of the conciliator, expenses of the conciliation, and the administrative expenses as set out in Appendix III hereto.

In any case where, in the course of the conciliation process, the Secretariat of the Court shall decide that the sum originally paid is insufficient to cover the likely total costs of the conciliation, the Secretariat shall require the provision of an additional amount which shall be paid in equal shares by the parties.

Upon termination of the conciliation, the Secretariat shall settle the total costs of the process and advise the parties in writing.

All the above costs shall be borne in equal shares by the parties except and insofar as a settlement agreement provides otherwise.

A party's other expenditures shall remain the responsibility of that party.

Article 10

Unless the parties agree otherwise, a conciliator shall not act in any judicial or arbitration proceeding relating to the dispute which has been the subject of the conciliation process whether as an arbitrator, representative or counsel of a party.

The parties mutually undertake not to call the conciliator as a witness in any such proceedings, unless otherwise agreed between them.

Article 11

The parties agree not to introduce in any judicial or arbitration proceeding as evidence or in any manner whatsoever:

(a)   any views expressed or suggestions made by any party with regard to the possible settlement of the dispute;

(b)   any proposals put forward by the conciliator;

(c)   the fact that a party had indicated that it was ready to accept some proposal for a settlement put forward by the conciliator.

Rules of Arbitration

Article 1
International Court of Arbitration

1.   The International Court of Arbitration of the International Chamber of Commerce is the arbitration body attached to the International Chamber of Commerce. Members of the Court are appointed by the Council of the International Chamber of Commerce. The function of the Court is to provide for the settlement by arbitration of business disputes of an international character in accordance with these Rules.

2.   In principle, the Court meets once a month. It draws up its own internal regulations.

3.   The Chairman of the International Court of Arbitration or his deputy shall have power to take urgent decisions on behalf of the Court, provided that any such decision shall be reported to the Court at its next session.

4.   The Court may, in the manner provided for in its internal regulations, delegate to one or more groups of its members the power to take certain decisions provided that any such decision shall be reported to the Court at its next session.

5.   The Secretariat of the International Court of Arbitration shall be at the Headquarters of the International Chamber of Commerce.

Article 2
The arbitral tribunal

1.   The International Court of Arbitration does not itself settle disputes. Insofar as the parties shall not have provided otherwise, it appoints, or confirms the appointments of, arbitrators in accordance with the provisions of this Article. In making or confirming such appointment, the Court shall have regard to the proposed arbitrator's nationality, residence and other relationships with the countries of which the parties or the other arbitrators are nationals.

2.   The disputes may be settled by a sole arbitrator or by three arbitrators. In the following Articles the word "arbitrator" denotes a single arbitrator or three arbitrators as the case may be.

3.   Where the parties have agreed that the disputes shall be settled by a sole arbitrator, they may, by agreement, nominate him for confirmation by the Court. If the parties fail so to nominate a sole arbitrator within 30 days from the date when the Claimant's Request for

Arbitration has been communicated to the other party, the sole arbitrator shall be appointed by the Court.

4.   Where the dispute is to be referred to three arbitrators, each party shall nominate in the Request for Arbitration and the Answer thereto respectively one arbitrator for confirmation by the Court. Such person shall be independent of the party nominating him. If a party fails to nominate an arbitrator, the appointment shall be made by the Court.

The third arbitrator, who will act as chairman of the arbitral tribunal, shall be appointed by the Court, unless the parties have provided that the arbitrators nominated by them shall agree on the third arbitrator within a fixed time-limit. In such a case the Court shall confirm the appointment of such third arbitrator. Should the two arbitrators fail, within the time-limit fixed by the parties or the Court, to reach agreement on the third arbitrator, he shall be appointed by the Court.

5.   Where the parties have not agreed upon the number of arbitrators, the Court shall appoint a sole arbitrator, save where it appears to the Court that the dispute is such as to warrant the appointment of three arbitrators. In such a case the parties shall each have a period of 30 days within which to nominate an arbitrator.

6.   Where the Court is to appoint a sole arbitrator or the chairman of an arbitral tribunal, it shall make the appointment after having requested a proposal from a National Committee of the ICC that it considers to be appropriate. If the Court does not accept the proposal made, or if said National Committee fails to make the proposal requested within the time-limit fixed by the Court, the Court may repeat its request or may request a proposal from another appropriate National Committee.

Where the Court considers that the circumstances so demand, it may choose the sole arbitrator or the chairman of the arbitral tribunal from a country where there is no National Committee, provided that neither of the parties objects within the time-limit fixed by the Court.

The sole arbitrator or the chairman of the arbitral tribunal shall be chosen from a country other than those of which the parties are nationals. However, in suitable circumstances and provided that neither of the parties objects within the time-limit fixed by the Court, the sole arbitrator or the chairman of the arbitral tribunal may be chosen from a country of which any of the parties is a national.

Where the Court is to appoint an arbitrator on behalf of a party which has failed to nominate one, it shall make the appointment after having requested a proposal from the National Committee of the country of which the said party is a national. If the Court does not accept the proposal made, or if said National Committee fails to make the proposal requested within the time-limit fixed by the Court, or if the country of which the said party is a national has no National Committee, the Court shall be at liberty to choose any person whom it regards as suitable, after having informed the National Committee of the country of which such person is a national, if one exists.

7.   Every arbitrator appointed or confirmed by the Court must be and remain independent of the parties involved in the arbitration.

Before appointment or confirmation by the Court, a prospective arbitrator shall disclose in writing to the Secretary General of the Court any facts or circumstances which might be of such a nature as to call into question the arbitrator's independence in the eyes of the parties. Upon receipt of such information, the Secretary General of the Court shall provide it to the parties in writing and fix a time-limit for any comments from them.

An arbitrator shall immediately disclose in writing to the Secretary General of the Court and the parties any facts or circumstances of a similar nature which may arise between the arbitrator's appointment or confirmation by the Court and the notification of the final award.

8.   A challenge of an arbitrator, whether for an alleged lack of independence or otherwise, is made by the submission to the Secretary General of the Court of a written statement specifying the facts and circumstances on which the challenge is based.

For a challenge to be admissible, it must be sent by a party either within 30 days from receipt by that party of the notification of the appointment or confirmation of the arbitrator by the Court; or within 30 days from the date when the party making the challenge was informed of the facts and circumstances on which the challenge is based, if such date is subsequent to the receipt of the aforementioned notification.

9.   The Court shall decide on the admissibility, and at the same time if need be on the merits, of a challenge after the Secretary General of the Court has accorded an opportunity for the arbitrator concerned, the parties and any other members of the arbitral tribunal to comment in writing within a suitable period of time.

10.   An arbitrator shall be replaced upon his death, upon the acceptance by the Court of a challenge, or upon the acceptance by the Court of the arbitrator's resignation.

11.   An arbitrator shall also be replaced when the Court decides that he is prevented *de jure* or *de facto* from fulfilling his functions, or that he is not fulfilling his functions in accordance with the Rules or within the prescribed time-limits.

When, on the basis of information that has come to its attention, the Court considers applying the preceding subparagraph, it shall decide on the matter after the Secretary General of the Court has provided such information in writing to the arbitrator concerned, the parties and any other members of the arbitral tribunal, and accorded an opportunity to them to comment in writing within a suitable period of time.

12.   In each instance where an arbitrator is to replaced, the procedure indicated in the preceding paragraphs 3, 4, 5 and 6 shall be followed. Once reconstituted, and after having invited the parties to comment, the arbitral tribunal shall determine if and to what extent prior proceedings shall again take place.

13.   Decisions of the Court as to the appointment, confirmation, challenge or replacement of an arbitrator shall be final.

The reasons for decisions by the Court as to the appointment, confirmation, challenge, or replacement of an arbitrator on the grounds that he is not fulfilling his functions in accordance with the Rules or within the prescribed time-limits, shall not be communicated.

Article 3
Request for Arbitration

1.   A party wishing to have recourse to arbitration by the International Chamber of Commerce shall submit its Request for Arbitration to the Secretariat of the International Court of Arbitration, through its National Committee or directly. In this latter case the Secretariat shall bring the Request to the notice of the National Committee concerned.

The date when the Request is received by the Secretariat of the Court shall, for all purposes, be deemed to be the date of commencement of the arbitral proceedings.

2.   The Request for arbitration shall *inter alia* contain the following information:

      a)   names in full, description, and addresses of the parties,

      b)   a statement of the Claimant's case,

      c)   the relevant agreements, and in particular the agreement to arbitrate, and such documentation or information as will serve clearly to establish the circumstances of the case,

      d)   all relevant particulars concerning the number of arbitrators and their choice in accordance with the provisions of Article 2 above.

3.   The Secretariat shall send a copy of the Request and the documents annexed thereto to the Defendant for his Answer.

Article 4
Answer to the Request

1.   The Defendant shall within 30 days from the receipt of the documents referred to in paragraph 3 of Article 3 comment on the proposals made concerning the number of arbitrators and their choice and, where appropriate, nominate an arbitrator. He shall at the same time set out his defence and supply relevant documents. In exceptional circumstances the Defendant may apply to the Secretariat for an extension of time for the filing of his defence and his documents. The application must, however, include the Defendant's comments on the proposals made with regard to the number of arbitrators and their choice and also, where appropriate, the nomination of an arbitrator. If the Defendant fails so to do, the Secretariat shall report to the International Court of Arbitration, which shall proceed with the arbitration in accordance with these Rules.

2.   A copy of the Answer and of the documents annexed thereto, if any, shall be communicated to the Claimant for his information.

Article 5
Counter-claim

1.   If the Defendant wishes to make a counter-claim, he shall file the same with the Secretariat, at the same time as his Answer as provided for in Article 4.

2.   It shall be open to the Claimant to file a Reply with the Secretariat within 30 days from the date when the counter-claim was communicated to him.

Article 6
Pleadings and written statements, notifications or communications

1.   All pleadings and written statements submitted by the parties, as well as all documents annexed thereto, shall be supplied in a number of copies sufficient to provide one copy for each party, plus one for each arbitrator, and one for the Secretariat.

2.   All notifications or communications from the Secretariat and the arbitrator shall be validly made if they are delivered against receipt or forwarded by registered post to the address or last known address of the party for whom the same are intended as notified by the party in question or by the other party as appropriate.

3.   Notification or communication shall be deemed to have been effected on the day when it was received, or should, if made in accordance with the preceding paragraph, have been received by the party itself or by its representative.

4.   Periods of time specified in the present Rules or in the Internal Rules or set by the International Court of Arbitration pursuant to its authority under any of these Rules shall start to run on the day following the date a notification or communication is deemed to have been effected in accordance with the preceding paragraph.   When, in the country where the notification or communication is deemed to have been effected, the day next following such date is an official holiday or a non-business day, the period of time shall commence on the first following working day.   Official holidays and non-working days are included in the calculation of the period of time.   If the last day of the relevant period of time granted is an official holiday or a non-business day in the country where the notification or communication is deemed to have been effected, the period of time shall expire at the end of the first following working day.

Article 7
Absence of agreement to arbitrate

Where there is no *prima facie* agreement between the parties to arbitrate or where there is an agreement but it does not specify the International Chamber of Commerce, and if the Defendant does not file an Answer within the period of 30 days provided by paragraph 1 of

Article 4 or refuses arbitration by the International Chamber of Commerce, the Claimant shall be informed that the arbitration cannot proceed.

Article 8
Effect of the agreement to arbitrate

1.   Where the parties have agreed to submit to arbitration by the International Chamber of Commerce, they shall be deemed thereby to have submitted *ipso facto* to the present Rules.

2.   If one of the parties refuses or fails to take part in the arbitration, the arbitration shall proceed notwithstanding such refusal or failure.

3.   Should one of the parties raise one or more pleas concerning the existence or validity of the agreement to arbitrate, and should the International Court of Arbitration be satisfied of the *prima facie* existence of such an agreement, the Court may, without prejudice to the admissibility or merits of the plea or pleas, decide that the arbitration shall proceed. In such a case any decision as to the arbitrator's jurisdiction shall be taken by the arbitrator himself.

4.   Unless otherwise provided, the arbitrator shall not cease to have jurisdiction by reason of any claim that the contract is null and void or allegation that it is inexistent provided that he upholds the validity of the agreement to arbitrate. He shall continue to have jurisdiction, even though the contract itself may be inexistent or null and void, to determine the respective rights of the parties and to adjudicate upon their claims and pleas.

5.   Before the file is transmitted to the arbitrator, and in exceptional circumstances even thereafter, the parties shall be at liberty to apply to any competent judicial authority for interim or conservatory measures, and they shall not by so doing be held to infringe the agreement to arbitrate or to affect the relevant powers reserved to the arbitrator.

Any such application and any measures taken by the judicial authority must be notified without delay to the Secretariat of the International Court of Arbitration. The Secretariat shall inform the arbitrator thereof.

Article 9
Advance to cover costs of arbitration

1.   The International Court of Arbitration shall fix the amount of the advance on costs in a sum likely to cover the costs of arbitration of the claims which have been referred to it.

Where, apart from the principal claim, one or more counter-claims are submitted, the Court may fix separate advances on costs for the principal claim and the counter-claim or counter-claims.

2.   The advance on costs shall be payable in equal shares by the Claimant or Claimants and the Defendant or Defendants. However, any one party shall be free to pay the whole of the

advance on costs in respect of the claim or the counter-claim should the other party fail to pay its share.

3.   The Secretariat may make the transmission of the file to the arbitrator conditional upon the payment by the parties or one of them of the whole or part of the advance on costs to the International Chamber of Commerce.

4.   When the Terms of Reference are communicated to the Court in accordance with the provisions of Article 13, the Court shall verify whether the requests for the advance on costs have been complied with.

The Terms of Reference shall only become operative and the arbitrator shall only proceed in respect of those claims for which the advance on costs has been duly paid to the International Chamber of Commerce.

Article 10
Transmission of the file to the arbitrator

Subject to the provisions of Article 9, the Secretariat shall transmit the file to the arbitrator as soon as it has received the Defendant's Answer to the Request for Arbitration, at the latest upon the expiry of the time-limits fixed in Articles 4 and 5 above for the filing of these documents.

Article 11
Rules governing the proceedings

The rules governing the proceedings before the arbitrator shall be those resulting from these Rules and, where these Rules are silent, any rules which the parties (or, failing them, the arbitrator) may settle, and whether or not reference is thereby made to a municipal procedural law to be applied to arbitration.

Article 12
Place of arbitration

The place of arbitration shall be fixed by the International Court of Arbitration, unless agreed upon by the parties.

Article 13
Terms of Reference

1.   Before proceeding with the preparation of the case, the arbitrator shall draw up, on the basis of the documents or in the presence of the parties and in the light of their most recent submissions, a document defining his Terms of Reference. This document shall include the following particulars:

a)   the full names and description of the parties,

b)   the addresses of the parties to which notifications or communications arising in the course of the arbitration may validly be made,

c)   a summary of the parties' respective claims,

d)   definition of the issues to be determined,

e)   the arbitrator's full name, description and address,

f)   the place of arbitration,

g)   particulars of the applicable procedural rules and, if such is the case, reference to the power conferred upon the arbitrator to act as amiable compositeur,

h)   such other particulars as may be required to make the arbitral award enforceable in law, or may be regarded as helpful by the International Court of Arbitration or the arbitrator.

2.   The document mentioned in paragraph 1 of this Article shall be signed by the parties and the arbitrator. Within two months of the date when the file has been transmitted to him, the arbitrator shall transmit to the Court the said document signed by himself and by the parties. The Court may, pursuant to a reasoned request from the arbitrator or if need be on its own initiative, extend this time-limit if it decides it is necessary to do so.

Should one of the parties refuse to take part in the drawing up of the said document or to sign the same, the Court, if it is satisfied that the case is one of those mentioned in paragraphs 2 and 3 of Article 8, shall take such action as is necessary for its approval. Thereafter the Court shall set a time-limit for the signature of the statement by the defaulting party and on expiry of that time-limit the arbitration shall proceed and the award shall be made.

3.   The parties shall be free to determine the law to be applied by the arbitrator to the merits of the dispute. In the absence of any indication by the parties as to the applicable law, the arbitrator shall apply the law designated as the proper law by the rule of conflict which he deems appropriate.

4.   The arbitrator shall assume the powers of an amiable compositeur if the parties are agreed to give him such powers.

5.   In all cases the arbitrator shall take account of the provisions of the contract and the relevant trade usages.

Article 14
The arbitral proceedings

1.   The arbitrator shall proceed within as short a time as possible to establish the facts of the case by all appropriate means. After study of the written submissions of the parties and of all documents relied upon, the arbitrator shall hear the parties together in person if one of them so requests; and failing such a request he may of his own motion decide to hear them.

In addition, the arbitrator may decide to hear any other person in the presence of the parties or in their absence provided they have been duly summoned.

2.   The arbitrator may appoint one or more experts, define their Terms of Reference, receive their reports and/or hear them in person.

3.   The arbitrator may decide the case on the relevant documents alone if the parties so request or agree.

Article 15

1.   At the request of one of the parties or if necessary on his own initiative, the arbitrator, giving reasonable notice, shall summon the parties to appear before him on the day and at the place appointed by him and shall so inform the Secretariat of the International Court of Arbitration.

2.   If one of the parties, although duly summoned, fails to appear, the arbitrator, if he is satisfied that the summons was duly received and the party is absent without valid excuse, shall have power to proceed with the arbitration, and such proceedings shall be deemed to have been conducted in the presence of all parties.

3.   The arbitrator shall determine the language or languages of the arbitration, due regard being paid to all the relevant circumstances and in particular to the language of the contract.

4.   The arbitrator shall be in full charge of the hearings, at which all the parties shall be entitled to be present. Save with the approval of the arbitrator and of the parties, persons not involved in the proceedings shall not be admitted.

5.   The parties may appear in person or through duly accredited agents. In addition, they may be assisted by advisers.

Article 16

The parties may make new claims or counter-claims before the arbitrator on condition that these remain within the limits fixed by the Terms of Reference provided for in Article 13 or that they are specified in a rider to that document, signed by the parties and communicated to the International Court of Arbitration.

Article 17
Award by consent

If the parties reach a settlement after the file has been transmitted to the arbitrator in accordance with Article 10, the same shall be recorded in the form of an arbitral award made by consent of the parties.

Article 18
Time-limit for award

1. The time-limit within which the arbitrator must render his award is fixed at six months. Once the terms of Article 9(4) have been satisfied, such time-limit shall start to run from the date of the last signature by the arbitrator or of the parties of the document mentioned in Article 13, or from the expiry of the time-limit granted to a party by virtue of Article 13(2), or from the date that the Secretary General of the International Court of Arbitration notifies the arbitrator that the advance on costs is paid in full, if such notification occurs later.

2. The Court may, pursuant to a reasoned request from the arbitrator or if need be on its own initiative, extend this time-limit if it decides it is necessary to do so.

3. Where no such extension is granted and, if appropriate, after application of the provisions of Article 2(11), the Court shall determine the manner in which the dispute is to be resolved.

Article 19
Award by three arbitrators

When three arbitrators have been appointed, the award is given by a majority decision. If there be no majority, the award shall be made by the Chairman of the arbitral tribunal alone.

Article 20
Decision as to costs of arbitration

1. The arbitrator's award shall, in addition to dealing with the merits of the case, fix the costs of the arbitration and decide which of the parties shall bear the costs or in what proportions the costs shall be borne by the parties.

2. The costs of the arbitration shall include the arbitrator's fees and the administrative costs fixed by the International Court of Arbitration in accordance with the scale annexed to the present Rules, the expenses, if any, of the arbitrator, the fees and expenses of any experts, and the normal legal costs incurred by the parties.

3. The Court may fix the arbitrator's fees at a figure higher or lower than that which would result from the application of the annexed scale if in the exceptional circumstances of the case this appears to be necessary.

Article 21
Scrutiny of award by the Court

Before signing an award, whether partial or definitive, the arbitrator shall submit it in draft form to the International Court of Arbitration. The Court may lay down modifications as to the form of the award and, without affecting the arbitrator's liberty of decision, may also draw his attention to points of substance. No award shall be signed until it has been approved by the Court as to its form.

Article 22
Making of award

The arbitral award shall be deemed to be made at the place of the arbitration proceedings and on the date when it is signed by the arbitrator.

Article 23
Notification of award to parties

1.   Once an award has been made, the Secretariat shall notify to the parties the text signed by the arbitrator; provided always that the costs of the arbitration have been fully paid to the International Chamber of Commerce by the parties or by one of them.

2.   Additional copies certified true by the Secretary General of the International Court of Arbitration shall be made available, on request and at any time, to the parties but to no one else.

3.   By virtue of the notification made in accordance with paragraph 1 of this article, the parties waive any other form of notification or deposit on the part of the arbitrator.

Article 24
Finality and enforceability of award

1.   The arbitral award shall be final.

2.   By submitting the dispute to arbitration by the International Chamber of Commerce, the parties shall be deemed to have undertaken to carry out the resulting award without delay and to have waived their right to any form of appeal insofar as such waiver can validly be made.

Article 25
Deposit of award

An original of each award made in accordance with the present Rules shall be deposited with the Secretariat of the International Court of Arbitration.

The arbitrator and the Secretariat of the Court shall assist the parties in complying with whatever further formalities may be necessary.

Article 26
General rule

In all matters not expressly provided for in these Rules, the International Court of Arbitration and the arbitrator shall act in the spirit of these Rules and shall make every effort to make sure that the award is enforceable at law.

* * *

INTERNATIONAL CHAMBER OF COMMERCE RECOMMENDATIONS TO COMBAT EXTORTION AND BRIBERY IN BUSINESS TRANSACTIONS*

The Recommendations to Combat Extortion and Bribery in Business Transactions were prepared by an ad hoc Commission of the International Chamber of Commerce. The Commission presented its report to the International Chamber of Commerce Council in November 1977. After further negotiations, the Council adopted the Code on 2 December 1977.

Part I
Foreword

International debate has focused recently on extortion and bribery in business transactions. This has spurred many governments, as well as the United Nations, to consider ways and means of combating such practices more vigorously than heretofore, by both national and international action. Simultaneously, the international business community has given high priority to the consideration of the issues involved, and to action required to solve them.

With this in mind, the ICC set up in December 1975 and *ad hoc* Commission, under the chairmanship of Lord Shawcross (United Kingdom), composed of personalities from both developed and developing countries, having held or holding high positions in business or in government. The Commission investigated the extent to which individual countries have enacted legislation to prohibit extortion and bribery. The results of this survey have clearly shown that while such laws exist in most countries, the effectiveness of their enforcement varies considerably.

In some countries, corruption does not appear to constitute a fundamental problem in business or political life. That is not to say that corruption does not occur; but the authorities are vigilant to detect it, it is regarded with grave social disapprobation and, when detected, it is severely punished. In other countries, corruption appears to be almost so common as to have been accepted as away of life which the national authorities seem unable or lack the political will to overcome.

Public opinion has sometimes tended to assume that corruption is generally initiated by enterprises. This is not so, and it ignores the often subtle but effective pressure by recipients of bribes or agents acting on their behalf.

The truth is that much bribery is in fact the response to extortion. Enterprises have too

---

*Source: International Chamber of Commerce (1977). *Rules of Conduct on Extortion and Bribery in Business Transactions*, ICC Doc. 192/44 (Paris: ICC). The Code is also reproduced in *International Legal Materials* (1978), vol. 17, pp. 417-421 [Note added by the editor].

often had the experience, in many countries, of having to choose between giving in to extortion or not doing business. At the least, it is true to say that there would be no bribes if there were no willing and often demanding receivers.

What then is the solution? Neither governments nor business can alone deal effectively with this problem. Therefore, complementary and mutually reinforcing action by both governments and the business community is essential. This action should be on the following lines:

a) By governments:

All governments should enact stringent and, as far as possible, comparable laws, where they do not already exist, prohibiting and punishing all forms of corruption, whether commercial or political. But this alone is not enough. There must be both the political will and the administrative machinery to enforce such laws. And it may be that in some cases these will only be established by means of intergovernmental agreement as to their necessity, as well as by the exposure of countries which fail to live up to the proper standards. Therefore, the ICC presents in Part II of this Report a set of recommendations for action to be taken by individual governments and as to matters to be included in the intergovernmental treaty on corruption which is currently being drafted under the aegis of the United Nations.

b) By the business community:

The ICC considers that the international business community has a corresponding responsibility to make its own contribution toward the effective elimination of extortion and bribery.

In this connection, it should be stressed that the promotion of self-regulation in international trade has always been one of the major objectives of the ICC, as reflected over the years in the publication of its Codes of Fair Practices in Marketing, its Guidelines for International Investment, and its Environmental Guidelines for Industry. Therefore, the ICC presents in Part III of this Report Rules of Conduct to Combat Extortion and Bribery. The by-laws of the Panel to be set up within the ICC to interpret, promote and oversee the application of the Rules of Conduct will be adopted by the Council of the ICC in June 1978.

The ICC is confident that the provisions of these Rules of Conduct, which, taken as a whole, are more stringent than those which the law imposes in many countries, will be widely adopted on a voluntary basis by enterprises of all sizes and in all countries, irrespective of their stage of economic development.

Part II
Recommendations to Governments

I.   Affirmation by Governments of their commitment against extortion and bribery

Basic criminal statutes of most countries clearly prohibit extortion and bribery. In the interest of gradual harmonization of standards of criminal legislation in this field, each government should review its statutes to ensure that they effectively prohibit, within its territorial jurisdiction, all aspects of both the giving and the taking of bribes, including promises and solicitation of bribes, as well as so-called facilitating payments to expedite the performance of functions which governmental officials have a duty to perform. Where no such legislation exists, the governments concerned should introduce it; in those countries where corruption is already clearly prohibited, the relevant legislation should be perfected.

Each national government should affirm its commitment to enforce vigorously its legislation in this area.

The ICC recommends that an international treaty be drawn up as a matter of urgency under the aegis of the United Nations so as to induce the various governments to take the necessary measures and to promote cooperation between governments which would facilitate the elimination of corruption. Bodies such as the ICC which have consultative status with the United Nations should be requested to give their views on the content of such a treaty.

Such a treaty should provide for:

a)   the implementation of the governmental measures recommended below;
b)   international cooperation and judicial assistance in dealing with extortion and bribery;
c)   cooperation by all States in the investigation and prosecution of offenders; to this effect, appropriate provisions should be included in all existing or future extradition treaties.

II.   National measures

In order to deal with the problem of extortion and bribery, governments should, within the limits of their territorial jurisdiction, take the following measures, if they have not already done so.

A.   Preventive Measures

1.   Disclosure procedures

a)   For the sake of transparency and within the limits defined in national legislation, such procedures should provide for periodic reports to an authorized government body of measures taken by governments to supervise government officials involved directly or indirectly in commercial transactions.

b) For enterprises engaged in transactions with any government or with any enterprise owned or controlled by government, disclosure procedures should provide for access, upon specific request, by the appropriate government authorities to information as to agents dealing directly with public bodies or officials and as to the payments to which such agents are entitled.

2. Economic regulations

When laying down any economic regulations or legislation, Governments should, as far as possible, avoid the introduction of systems under which the carrying out of business requires the issue of individual authorizations, permits, etc. Experience shows that, in contrast with a legal framework within which business can operate freely, such systems offer scope for extortion and bribery, since the conclusion of business deals then often depends on decisions taken at a level at which it is almost impossible to ensure effective control and supervision.

3. Transactions with governments and inter-governmental organizations

Such transactions should be subject to special safeguards to minimize the opportunities for their being influenced by extortion or bribery. the system for awarding government contracts might include disclosure, to an appropriate government entity independent of the one directly concerned in the transaction, of the criteria and conclusions upon which the award is based. The ICC supports the growing practice of making government contracts dependent on undertakings to refrain from bribery, and recommends that such contracts should include appropriate provisions to ensure compliance with international, national or enterprise codes against extortion and bribery.

4. Political contributions

The ICC recognizes that political contributions are usually legitimate and proper. However, undisclosed political contributions may on occasion serve as a vehicle for extortion and bribery. Therefore, where payments by enterprises to political parties, political committees or individual politicians are permitted by the applicable national legislation, governments should consider, having regard to all the circumstances prevailing within each country, enacting legislation which ensures that such payments are publicly recorded by the payors and accounted for by the recipients.

B. Enforcement Measures

Governments should ensure that adequate machinery exists for surveillance and investigation, and should ensure the prosecution with appropriate penalties, of those who, within their territorial jurisdiction, offer, give, demand, solicit or receive bribes in violation of their laws. Governments should periodically publish statistical or other information in respect of such prosecutions.

C.   Auditing

Governments, if they have not already done so, should consider the enactment of appropriate legislation providing for auditing by independent professional auditors of the accounts of enterprises which are economically significant.

III.   International Cooperation and Judicial Assistance

Pending the establishment of a multilateral treaty under the aegis of the United Nations as recommended under Section I above, States should agree, under appropriate provisions for confidentiality, to exchange through law enforcement agencies relevant and material information for the purpose of criminal investigation and prosecution of cases of extortion and bribery. They should also continue to cooperate bilaterally on matters involving extortion and bribery.

PART III
Rules of Conduct to Combat Extortion and Bribery

INTRODUCTION

These Rules of Conduct are intended as a method of self-regulation. Their voluntary acceptance by business enterprises will not only promote high standards of integrity in business transactions, whether between enterprises and public bodies or between enterprises themselves, but will also form a valuable defensive protection to those enterprises which are subjected to attempts at extortion.

Thus, such enterprises will be able to draw attention to the existence of the ICC Panel, the functions of which are outlined in Article 11 hereafter.

The ICC is only too well aware that extortion and bribery cannot be eliminated by a stroke of the pen overnight. Much of the evil, particularly in cases involving minor amounts, is the result of social conditions which may take time to ameliorate. This is also the case with so-called facilitating payments, usually in regard to documentation, dock or customs clearances and similar matters, where minor officials in many countries habitually demand payments to supplement often inadequate salaries. The remedy for this state of affairs lies primarily in the hands of governments and, since the greater threat to competition comes from extortion and bribery relating to business transactions, it is not the present intention that the Panel should concern itself with particular instances of facilitating payments.

For the rest it is the hope of the ICC that all business enterprises, whether international or domestic, will faithfully follow the spirit of the Rules of Conduct.

These Rules of Conduct are of a general nature constituting what is considered good commercial practice in the matters to which they relate but without direct legal effect. They do not derogate from applicable local laws, and since national legal systems are by no means uniform, they must be read *mutatis mutandis* subject to such systems.

BASIC PRINCIPLE

All enterprises should conform to the relevant laws and regulations of the countries in which they are established and in which they operate, and should observe both the letter and the spirit of these Rules of Conduct.

For the purposes of these Rules of Conduct, the term "enterprise" refers to any person or entity engaged in business, whether or not organised for profit, including any entity controlled by a State or a territorial subdivision thereof; it includes, where the context so indicates, a parent or subsidiary.

BASIC RULES

Article 1
Extortion

No one may demand or accept a bribe.

Article 2
Bribery

No enterprise may, directly or indirectly, offer or give a bribe in order to obtain or retain business, and any demand for such a bribe must be rejected.

Article 3
"Kickbacks"

Enterprises should take measures reasonably within their power to ensure that no part of any payment made by them in connection with any commercial transaction is paid back to their employees or to any other person not legally entitled to the same.

Article 4
Agents

Enterprises should take measures reasonably within their power to ensure:

a) that any payment made to any agent represents no more than an appropriate remuneration for the services rendered by him; and

b) that no part of any such payment is passed on by the agent as a bribe or otherwise in contravention of these Rules of Conduct.

Article 5
Financial Recording

1.   All financial transactions must be properly and fairly recorded in appropriate books of account available for inspection by boards and auditors.

2.   There must be no "off the books" or secret accounts, nor may any documents be issued which do not properly and fairly record the transactions to which they relate.

GUIDELINES FOR IMPLEMENTATION

Article 6
Responsibilities of Enterprises

The body or individual which or who under the applicable law has the ultimate responsibility for the enterprises with which it or he is concerned should:

(a)   take reasonable steps, including the establishment and maintenance of proper systems of control, to prevent any payments being made by or on behalf of the enterprise which contravene these Rules of Conduct.

(b)   periodically review compliance with these Rules of Conduct and establish procedures for obtaining appropriate reports for the purposes of such review.

(c)   take appropriate action against any director or employee contravening these Rules of Conduct.

Article 7
Auditing

Enterprises should take all necessary measures to establish independent systems of auditing in order to bring to light any transactions which contravene the present Rules of Conduct.   Appropriate corrective action must then be taken.

Article 8
Agents

Enterprises should maintain a record of the names and terms of employment of all agents whose remuneration exceeds US $ 50,000 a year and who are employed by them in connection with transactions with public bodies or State enterprises.   This record should be available for inspection by auditors and upon specific request by appropriate governmental authorities.

Article 9
Political Contributions

Contributions to political parties or committees or to individual politicians may only be made in accordance with the applicable local law and must be accorded such publicity as that law requires.

Article 10
Company Codes

These Rules of Conduct being of a general nature, enterprises should, where appropriate, draw up their own codes consistent with the ICC Rules and apply them to the particular circumstances in which their business is carried out. Such codes may usefully include examples and should enjoin employees or agents who find themselves subjected to any form of extortion or bribery immediately to report the same to senior management.

Article 11
Panel

a)   The ICC is establishing a Panel to interpret, promote, and oversee the application of, these Rules of Conduct.

b)   In particular, the Panel will periodically review matters relating to the Rules of Conduct and the experience gained in their application as well as developments in fighting extortion and bribery in business transactions.

c)   The Panel may consider the interpretation and the clarification of the Rules of Conduct, and may suggest modifications thereto, as occasion requires.

d)   The Panel will periodically report to the Council of the ICC on its activities.

e)   The Panel may, in appropriate circumstances, consider alleged infringements of the Rules of Conduct.

Committee to Elaborate By-Laws

The President of the ICC will nominate a small Committee to elaborate the by-laws of the Panel, taking into account the Report of the Commission on Ethical Practices, the alternative draft No. 192/INT. 12 and all other relevant material. The Committee can examine *inter alia*:

(a) the scope of the examination by the Panel of alleged infringements of the Rules of Conduct, the procedure therefore and limitations thereon;

(b) criteria to be employed in evaluating claims of violations to be considered by the Panel;

(c) whether and to what extent findings and opinions of the Panel may be published by the Panel without the consent of parties affected, and

(d) such other matters as the Committee shall consider necessary or appropriate in the discharge of the functions of the Panel.

The Committee will report to the Council so as to enable it to reach a decision in June 1978, and to that effect National Committees will receive the report of the Committee, for consideration, at least 45 days before the Council's session. Upon approval by the Council of the by-laws of the Panel, the Panel will be promptly elected by the Council upon the recommendations of the President of the ICC.

*   *   *

THE BUSINESS CHARTER FOR SUSTAINABLE DEVELOPMENT:
PRINCIPLES FOR ENVIRONMENTAL MANAGEMENT[*]

The Business Charter for Sustainable Development: Principles for Environmental Management was adopted at the 64th Session of the International Chamber of Commerce Executive Board on 27 November 1990, and first published in April 1991. It was prepared for the ICC Commission on Environment.

Introduction

Sustainable development involves meeting the needs of the present without compromising the ability of future generations to meet their own needs.

Economic growth provides the conditions in which protection of the environment can best be achieved, and environmental protection, in balance with other human goals, is necessary to achieve growth that is sustainable.

In turn, versatile, dynamic, responsive and profitable businesses are required as the driving force for sustainable economic development and for providing managerial, technical and financial resources to contribute to the resolution of environmental challenges. Market economies, characterised by entrepreneurial initiatives, are essential to achieving this.

Business thus shares the view that there should be a common goal, not a conflict, between economic development and environmental protection, both now and for future generations.

Making market forces work in this way to protect and improve the quality of the environment -- with the help of performance-based standards and judicious use of economic instruments in a harmonious regulatory framework -- is one of the greatest challenges that the world faces in the next decade.

The 1987 report of the World Commission on Environment and Development, "Our Common Future", expresses the same challenge and calls on the cooperation of business in tackling it. To this end, business leaders have launched actions in their individual enterprises as well as through sectoral and cross sectoral associations.

In order that more businesses join this effort and that their environmental performance continues

---

[*]Source: International Chamber of Commerce (1991). *The Business Charter for Sustainable Development. Principles for Environmental Management* (Paris: International Chamber of Commerce) ICC Publication No. 210/356 A [Note added by the editor].

to improve, the International Chamber of Commerce hereby calls upon enterprises and their associations to use the following Principles as a basis for pursuing such improvement and to express publicly their support for them. Individual programmes developed to implement these Principles will reflect the wide diversity among enterprises in size and function.

The objective is that the widest range of enterprises commit themselves to improving their environmental performance in accordance with these Principles, to having in place management practices to effect such improvement, to measuring their progress, and to reporting this progress as appropriate internally and externally.

Note: The term environment as used in this document also refers to environmentally related aspects of health, safety and product stewardship.

PRINCIPLES

1. Corporate priority

To recognise environmental management as among the highest corporate priorities and as a key determinant to sustainable development; to establish policies, programmes and practices for conducting operations in an environmentally sound manner.

2. Integrated management

To integrate these policies, programmes and practices fully into each business as an essential element of management in all its functions.

3. Process of improvement

To continue to improve corporate policies, programmes and environmental performance, taking into account technical developments, scientific understanding, consumer needs and community expectations, with legal regulations as a starting point; and to apply the same environmental criteria internationally.

4. Employee education

To educate, train and motivate employees to conduct their activities in an environmentally responsible manner.

5. Prior assessment

To assess environmental impacts before starting a new activity or project and before decommissioning a facility or leaving a site.

6.   **Products and services**

To develop and provide products or services that have no undue environmental impact and are safe in their intended use, that are efficient in their consumption of energy and natural resources, and that can be recycled, reused, or disposed of safely.

7.   **Customer advise**

To advise, and where relevant educate, customers, distributors and the public in the safe use, transportation, storage and disposal of products provided; and to apply similar considerations to the provision of services.

8.   **Facilities and operations**

To develop, design and operate facilities and conduct activities taking into consideration the efficient use of energy and materials, the sustainable use of renewable resources, the minimisation of adverse environmental impact and waste generation, and the safe and responsible disposal of residual wastes.

9.   **Research**

To conduct or support research on the environmental impacts of raw materials, products, processes, emissions and wastes associated with the enterprise and on the means of minimizing such adverse impacts.

10.   **Precautionary approach**

To modify the manufacture, marketing or use of products or services or the conduct of activities, consistent with scientific and technical understanding, to prevent serious or irreversible environmental degradation.

11.   **Contractors and suppliers**

To promote the adoption of these principles by contractors acting on behalf of the enterprise, encouraging and, where appropriate, requiring improvements in their practices to make them consistent with those of the enterprise, and to encourage the wider adoption of these principles by suppliers.

12.   **Emergency preparedness**

To develop and maintain, where significant hazards exist, emergency preparedness plans in conjunction with the emergency services, relevant authorities and the local community, recognizing potential transboundary impacts.

13.   Transfer of technology

To contribute to the transfer of environmentally sound technology and management methods throughout the industrial and public sectors.

14.   Contributing to the common effort

To contribute to the development of public policy and to business, governmental and intergovernmental programmes and educational initiatives that will enhance environmental awareness and protection.

15.   Openness to concerns

To foster openness and dialogue with employee and the public, anticipating and responding to their concerns about the potential hazards and impact of operations, products, wastes or services, including those of transboundary or global significance.

16.   Compliance and reporting

To measure environmental performance; to conduct regular environmental audits and assessments of compliance with company requirements, legal requirements and these principles; and periodically to provide appropriate information to the Board of Directors, shareholders, employees, the authorities and the public.

*   *   *

THE CERES PRINCIPLES*

In 1988, a group of investors set up a set of criteria to help assess corporate environmental performance. The resulting Valdez Principles were adopted by the Coalition for Environmentally Responsible Economies (CERES). The amended version of the Valdez Principles was adopted by the CERES Board of Directors on 28 April 1992.

Introduction

By adopting these Principles, we publicly affirm our belief that corporations have a responsibility for the environment, and must conduct all aspects of their business as responsible stewards of the environment by operating in a manner that protects the Earth. We believe that corporations must not compromise the ability of future generations to sustain themselves.

We will update our practices constantly in light of advances in technology and new understandings in health and environmental science. In collaboration with CERES, we will promote a dynamic process to ensure that the Principles are interpreted in a way that accommodates changing technologies and environmental realities. We intend to make consistent, measurable progress in implementing these Principles and to apply them to all aspects of our operations throughout the world.

Protection of the Biosphere

We will reduce and make continual progress toward eliminating the release of any substance that may cause environmental damage to the air, water, or the earth or its inhabitants. We will safeguard all habitats affected by our operations and will protect open spaces and wilderness, while preserving biodiversity.

Sustainable Use of Natural Resources

We will make sustainable use of renewable natural resources, such as water, soils and forests. We will conserve nonrenewable natural resources through efficient use and careful planning.

Reduction and Disposal of Wastes

We will reduce and where possible eliminate waste through source reduction and recycling. All waste will be handled and disposed of through safe and responsible methods.

---

*Source: CERES (1995). *CERES Principles* (CERES: Boston) [Note added by the editor].

Energy Conservation

We will conserve energy and improve the energy efficiency of our internal operations and of the goods and services we sell. We will make every effort to use environmentally safe and sustainable energy sources.

Risk Reduction

We will strive to minimize the environmental, health and safety risks to our employees and the communities in which we operate through safe technologies, facilities and operating procedures, and by being prepared for emergencies.

Safe Products and Services

We will reduce and where possible eliminate the use, manufacture or sale of products and services that cause environmental damage or health or safety hazards. We will inform our customers of the environmental impacts of our products or services and try to correct unsafe use.

Environmental Restoration

We will promptly and responsibly correct conditions we have caused that endanger health, safety or the environment. To the extent feasible, we will redress injuries we have caused to persons or damage we have caused to the environment and will restore the environment.

Informing the Public

We will inform in a timely manner everyone who may be affected by conditions caused by our company that might endanger health, safety or the environment. We will regularly seek advice and counsel through dialogue with persons in communities near our facilities. We will not take any action against employees for reporting dangerous incidents or conditions to management or to appropriate authorities.

Management Commitment

We will implement these Principles and sustain a process that ensures that the Board of Directors and Chief Executive Officer are fully informed about pertinent environmental issues and are fully responsible for environmental policy. In selecting our Board of Directors, we will consider demonstrated environmental commitment as a factor.

Audits and Reports

We will conduct an annual self-evaluation of our progress in implementing these Principles. We will support the timely creation of generally accepted environmental audit procedures. We will annually complete the CERES Report, which will be made available to the public.

Disclaimer

These Principles establish an environmental ethic with criteria by which investors and others can assess the environmental performance of companies. Companies that endorse these Principles pledge to go voluntarily beyond the requirements of the law. The terms may and might in Principles one and eight are not meant to encompass every imaginable consequence, no matter how remote. Rather, these Principles obligate endorsers to behave as prudent persons who are not governed by conflicting interests and who possess a strong commitment to environmental excellence and to human health and safety. These Principles are not intended to create new legal liabilities, expand existing rights or obligations, waive legal defenses, or otherwise affect the legal position of any endorsing company, and are not intended to be used against an endorser in any legal proceeding for any purpose.

*   *   *

CONSUMER CHARTER FOR GLOBAL BUSINESS*

The Consumer Charter for Global Business was published by Consumers International (formerly the International Organisation of Consumers Unions) in 1995. The text of the Intent of the Charter was still under discussion at the time of publication and therefore has not been reproduced in this volume.

1. Ethical Standards

Consumers have a right to expect:

1.1 That corporations will conduct all of their operations, including all stages of the production, distribution and marketing process, in such a way that the interest of consumers of the end product or service are considered at every stage.

1.2 That corporations will conduct all their operations (listed in Section 1.1) in such a way to, as a minimum, comply with the provisions of the OECD Councils' Recommendation on Bribery in International Business Transactions.

1.3 That corporations will, from time-to-time, provide all necessary information regarding their compliance with this Charter to Consumers International so that it can examine the conduct of the corporation in regards of this Charter. Where information is deemed to be commercially sensitive by the corporation, the denial of such information must be notified to Consumers International and an explanation of the information's sensitivity must be provided.

1.1 That corporations have published statements of ethics or conduct. These statements shall apply to all countries in which the corporation operates and shall be publicly available and presented in a clear and concise manner.

2. Competition Issues

Consumers have a right to expect:

2.1 That corporations will encourage the development and maintenance of fair, transparent and open competition. In light of this commitment, corporations agree to:

a) as a minimum standard abide by local and national competition and anti-trust laws in each

---

*Source: Consumers International (1995). *A Consumer Charter for Global Business* (Consumers International: London) [Note added by the editor].

country in which they operate;

b) ensure that all parts of the corporation are aware of local competition rules and comply fully with their provisions;

c) that where competition or anti-trust laws are not in operation, corporations will base their operating procedures on international standards of business practice (including the UN Code of Conduct on Restrictive Business Practices).

In light of this commitment, corporations agree to:

d) notify Consumers International of any legal action brought against them, or initiated by them against a competitor, for anti-competitive practices.

2.2 In light of the provisions of Article 2.1, corporations agree:

a) not to enter into arrangements or agreements with competing corporations that, whether directly or indirectly, result in an agreement to fix prices on any product or service. Such prices include the retail, wholesale or consumer price, export prices and import prices or any price charged to a third party;

b) not to enter into any agreement with a competing corporation whose effect, whether direct or indirect, involves the division of territory, be it national or international, into zones of operation. For the purposes of this Charter a zone of operation can be any geographical area in which corporations operate;

c) that when transferring goods or services within the legal body of their corporation, they price these goods and services as if the subsidiary were a separate corporation (the so-called `arms length' principle) and not to use any other method of pricing calculation as a means of avoiding the payment of taxes on their body;

d) not to enter into any agreement that results, either directly or indirectly, in a monopoly position for that corporation in its home market.

3. Marketing Practices

Consumers have a right to expect:

3.1 That all goods and services produced and distributed by the corporation shall be marketed or promoted in such a way that:

a) all claims made in the advertising or promotion are independently verifiable;

b) all claims made in the advertising or promotion in any particular country are consistent with levels of honesty and truthfulness that are either legally established or that any reasonable person would set;

c) marketing campaigns or promotions do not mislead consumers;

d) such campaigns or promotions do not abuse the trust of consumers or exploit any lack of knowledge or experience on their part.

3.2 That the corporation shall, as a minimum level, abide by the laws and regulations concerning the promotion and advertising of goods and services operating in the country concerned.

3.3. That corporations will also observe relevant internationally agreed codes which control the promotion of specific products, such as the WHO Code on Breast Milk Substitutes and the WHO Ethical Criteria for Medical Drug Promotion, and that where laws or regulations regarding advertising and promotion do not exist, the corporation will base its operating procedures on international standards of business practices.

3.4 That corporations will take particular case when marketing their products and services to children. Advertising of harmful products (such as tobacco and alcohol) should not, in any manner, be aimed at children.

4. Product Standards

Consumers have the right to expect:

4.1 That all goods and services produced distributed or marketed by a corporation are:

a) capable of use for the purposes claimed;

b) safe, both for the use intended and for any reasonable use made;

c) durable and reliable and offer levels of utility and suitability that, as a minimum, conform to standards defined in laws or regulations, or would be construed as reasonable by an ordinary person;

d) regularly monitored and tested by the corporation to ensure that they conform to the standards listed above.

4.2 That all goods and services produced, distributed or marketed by corporations are designed and manufactured:

a) to generally accepted international levels, or:

b) as a minimum, to standards no less stringent than those of comparable enterprises in the country concerned.

4.3 That all goods produced, distributed and marketed by the corporation are:

a) produced in such a manner that causes as little damage as possible to the environment, both directly and indirectly;

b) distributed in such a manner as to minimise damage to the environment, both directly and indirectly.;

c) transported in such a manner that minimises damage to the environment, both directly and indirectly;

d) corporations will, insofar as it is reasonable, ensure that their products are disposed of in a manner that is consistent with the principle of environmental sustainability.

5. Labelling of Products

Consumers have the right to expect:

5.1 That corporations will provide information regarding purchase and use (for products and services) and content, maintenance, storage and disposal (for products) in such a way that:

a) any information is comprehensible, that is, written clearly and legibly and in the officially recognised language(s) operating in each country;

b) any information displayed is clearly visible and in an obvious position on the product;

c) all information relating to possible misuse of the product is displayed prominently and clearly and in language and symbols that are clearly recognisable.

5.2 That corporations will provide information regarding the reusability or recycling of the product. Such information shall be displayed prominently and in a clear manner on the product or service concerned, and in the officially recognised language(s) operating in each country.

5.3 That corporations will only use environmental symbols on their labelling that are independently developed and standardised.

5.4 That where a product or service, in either a direct or indirect manner, is potentially harmful to the consumer of that product or service:

a) all information pertaining to that potential harm is comprehensible, and displayed clearly, legibly and prominently on the product or its made available prior to the provision of the service concerned;

b) all labelling relating to the use of the product or the provision of the service exhibits a nationally, or where none exists, an internationally recognised symbol indicating the nature of the danger, the means by which that danger can be avoided and the remedy needed to treat any harmful effect of the product or service.

6. Provision of Information

Consumers have a right to expect:

6.1 That corporations will provide the same level and detail of information on the appropriate use and storage of their products in all the countries in which they operate.

6.2 That corporations will provide consumers with information on the appropriate recycling, re-usability and disposal of their products.

6.3 That corporations will make available to Consumers International upon request, information on those international standards which they observe in each country of operation.

6.4 That corporations will provide Consumers International with an bi-annual report outlining measures adopted by each of their subsidiaries to prevent environmental pollution.

7. Complaints procedures

Consumers have a right to expect:

7.1 That corporations will establish and operate a system of informal redress through conciliation for the fair settlement of consumers' just claims. This will include fair compensation for unsatisfactory goods or services.

7.2 That corporations will institute procedures to enable consumers to enforce their statutory or contractual rights against a corporation.

8. Guarantees

8.1 That corporations will provide consumers with some form of guarantee relating to their product.

8.2 That such a guarantee is additional to any statutory obligation and does not prejudice the rights of a consumer to enforce their contractual rights against the producer or retailer of the product.

8.3 That it is clearly stated that such a guarantee is binding for the corporation giving it whether or not it has a direct contractual relationship with the consumer.

DEFINITION

A corporation is a legally established entity involved in the production, distribution, marketing or promotion of a good or service. For the purposes of this Charter it shall include public bodies that carry out the functions listed. A corporation may, or may not, operate in more than one country.

*   *   *

Pacific Basin Charter on International Investments[*]

The Pacific Basin Charter on International Investments was drafted by the Pacific Basin Economic Council (PBEC). The PBEC Committee on Foreign Direct Investment approved the Charter on 16 November 1995.

Preamble

We, the members of the Pacific Basin Economic Council (PBEC) and as members of the international business community from Australia, Canada, Chile, People's Republic of China, Colombia, Fiji, Hong Kong, Indonesia, Japan, Republic of Korea, Malaysia, Mexico, New Zealand, Peru, Republic of the Philippines, Russia, Chinese Taipei, Thailand, United States of America, and the Pacific region, recognizing the vast demands for an increasing flow of private investment capital among economies, and the fundamental importance of improving the investment environment in all Pacific economies, hereby endorse, and invite other organizations - public and private - to embrace a Pacific Basin Charter on International Investments.

We advance the principles of this Charter with high aspirations that they will be increasingly accepted and applied by governments and international business in the Pacific Basin and with a firm belief that these steps will foster more rapid and sound economic and social progress - as well as strengthen business enterprise - in the Pacific economies. Our objective in this initiative is to fulfill a responsibility to governments and private enterprises by indicating the basis on which we believe sound and constructive investment can be attracted and play a constructive part in the economic process in economies subscribing to private enterprise concepts.

We believe that, in line with goals established by the United Nations, the application of the principles of this Charter will increase the contribution of international business toward meeting the needs and aspirations of all peoples and, in particular, will facilitate the flow of capital, both private and public, to the benefit of all economies. In pursuance of that objective both international investors and governments should respect and honor the contractual obligations they freely undertake.

Both international investors and governments should promote and maintain mutual dialogues through which international investments would be furthered in accordance with the principles of this Charter.

International investors should maintain high standards of conduct in all the relationships with

---

[*]Source: The text of the Pacific Basin Charter on International Investments was provided by the Pacific Basin Economic Council, United States.

governments and other parties, thereby maintaining their enterprises as national and international corporate citizens of high standing and integrity.

BASIC PRINCIPLES

Responsibilities

International investors, in pursuit of their business objectives, should proceed in ways which will contribute to economic and social development, particularly in host economies, and they should maintain a sensitivity to changing domestic goals and aspirations in all economies with which they are concerned.

Governments wishing to receive international investments, realizing that such investments must be profitable, should develop policies conducive to successful business enterprise which will be consistent with the achievement of their domestic economic and social goals.

Governments of economies from which private capital flows abroad should strive to develop agreements with other governments aimed at encouraging private investments and the growth of international business in mutual interests of the economies concerned.

Policies

International investors should fully recognize the sovereign rights and responsibilities of economies and must accept reasonable obligations that are placed upon business enterprises in the domestic interest, and should act in all ways as a good corporate citizen of the host economy.

Recognizing that performance requirements can distort or limit expansion of trade and investment, governments should refrain from their use.

All enterprises operating in a given economy should have equality of access to domestic markets and resources.

Governments should publicly announce their laws, regulations, administrative guidelines and policies on encouragement and/or limitations on international investments and should make explicit their development priorities and the guidelines which transnational enterprises are expected to meet. These policies and guidelines should be maintained with reasonable consistency and applied to all on an equal basis.

Governments should ensure that their announced policies are applied on a fair basis and that they do not serve to abrogate on a unilateral basis investment agreements entered into in good faith.

Governments should publicly announce policies on the encouragement and/or limitation of international investment, both incoming and outgoing.

Governments - especially those of economies in a creditor or favourable foreign exchange situation - should stimulate and encourage the flow of private investments abroad.

Host governments should treat international investors impartially, in accordance with national and international law.

In selecting projects and in operating their enterprises, international investors should give emphasis to activities that provide long-term net additions to the host economy. They should also utilize and assist in the development of local resources, human and physical, as well as local industrial capabilities to the fullest extent possible.

The terms of investment agreements should be altered only by mutual agreement between the parties, and not by the unilateral act of either government or the investor.

Both international investors and governments in their mutual interest should give special emphasis in their planning and operations (including transfers of funds) to continuity, growth and sound long-range development of international investment projects. Governments wishing incoming international investments only for limited periods of time should announce their policies clearly and explicitly in this respect.

Governments and international investors should support the principle of multinational efforts to create and maintain a feasible and mutually acceptable international investment insurance or reinsurance program.

International investors and governments should ensure that investment projects will have minimum adverse effect on the environment.

Governments should simplify entry and exit procedures to assist international investors in familiarizing themselves with international, industrial, technical and commercial situations, to permit trainees to receive technical and job training in relevant economies, and to allow entry of foreign technical and managerial personnel.

Governments and investors should support efforts of the World Trade Organization to establish model investment policies which serve to promote the free flow of international investment.

OPERATIONS

Ownership, Management, Employment

Host governments should adopt policies which permit international investors to own and manage their enterprises to the extent necessary to maximize their ability to obtain an adequate return on the investment and thus to contribute to the host economy. Ample opportunities should be available to domestic investors so that they may participate through joint ventures or otherwise, in ownership and management of international enterprises operating in their economies.

International investors should train and utilize local personnel in their enterprises so that such personnel might enhance to the greatest possible extent their technical, managerial and other potential employment skills. Nevertheless, particularly during the early stages of development, international investors should be permitted to employ foreign personnel, particularly when such personnel have technological or other knowledge necessary for the success of the enterprise.

Governments should levy taxes on international investors and their employees from abroad on a basis no less favourable than those levied on domestic investors and their local employees. Governments should strive through international agreements to avoid double taxation between economies.

Capital transmitted to an economy through recognized banking channels, dividends or profits thereon, as well as license and royalty fees owed outside the host economy, should be freely transferable by international investors. In international transfers of funds, governments and international investors should proceed in a manner consistent with the Articles of the International Monetary Fund and with international banking practices, and as may be fair and reasonable to both parties concerned.

International investors should observe all policies and requirements of governments pertaining to the protection of life and property. Governments should ensure that adequate protection of this type is available to international investors.

Property

Only when a host government finds it necessary in the furtherance of a public purpose, should it expropriate an enterprise belonging to international investors. When expropriation, or any other measure having a similar effect is carried out, it should be done so on a nondiscriminatory basis and provide for full and prompt settlement to the international investors. In the event of disagreements as to the amount of compensation, it should be established without right of appeal by submission to an arbitrator acceptable to both parties. The arbitrator should take into account, inter alia, potential earnings of the enterprise so taken as if it were the subject of a Buy and Sell Agreement between consenting parties.

Legislation

International investors should comply fully with legislation, regulations and international agreements within and among the governments concerned.

Legislation affecting international investment should be fair and reasonable among all types of investors.

Governments should respect the jurisdictional integrity of those economies in which its nationals operate and should not attempt to extend to international enterprises the jurisdiction of their laws and regulations in such a way as to influence business activities in other economies.

Technology

Governments and international investors should **stimulate** the flow of technology and sound managerial concepts and practices across international boundaries which will serve to improve the technical and managerial capabilities of recipient economies.

Governments should recognize the rights of international investors to receive reasonable payment covering the use of their proprietary technology.

Information Disclosure

Host governments should not require more information from an enterprise belonging to an international investor than it does from one belonging to a domestic investor, it always being remembered that the requirement for unwarranted **public** disclosure can affect the competitive position of such enterprises.

Consultations

Governments and international investors should give sympathetic consideration to, and adequate opportunity for, consultations on any policy or operating problems raised by one party with the other. In the event a mutually satisfactory solution to given problems cannot be reached, the parties concerned should seek suggestions from a mutually acceptable third party such as the International Center for the Settlement of Investment Disputes.

The Future

The preceding principles are intended as basic guidelines in the international investment process. Additions, modifications, amplifications may be appropriate from time to time to reflect changing conditions and circumstances. The Charter can be altered through the same review process as applied to its original establishment. Action can be initiated (if considered advisable) on development of a series of Supplements. These would elaborate on various topics in the Charter, e.g. responsibilities, investment policies, investment agreements, ownership and management, personnel, taxation, capital markets, foreign exchange, protection of life and property, marketing, legislation and technology.

*   *   *

SELECT LIST OF PUBLICATIONS OF THE UNCTAD DIVISION ON TRANSNATIONAL CORPORATIONS AND INVESTMENT

World Investment Report 1995: Transnational Corporations and Competitiveness. 491p. Sales No. E.95.II.A.9. $45.

World Investment Report 1995: Transnational Corporations and Competitiveness. Overview. 68p. Free-of-charge. *(Arabic/Chinese/English/French/Russian/Spanish)*

World Investment Report 1994: Transnational Corporations, Employment and the Workplace. 482p. Sales No. E.94.II.A.14. $45.

World Investment Report 1994: Transnational Corporations, Employment and the Workplace. An Executive Summary. 34p. Free-of-charge. *(English/Chinese/Japanese)*

Liberalizing International Transactions in Services: A Handbook. 182p. Sales No. E.94.II.A.11. $45. (Joint publication with the World Bank)

World Investment Directory. Volume IV: Latin America and the Caribbean. 478p. Sales No. E.94.II.A.10. $65.

World Investment Report 1993: Transnational Corporations and Integrated International Production. 290p. Sales No. E.93.II.A.14. $45.

World Investment Report 1993: Transnational Corporations and Integrated International Production. An Executive Summary. 31p. ST/CTC/159. Free-of-charge.

Intellectual Property Rights and Foreign Direct Investment (Current Studies, Series A, No. 24.) 108p. Sales No. E.93.II.A.10. $20.

World Investment Directory 1992. Volume III: Developed Countries. 532p. Sales No. E.93.II.A.9. $75.

World Investment Directory 1992. Volume II: Central and Eastern Europe. 432p. Sales No. E.93.II.A.1. $65. (Joint publication with ECE)

World Investment Report 1992: Transnational Corporations as Engines of Growth: An Executive Summary. 30p. Sales No. E.92.II.A.24. Free-of-charge.

World Investment Report 1992: Transnational Corporations as Engines of Growth. 356p. Sales No. E.92.II.A.19. $45.

Bilateral Investment Treaties. 1959-1991. 46p. Sales No. E.92.II.A.16. $22. (Joint publication with the International Chamber of Commerce).

World Investment Directory 1992. Volume I: Asia and the Pacific. 356p. Sales No. E.92.II.A.11. $65.

Formulation and Implementation of Foreign Investment Policies: Selected Key Issues (Current Studies, Series A, No. 10), 84p. Sales No. E.92.II.A.21. $12.

The Determinants of Foreign Direct Investment: A Survey of the Evidence. 84p. Sales No. E.92.II.A.2. $12.50.

Government Policies and Foreign Direct Investment (UNCTC Current Studies, Seires A, No. 17) 66p., Sales No. E.91.II.A.20. $12.50.

The Impact of Trade-related Investment Measures on Trade and Development. (A joint publication by the United Nations Centre on Transnational Corporations and the Untied Nations Conference on Trade and Development), 104 p., Sales No. E.91.II.A.19. $17.50.

World Investment Report 1991: The Triad in Foreign Direct Investment. 108 p., Sales No.E.91.II.A.12 (out of print).

New Issues in the Uruguay Round of Multilateral Trade Negotiations (Current Studies, Series A, No. 19) 52p. Sales No. E.90.II.A.15. $12.50.

The New Code Environment (UNCTC Current Studies, Series A, No. 16), 54p., $7.50, Sales No. E.90.II.A.7. $7.50.

Key Concepts in International Investment Arrangements and Their Relevance to Negotiations on International Transactions in Services (UNCTC Current Studies, Series A, No. 13), 66 p., Sales No. E.90.II.A.3. $9.00.

Transnational Corporations and International Economic Relations: Recent Developments and Selected Issues (UNCTC Current Studies, Series A, No. 11) 50 p., Sales No. E.89.II.A.15. $7.50.

Transnational Corporations in World Development: Trends and Prospects, Sales No. E.88.II.A.15. $11.00 (out of print).

Bilateral Investment Treaties. 188 p., Sales No. E.88.II.A.1. $ 20.00.

The United Nations Code of Conduct on Transnational Corporations (UNCTC Current Studies, Series A, No. 4), 80p., Sales No. 86.II.A.15.

The Question of a Reference to International Obligations in the United Nations Code of Conduct on Transnational Corporations: A Different View (UNCTC Current Studies, Series A, No. 2), 17p., Sales No. E.86.II.A.11. $4.00.

The Question of a Reference to International Law in the United Nations Code of Conduct on Transnational Corporations (UNCTC Current Studies, Series A, No.1), 22p., Sales No. E.86.II.A.5. $4.00.

Transnational Corporations: Material Relevant to the Formulation of a Code of Conduct, 114p., $7.00 (out of print).

Transnational Corporations: Issues Involved in the Formulation of a Code of Conduct, 41p., No.E.77.II.A.5., $3.00 (out of print).

Transnational Corporations: Transfer Pricing and Taxation in The United Nations Library on Transnational Corporations, volume fourteen (published by Routledge on behalf of the United Nations, 1994), 330p.

Transnational Corporations and National Law in The United Nations Library on Transnational Corporations, volume nineteen (published by Routledge on behalf of the United Nations, 1994), 332p.

Transnational Corporations: The International Legal Framework in The United Nations Library on Transnational Corporations, volume twenty (published by Routledge on behalf of the United Nations, 1994), 545p.

National Legislation and Regulations Relating to Transnational Corporations, Vol. VIII, (Geneva, United Nations, 1994), 263 p., $36.00, Sales No. E.94.II.A.18.

National Legislation and Regulations Relating to Transnational Corporations, Vol. VII, (New York, United Nations, 1989), 320 p., $36.00, Sales No. E.89.II.A.9.

National Legislation and Regulations Relating to Transnational Corporations, Vol. VI, (New York, United Nations, 1988), 322 p., $45.00, Sales No. E.87.II.A.6 (out of print). (Also published in English by Graham and Trotman, London/Dordrecht/Boston, 1988, 322 p., $45.00).

National Legislation and Regulations Relating to Transnational Corporations, Vol. V, (New York, United Nations, 1986), 246 p., $23.00, Sales No. E.86.II.A.3 (out of print).

National Legislation and Regulations Relating to Transnational Corporations, Vol. IV, (New York, United Nations, 1986), 241 p., $23.00, Sales No. E.85.II.A.14 (out of print).

National Legislation and Regulations Relating to Transnational Corporations, Vol. III, (New York, United Nations, 1989), 345 p., $33.00, Sales No. E.83.II.A.15 (out of print).

National Legislation and Regulations Relating to Transnational Corporations, Vol. II, (New York, United Nations, 1983), 338 p., $33.00, Sales No. E.83.II.A.7 (out of print).

National Legislation and Regulations Relating to Transnational Corporations, Vol. I (Part Two), (New York, United Nations, 1980), 114 p., $9.00, Sales No. E.80.II.A.5 and corrigendum.

National Legislation and Regulations Relating to Transnational Corporations, Vol. I (Part One), (New York, United Nations, 1978), 302 p., $16.00, Sales No. E.78.II.A.3 and corrigendum (out of print).

United Nations publications may be obtained from bookstores and distributors throughout the world. Please consult your bookstore or write to:

United Nations Publications

Sales Section	OR	Sales Section
Room DC2-0853		United Nations Office at Geneva
United Nations Secretariat		Palais des Nations
New York, N.Y. 10017		CH-1211 Geneva 10
U.S.A.		Switzerland
Tel: (1-212) 963-8302 or (800) 253-9646		Tel: (41-22) 917-1234
Fax: (1-212) 963-3489		Fax: (41-22) 917-0123

All prices are quoted in United States dollars.

For further information on the work of the Transnational Corporations and Investment Division, UNCTAD, please address inquiries to:

United Nations Conference on Trade and Development
Division on Transnational Corporations and Investment
Palais des Nations, Room E-8006
CH-1211 Geneva 10
Switzerland

Telephone: (41-22) 907-1124
Telefax: (41-22) 907-0194

*   *   *

QUESTIONNAIRE

INTERNATIONAL INVESTMENT INSTRUMENTS: A COMPENDIUM

Sales No. E.96.XXXX

In order to improve the quality and relevance of the work of the UNCTAD Division on Transnational Corporations and Investment, it would be useful to receive the views of readers on this and other similar publications. It would therefore be greatly appreciated if you could complete the following questionnaire and return to:

Readership Survey
UNCTAD Division on Transnational Corporations and Investment
United Nations Office in Geneva
Palais des Nations
Room E-8006
CH-1211 Geneva 10
Switzerland

1. Name and address of respondent (optional):

_____
_____
_____

2. Which of the following best describes your area of work?

Government   o   Public enterprise   o

Private enterprise   o   Academic or research institution   o

International organization   o   Media   o

Not-profit organization   o   Other (specify) _____

3. In which country do you work? _____

4. What is your assessment of the contents of this publication?

Excellent   o   Adequate   o

Good   o   Poor   o

5. How useful is this publication to your work?

Very useful   o   Of some use   o   Irrelevant   o

6. Please indicate the three things you liked best about this publication:

_____

_____

_____

7. Please indicate the three things you liked least about this publication:

_____

_____

_____

8. If you have read more than the present publication of the UNCTAD Division on Transnational Corporations and Investment, what is your overall assessment of them?

Consistently good   o   Usually good, but with
                                    some exceptions   o

Generally mediocre   o   Poor   o

9. On the average, how useful are these publications to you in your work?

Very useful   o   Of some use   o   Irrelevant   o

10. Are you a regular recipient of *Transnational Corporations* (formerly *The CTC Reporter*), UNCTAD-DTCI's tri-annual refereed journal?

Yes   O   No   O

If not, please check here if you would like to receive
a sample copy sent to the name and address you have
given above   O

*   *   *